Laptops
For Seniors

FOR

DUMMIES®

3RD EDITION

by Nancy Muir

Laptops For Seniors For Dummies,® 3rd Edition

Published by: **John Wiley & Sons, Inc.**, 111 River Street, Hoboken, NJ 07030-5774, www.wiley.com

Copyright © 2013 by John Wiley & Sons, Inc., Hoboken, New Jersey

Published simultaneously in Canada

For general information on our other products and services, please contact our Customer Care Department within the U.S. at 877-762-2974, outside the U.S. at 317-572-3993, or fax 317-572-4002. For technical support, please visit www.wiley.com/techsupport.

Wiley publishes in a variety of print and electronic formats and by print-on-demand. Some material included with standard print versions of this book may not be included in e-books or in print-on-demand. If this book refers to media such as a CD or DVD that is not included in the version you purchased, you may download this material at http://booksupport.wiley.com. For more information about Wiley products, visit www.wiley.com.

Library of Congress Control Number: 2013942770

ISBN 978-1-118-71105-7 (pbk); ISBN 978-1-118-71119-4 (ebk); ISBN 978-1-118-71124-8 (ebk); ISBN 978-1-118-71129-3 (ebk)

Manufactured in the United States of America

10 9 8 7 6 5 4 3 2 1

Contents at a Glance

Table of Contents

Introduction

Computers for consumers have come a long way in just 25 years or so. They're now at the heart of the way many people communicate, socialize, shop, and learn. They provide useful tools for tracking information, organizing finances, and being creative.

During the rapid growth of the personal computer, you might have been too busy to jump in and explore all computers have to offer, but you now realize how useful and fun working with a computer can be — and you've decided to opt for a laptop.

This book helps you get going with your laptop quickly and painlessly.

About This Book

This book is specifically written for mature people like you, folks who are relatively new to using a computer and want to discover the basics of buying a laptop, working with software, and getting on the Internet. In writing this book, I've tried to take into account the types of activities that might interest a 50+-year-old citizen discovering computers for the first time.

Conventions used in this book

This book uses certain conventions to help you find your way around:

➡ When you have to type something in a text box, I put it in **bold** type. Whenever I mention a website address, I put it in another font, `like this`. If you are reading this on an e-reader or tablet, you can click the links to access the websites. Figure references are also in bold to help you find them.

➡ For menu commands, I use the ⇨ symbol to separate menu choices. For example, choose Tools⇨Internet Options. The ⇨ symbol is just my way of saying "Open the Tools menu and then click Internet Options."

➡ Callouts for figures draw your attention to an action you need to perform. In some cases, points of interest in a figure might be circled. The text tells you what to look for; the circle makes it easy to find.

 Tip icons point out insights or helpful suggestions related to tasks in the step list.

Foolish Assumptions

This book is organized by sets of tasks. These tasks start from the very beginning, assume you know little about computers, and guide you through the most basic steps in easy-to-understand language. Because I assume you're new to laptops, the book provides explanations or definitions of technical terms to help you out.

All computers are run by software called an *operating system*, such as Windows. Because Microsoft Windows–based personal computers (PCs) are the most common type, the book focuses on Windows 8.1 functionality.

Why You Need This Book

Working with computers can be a daunting prospect to people who are coming to them later in life. You may have used computers to e-mail in your job or write a report, but you feel that your grandchildren run rings around you when it comes to the many uses of technology. But fear not: recent research refutes the adage that you can't teach an old dog new tricks. With the simple step-by-step approach of this book, even the technophobic can get up to speed with a laptop.

You can work through this book from beginning to end or simply open up a chapter to solve a problem or help you learn a new skill whenever you need it. The steps in each task get you where you want to go quickly, without a lot of technical explanation. In no time, you'll start picking up the skills you need to become a confident laptop user.

How This Book Is Organized

This book is conveniently divided into several handy parts to help you find what you need.

➠ **Part I: First Steps with Your Laptop:** If you need to buy a laptop or get started with the basics of using a computer, this part is for you. These chapters help you understand how a laptop differs from a desktop computer and the benefits of laptop portability. You get to explore the different specifications, styles, and price ranges for laptops and discover how to set up your laptop out of the box, including hooking it up to a printer. There's even a chapter on the important topic of power management so you can maximize the battery life of your laptop.

➠ **Part II: Exploring Windows:** These chapters provide information for exploring the Windows Start screen and Desktop when you first turn on your computer and customizing Windows to work the way you want it to. You get advice on using accessibility features that make using a laptop easier for those with vision, hearing, or dexterity challenges and discover how to set up printers and scanners. Finally, I provide information on using the Help system that's part of Windows.

➠ **Part III: Having Fun and Getting Things Done:** Here's where you start working with that new laptop. First, I cover how to work with applications and the files you create with them. Then, discover what you can do with pre-installed apps to get the latest weather, news, sports scores, and finance news and to connect with people. Chapters in this part also introduce you to built-in Windows applications you can use to work with digital photos and listen to music.

➡ **Part IV: Exploring the Internet:** It's time to get online! The chapters in this part help you understand what the Internet is and what tools and functions it makes available to you. Find out how to explore the Internet with a web browser; how to stay in touch with people via e-mail, instant messaging, chat, and blogs, and even how to make Internet phone calls. You work with SkyDrive, Microsoft's popular file sharing site. I also introduce you to the social web, provide an overview of social networking sites such as Facebook, introduce microblogging with such services as Twitter, look at sharing videos, and even offer guidelines for safely communicating and dating online.

➡ **Part V: Taking Care of Your Laptop:** Now that you have a laptop, you have certain responsibilities toward it (just like having a child or puppy). In this case, you need to protect your laptop from theft and protect the data on your computer, which you can do using Windows 8.1 and Internet Explorer 11 tools. In addition, you need to perform some routine maintenance tasks to keep your hard drive uncluttered and virus-free.

Beyond the Book

You can find additional features of this book online. Visit the web to find these extras:

➡ **Cheat Sheet:** Go to `www.dummies.com/cheat sheet/laptopsforseniors` to find this book's online Cheat Sheet, a collection of handy tips for your reference. This book's Cheat Sheet offers a checklist to use when shopping for a laptop, a table of Windows 8.1 keystroke shortcuts, a list of useful websites for you to check out, and care and maintenance tips for your laptop.

Discovering the Laptop Advantage

*L*aptop computers started as very expensive options for those who travelled for business and were willing to carry almost ten pounds of machine to be able to use a computer on the road.

Move forward in time, and you'll find that laptops have become a much more affordable, portable, and ubiquitous option that many are choosing as their only computer, whether they travel much or not. If you're thinking about joining the laptop revolution, it's time you understand the advantages a laptop can offer.

In this chapter, I introduce you to the key differences between a desktop computer and a laptop, the computing opportunities your laptop offers, and the different styles of laptops available.

Get ready to . . .

Understand the Difference between a Desktop and Laptop

The fact is that when it comes to performing computing tasks, a desktop and laptop are pretty much identical. They both have an operating system such as Windows 8.1 or Mac OS X. They both contain a hard drive where you store data and computer chips that process data, and they both run software and access the Internet.

Where a desktop and laptop differ is their physical appearance, size, and weight. Here's a rundown of the key differences:

➡ **Appearance:** A desktop computer is typically encased in a tower, into which you plug a separate monitor, keyboard, and mouse. (Some newer models have the brains of the computer incorporated into a monitor base.) A laptop has all its parts in one unit, as shown in **Figure 1-1.** The central processing unit (CPU) — chips, monitor, keyboard, and touchpad (a laptop version of a mouse) — all fit in one compact package that includes slots called ports for plugging in other devices (called peripherals), such as a little toggle that acts as a transmitter for a wireless mouse or printer.

➡ **Power source:** A laptop contains a battery that you charge by plugging it into a wall outlet. You can run the laptop off of a charged battery or plug the laptop into a wall outlet so battery charge isn't a concern.

➡ **Portability:** Having a battery and coming in a more compact package makes a laptop more portable (although some larger models are a bit hefty to tote around); a desktop stays put on a desktop as a rule.

➡ **Extras:** Very small laptops might not include a CD/DVD drive and therefore require an external drive, like the one shown in **Figure 1-2,** to be attached.

➡ **Dummies.com online articles:** To see online articles related to this book, check out www.dummies.com/extras/laptopsforseniors. Here you can find more information about accessories for your laptop, how to customize the Internet Explorer toolbar, tips for creating strong passwords for your online accounts and computer, and how to pin items to the Start screen in Windows 8.1.

➡ **Updates:** Technology changes all the time, and therefore tech books sometimes have updates. You can find updates for this book at www.dummies.com/extras/laptopsforseniors.

Get Going!

Whether you need to start from square one and buy yourself a laptop or you're ready to just start enjoying the tools and toys your current laptop makes available, it's time to get going, get online, and get laptop-savvy.

Part I
First Steps with Your Laptop

getting started with

Laptops

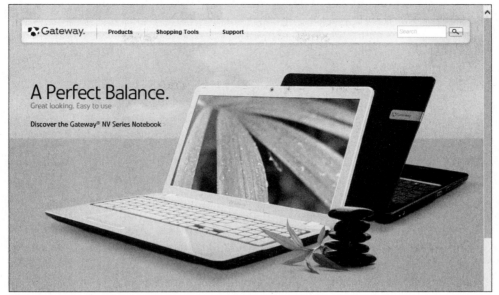

Figure 1-1

Figure 1-2

Tablets versus laptops

What's the difference between a laptop and tablet? Tablets, also called *slates*, are more like a hefty pad than a computer. There is no keyboard and no mouse. Instead, you tap the screen to make choices and enter text. The onscreen keyboard is still smaller than a laptop keyboard, but there are physical keyboard and mouse accessories that you can use with tablets to make input (typing text and commands) easier. Tablets also have super battery life at as much as 10 hours — almost a month in standby mode (when you're not actually using them). Tablets connect to the Internet using either Wi-Fi or 3G technologies (Wi-Fi is a network that is in close proximity to you; 3G is what your cellphone uses to connect virtually anywhere). 3G models require that you pay for your connection time.

Tablets, which are coming out from many manufacturers to compete with the iPad as of this writing, weigh about 1.5 pounds (more or less), and were first planned as devices for consuming media (watching videos and listening to music, to you and me). Whether used to read eBooks, play games such as Scrabble, browse the Internet, play music, or watch movies, these devices have proven incredibly popular. The big surprise since the launch of the iPad has been how big a hit tablets are with business and educational groups. Applications (called *apps*) range from credit card readers for retail businesses to eReaders such as Kindle and reasonably robust productivity tools such as word processors and spreadsheets.

However, tablets are pretty darn small. If you want a computing solution that's comfortable to work on at a desk for a few hours and pretty easy to take on the road, a laptop still has some advantages over a tablet.

Understand Different Types of Laptops

Today, there are several types of laptop that vary by size and weight, functionality, and the way you enter information into them. Here are some options available to you:

➠ The garden-variety laptop (also referred to as a *notebook computer*) runs around 5–8 pounds and has a monitor size ranging from about 13 inches to 16 or so. It's portable and can handle most computing tasks. *Multimedia/gaming laptops* are laptops that have more sophisticated graphics and sound cards.

➠ *Desktop replacements* are laptops with more heft. They might weigh more than 10 pounds and have larger monitors (perhaps as big as 20 inches). Their keyboards are roomier as well. However, although they aren't too difficult to move around your home, they aren't meant to be as portable as other types of laptops.

➠ *Ultrabooks* are thinner, lightweight laptops that have lower-power processors for longer battery life. Whereas laptops usually weigh in at about 4 to 7 pounds, ultrabooks (see Figure 1-3) weigh a mere 3 pounds or so and their screens come in at around 12 to 15 inches. Of course, their light weight has tradeoffs, mainly in the form of a smaller keyboard, no DVD drive, and a heftier price point.

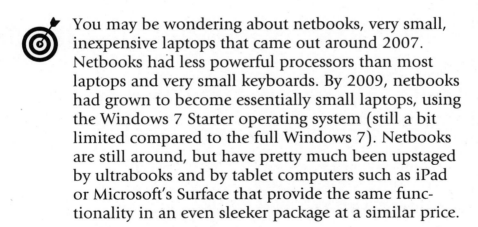 You may be wondering about netbooks, very small, inexpensive laptops that came out around 2007. Netbooks had less powerful processors than most laptops and very small keyboards. By 2009, netbooks had grown to become essentially small laptops, using the Windows 7 Starter operating system (still a bit limited compared to the full Windows 7). Netbooks are still around, but have pretty much been upstaged by ultrabooks and by tablet computers such as iPad or Microsoft's Surface that provide the same functionality in an even sleeker package at a similar price.

Many people own both a laptop and a tablet. If you decide to buy a tablet and choose an iPad, you might want to check out my book *iPad For Seniors For Dummies*, 5th Edition (John Wiley & Sons, Inc.).

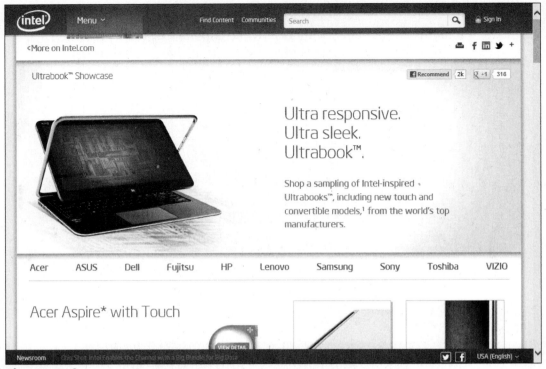

Figure 1-3

Explore All You Can Do with Your Laptop

Your laptop is a computer in a smaller package, so you can perform all the typical computing tasks with it. If you've never owned a computer of any type, your laptop purchase will open up a world of activities. Even if you're buying your laptop just to do e-mail (I hear this a lot from seniors!), do yourself a favor and explore a few other computing tasks that your laptop will allow you to do, such as these:

➡ **Run software programs to accomplish everyday tasks.** Utilize word processors to write letters or create flyers, spreadsheet software to organize your finances or household inventory, or photo-imaging software to work with your snapshots.

➡ **Work with financial activities.** From storing your checkbook and credit card records to doing your taxes, a computer can help you gain control over your finances. You can manage your investing, pay bills, and do your banking. Performing financial activities online can be very safe if you know the ins and outs of staying safe online (described in Chapter 21), and working online can be incredibly convenient, with your accounts available 24/7.

➡ **Keep in touch with friends and family.** The Internet makes it possible to communicate with other people via e-mail; share video images using *webcams* (tiny, inexpensive video cameras that capture and send your images to another computer); and make phone calls using a technology called VoIP (Voice over Internet Protocol) that uses your laptop and Internet connection to place calls. You can also chat with others by typing and sending messages using a technology called *instant messaging.* These messages are exchanged in real time so that you and your grandchild, for example, can see and reply to text immediately. Part IV of this book explains these topics in more detail.

➡ **Research any topic from the comfort of your home.** Online, you can find many reputable websites that give you information on anything from expert medical advice to the best travel deals. You can read news from around the corner or around the world. You can visit government websites to find out information about your taxes, Social Security, and more, or even go to entertainment sites to look up your local television listings.

➡ **Create greeting cards, letters, or home inventories.** Whether you're organizing your holiday card list or figuring out a monthly budget, computer programs can help. For example, **Figure 1-4** shows the Hallmark greeting card site with lots of options for creating electronic cards to send to your friends' e-mail inboxes.

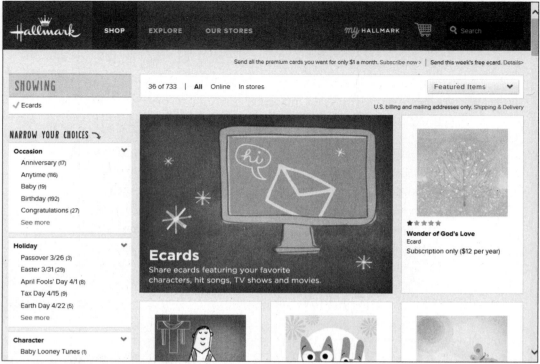

Figure 1-4

⟶ **Pursue hobbies such as genealogy or sports.** You can research your favorite teams online or connect with people who have the same interests. The online world is full of special-interest chat groups where you can discuss your interests with others.

⟶ **Play interactive games with others over the Internet.** You can play everything from shuffleboard to poker or action games in virtual worlds.

⟶ **Share and create photos, drawings, and videos.** If you have a digital camera or mobile phone with a camera, you can transfer photos to your laptop (doing this is called *uploading*) or copy photos off the Internet and share them in e-mails or use them to create your own artwork. If you're artistically inclined, you can create digital drawings. Many popular websites make sharing digital movies easy, too. If you have a digital video camera and editing software, you can use editing tools to make a movie and share it with others. Steven Spielberg, look out!

➡ **Shop online and compare products easily, day or night.** You can shop for anything from a garden shed to travel deals or a new camera. Using handy online features, you can easily compare prices from several stores or read customer product reviews. Websites such as www.nextag.com list product prices from a variety of vendors on one web page, as shown in Figure 1-5, so you can find the best deals. Beyond the convenience, all this information can help you save money.

Figure 1-5

Appreciate the Portability Factor

Because your laptop is portable, you can move it around your house or around town with relative ease. What does this portability allow you to do?

➡ You can access your e-mail account from anywhere to stay in touch with others or get work done away from home or the office. You can also store documents online so that you can access them from anywhere.

➡ Use public *hotspots* — locations that provide access to the Internet, such as airports and Internet cafés — to go online. For example, some hotels today provide Wi-Fi access free of charge, so you can work on your laptop from the lobby or your room.

➡ Even if you're staying in town, it might be fun to take your laptop to a local café and putter while sipping a latte.

 Check your laptop battery-life specifications. Recently, one laptop was shipped from Lenovo with a 30-hour battery life, but some still offer only about 2 hours. If you plan to use your laptop for an extended time away from a power source, be sure you've charged your battery (find out more about this in Chapter 4), and keep an eye on it. You could lose some work if you haven't saved it and the battery power runs out.

Buying a Laptop

*I*f you've never owned a laptop and now face purchasing one for the first time, deciding what model to get can be a somewhat daunting experience. There are lots of technical terms to figure out, various pieces of *hardware* (the physical pieces of your laptop, such as the monitor and keyboard) to become familiar with, and *software* (the programs that serve as the brains of the computer, helping you create documents and play games, for example) that you need to understand.

In this chapter, I introduce you to the world of activities your new laptop makes available to you, and I provide the information you need to choose just the right laptop for you. Remember as you read through this chapter that figuring out what you want to do with your laptop is an important step in determining which laptop you should buy. You have to consider how much money you want to spend, how you'll connect your laptop to the Internet, and how much power and performance you'll require from your laptop.

Understand Hardware and Software

Your computing experience is made up of interactions with hardware and software. The *hardware* is all the tangible computer equipment, such as the body of your laptop containing the hard drive, keyboard, and touchpad for pointing at and clicking on items onscreen. The *software* is what makes the hardware work or lets you get things done, such as writing documents with Microsoft Word or playing a Solitaire game. Think of the hardware as being like your television set, and think of the software as being like the shows that you watch on it.

The hardware on your laptop consists of

➡ **A central processing unit (CPU),** which is the very small, very high-tech semiconductor *chip* (integrated circuit) that acts as the brains of your computer. The CPU is stored in your laptop along with the other nuts and bolts of your computer.

➡ **A monitor,** which displays images on its screen similar to the way your TV screen displays programs. Your computer monitor shows you, for example, the Microsoft Windows 8.1 Desktop, a video you watch at an online entertainment site, or a document in a software program. Today, some laptops sport touchscreen monitors, which allow you to use your finger on the screen to provide input to the computer.

➡ **A keyboard,** which is similar to a typewriter keyboard. In addition to typing words and numbers, you can use a keyboard to give the computer commands such as selecting text or objects, copying, and pasting.

➡ **A touchpad,** which you also use to give your computer commands, but this little device offers a more tactile way to provide input. You move your laptop cursor on the screen by using a built-in pointing device, which might be in the form of a touchpad or a small button. Slide your fingertip around the touchpad.

This moves a pointer around onscreen. You position this pointer on an onscreen button or menu name, for example, and then click the left or side of your touchpad, which causes an action. You can also tap and drag your fingertip to select text or an object to perform an action on it (such as deleting a file or making a line of text bold). You also have the option of attaching a physical wireless mouse to your laptop; a small transmitter which you place in a USB port on your laptop enables the mouse input.

➠ **A webcam and speakers, and probably a microphone,** are likely to be built in to your laptop. A webcam allows you to produce video images you can share during video phone calls and instant messaging sessions. Speakers play back sounds, and a built-in microphone allows you to record audio files.

➠ **Ports to attach peripherals,** such as a printer or scanner. Your laptop comes with slots (called *ports*) where you plug in various peripherals (additional hardware). The type of port you'll use most often is called a USB port; it's a small slot useful for plugging in small sticks called *flash drives* on which you can store data, or devices that typically today sport a USB connector (such as digital cameras and smartphones).

Software (also known as *programs* or *applications*) is installed on your laptop hard drive, which resides in the laptop casing. Here are a few basics about software:

➠ **You use software to get your work done, run entertainment programs, and browse the Internet.** For example, Quicken is a financial-management program you can use to balance your checkbook or keep track of your home inventory for insurance purposes.

➠ **Some programs come preinstalled on your laptop; you can buy and install other programs as you**

need them. Computers have to have an operating system installed to be of any use at all because an operating system runs all the other programs. Also, some programs are included with your operating system — such as WordPad, a simple word processing program, which comes with Windows 8.1. But you're not limited to pre-installed software. You can purchase other software or download free software programs from the Internet. For example, you can find Skype (a free program that enables you to make online phone calls using your laptop) in the Windows Store or on the Internet and install it on your laptop yourself.

➡ **You can uninstall programs you no longer need.** Uninstalling unwanted programs helps to free up some space on your laptop, which helps it perform better.

➡ **Software programs called *utilities* exist to keep your laptop in shape.** An antivirus program is an example of a utility used to spot and erase computer viruses from your system. Your *operating system* (such as Windows 8.1, the operating system on which the steps in this book are based) also includes some utilities, such as Disk Cleanup to free up wasted space on your hard drive or the Windows Defender program. Windows Defender protects your laptop from unwanted intrusion by malicious programs called *spyware*. See Part V for details about using utilities.

Select a Type of Laptop

Just as there are many styles of shoes or mobile phones, you can find several styles of laptops. Some are smaller and more portable, whereas others are essentially desktop replacements with large screens and a bit of heft. Some use different operating systems to make everything run, and some excel at certain functions such as working with graphics or playing games. This task explains some features you should consider when choosing a laptop.

➡ **Operating system (OS):** An OS is the software that allows you to start and shut down your computer and work with all the other software programs, manage files, and connect to the Internet. Windows is probably the most common computer operating system, and this book focuses mainly on its features.

However, Mac laptops from Apple are also very popular. These use Apple-specific software including the Mac operating system, and many software applications written for Windows are also available for the Mac. You can also set up your Mac to run the Windows operating system, which gives you the best of both worlds.

Some computers run on a freely available operating system called Linux, which has functionality similar to Windows. Chromebooks from Google use the Linux-based Chrome operating system and come pre-loaded with lots of Google apps.

➡ **Computer design:** A *laptop* is a portable computer, weighing anywhere from two to ten pounds. The thinnest and lightest ones (as light as two pounds) are called *ultrabooks*. Touchscreen laptops allow you to write on the screen with a special stylus, or use an onscreen keyboard. The monitor, keyboard, and touchpad are built in to a laptop. Note that if the monitor is damaged, you have to pay quite a bit to have it repaired, or you can hook it up to an external monitor.

Figure 2-1 shows (from left to right) a laptop and ultrabook. Laptops are perfect if you want to use your computer mainly away from home or you have little space in your home for a larger computer. Consider their design and weight when purchasing a laptop.

Figure 2-1

➡ **Pictures and sound:** If you work with a lot of *visual elements* (for example, photographs, home movies, or computer games), consider a laptop that has a good graphics card. Games often involve sound, so a high-end sound card might also be useful. Laptops with more sophisticated sound and image capabilities are often referred to as *gaming* or *multimedia* models, and they typically require a large-capacity hard drive to handle these functions. Because the capabilities of these cards change all the time, I don't give you exact specifications for what's considered high-end; instead, ask the person you're buying the laptop from whether the system can handle sophisticated sound and graphics.

One clue that the model has better support for higher-end graphics is if it has a *discrete* (that is, a card separate from the CPU) graphics card versus one built in to the CPU (called *integrated graphics*).

Tablets such as iPad and Kindle Fire HD and Microsoft Surface offer many computing capabilities, such as reading and working on simple documents, connecting to the Internet to send and receive e-mail, playing games, listening to music, and so on. However, they have relatively small touchscreens (with a touchscreen, you provide input with your finger or a stylus), onscreen keyboards, which can be a bit challenging to use, no mouse, and often less in the way of file-management capabilities. If you just want to browse the web, read e-mail, listen to music, and play games, a tablet could be a way to go. If you want a broader range of capabilities with a larger screen size and can handle toting around a machine that weighs a few pounds, a laptop is the way to go. Many people have both a laptop and a tablet, and it's easy to share files and settings between them. They do complement each other nicely if that approach fits your budget.

Choose a Version of Windows

As mentioned in an earlier task, your laptop's operating system (software that runs all the programs and organizes the data on your computer) will be one of your first choices. This book focuses on computers running the current version of Windows, which is called Windows 8.1. Windows 8 and 8.1 have been a radical departure from previous Windows operating systems, so if you opt for an earlier version of Windows, such as Windows 7, you would need to buy the Windows 7 edition of this book.

Windows 8.1 comes in two different versions for home and small business users. The two versions of Windows 8.1 are

➠ **Windows 8.1:** Includes entertainment tools such as Windows Media Center for playing music and movies. If you want to do more than look at photos, you'll find that this version of Windows 8.1 is good at working with design and image manipulation programs such as Photoshop. Also, if you choose a laptop, be aware that Windows 8.1 includes great features for managing the battery power of your computer. If you consider yourself primarily a home user, you should consider this version of Windows 8.1.

➡ **Windows 8.1 Enterprise:** Is great for small businesses or if you work from home. This version of
Windows has ultimate security features and you can
also use a Media Pack add-on with this version to get
richer multimedia features.

Determine a Price Range

You can buy a laptop for anywhere from about U.S. $299 to $5,000 or
more, depending on your budget and computing needs. You may start
with a base model, but extras such as a larger monitor or higher-end
graphics card can soon add hundreds to the base price.

You can shop in a retail store for a laptop or shop online using a
friend's computer (and perhaps get his help if you're brand new to
using a computer). Consider researching different models and prices
online and using that information to negotiate your purchase in the
store if you prefer shopping at the mall. Be aware, however, that most
retail stores have a small selection compared to all you can find online
on a website such as Newegg (www.newegg.com).

Buying a laptop can be confusing, but here are some guidelines to
help you find a laptop at the price that's right for you:

➡ **Determine how often you will use your computer.** If
you'll be working on it eight hours a day running a
home business, you will need a better-quality laptop
to withstand the use and provide good performance.
If you turn on the computer once or twice a week, it
doesn't have to be the priciest model in the shop.

➡ **Consider the features that you need.** Do you want
(or have room for) a heftier laptop with an 18-inch
monitor? Do you need the laptop to run very fast
and run several programs at once, or do you need to
store tons of data? (Computer speed and storage are
covered later in this chapter.) Understand what you
need before you buy. Each feature or upgrade adds
to your laptop's price.

➡ **Shop wisely.** If you shop around, you'll find that the price for the same laptop model can vary by hundreds of dollars at different stores. See if your memberships in organizations such as AAA, AARP, or Costco make you eligible for better deals. Consider shipping costs if you buy online, and keep in mind that many stores charge a restocking fee if you return a laptop you aren't happy with. Some stores offer only a short time period in which you can return a laptop, such as 14 days.

➡ **Buying used or refurbished is an option, though new laptops have reached such a low price point that this might not save you much.** In addition, technology goes out of date so quickly that you might be disappointed with buying an older model which might not support newer software or peripheral devices such as Bluetooth headphones. Instead, consider going to a company that produces customized, non-name-brand laptops at lower prices — perhaps even your local computer repair shop. You might be surprised at the bargains you can find (but make sure you're dealing with reputable people before buying).

➡ **Online auctions such as eBay are a source of new or slightly used laptops at a low price.** However, be sure you're dealing with a reputable store or person by checking reviews that others have posted about them or contacting the Better Business Bureau. Be careful not to pay by check (this gives a complete stranger your bank account number), but instead use the auction site's tools to have a third party such as PayPal handle the money until the goods are delivered in the condition promised. Check the auction site for guidance on staying safe when buying auctioned goods.

Some websites, such as Epinions (`www.epinions.com`), allow you to compare several models of laptops side by side. Others such as Nextag (`www.nextag.com`) allow you to compare prices on a particular model from multiple stores. For helpful computer reviews, visit sites such as CNET (`www.cnet.com`) or Epinions.

Select Monitor Features

Monitors are the window to your computer's contents. A good monitor (also known as a *screen*) can make your computing time easier on your eyes. The crisper the image, the more impressive the display of your vacation photos or that video of your last golf game will be.

Consider these factors when choosing your laptop:

➡ **Size:** Monitors for the average laptop user come in several sizes, from tiny 9-inch screens on smaller laptops to 28-inch screens on desktop replacement models. Laptops with larger screens are typically more expensive. A laptop with a larger monitor takes up more space on your desk than a laptop with a smaller monitor.

➡ **Image quality:** The quality can vary greatly. You will see terms such as LCD (liquid crystal display; also referred to as *flat panel*), flat screen, brightness, and resolution.

Look for a laptop with an LCD monitor, preferably with a screen (see **Figure 2-2**) that reduces glare.

➡ **Resolution:** A monitor's resolution represents the number of pixels that form the images you see on the screen. The higher the resolution, the crisper the image. You should look for a laptop that can provide at least a 1,024 × 768 pixel resolution.

Figure 2-2

➡ **Touchscreen technology:** Windows 8.1 provides support for using a touchscreen interface, which allows you to use your fingers to provide input by tapping or swiping on the screen itself. If you opt for a touchscreen device, you can still use your keyboard and mouse to provide input, but touchscreen technology can add a wow factor when performing tasks such as using painting software, browsing the web, or flipping the pages in an electronic book (e-book).

Opt for Longer Battery Life

Because you're likely to use your laptop away from home now and then, the amount of time it retains a battery charge can be important. Though many laptops still only last a couple of hours on one charge, newer models are beginning to offer battery lives of six to ten hours and technologies to extend battery life even more are evolving at a rapid pace.

 The most popular type of battery for laptops today is Lithium Ion (LiON). Nickel Metal Hydride (NiMH) is an older technology with much less capacity.

Check the battery life rating when looking at a laptop and decide if you might need more hours, for example, to use the laptop on a long airplane flight, if the power goes out for hours in your area during storms, or for other situations when power just won't be available.

Choose an Optical Drive

You've probably played a movie from a DVD from your local video store or from services such as Netflix. Laptops can also read data from or play movies or music from DVDs or store data on them (called *burning*). Your laptop is likely to come with an *optical drive*, which is a small drawer that pops out, allowing you to place a DVD in a tray, push the drawer back into the laptop, and access the contents of the DVD. If you buy a software program, it may come on a CD or DVD, so you also need this drive to install software. However, very small laptops such as ultrabooks have no DVD drives to keep their size and weight down. In that case, you can buy an external DVD drive and plug it into a port on your laptop.

When you buy a laptop with a built-in DVD drive or use an external drive, keep these things in mind about optical drives:

- ➡ **DVDs versus CDs:** DVDs have virtually replaced CDs as the computer storage medium of choice, but you might still find a CD floating around with music or data on it that you need to read. For that reason, you might want a DVD/CD combo drive.

- ➡ **DVD drives:** DVD drives are rated as read (R), write (W), or read-writable (RW). A *readable* DVD drive only allows you to only look at data on your discs, but not save data to them. A *writeable* DVD drive allows you to save data (or images, or music) to discs. A *read-writeable* DVD drive lets you both read and write to DVDs.

- ➡ **DVD standards:** In the earliest days of DVDs, there were two different standards, + and –. Some drives could play DVDs formatted + but not those formatted –, for example. Today, you should look for a DVD drive that is specified as +/– so that it can deal with any DVD you throw at it.

➡ **Blu-ray discs:** If you want to be able to play the latest optical discs, get a laptop with a Blu-ray player. Blu-ray is a great medium for storing and playing back feature-length movies because it can store 50GB, which is the size of most movies.

One of the first things you should do when you buy a laptop, if it doesn't come with recovery discs, is to burn recovery discs you can use if you have to restore the laptop to its factory settings. You might need to do this, for example, if a virus corrupts your system data. Your laptop should offer this as an option when you first start it, but if it doesn't, check your laptop help system or the manufacturer's website to find out how to burn recovery discs, which allow you to return your system to factory settings if you have a major crash.

So much can be done from the Internet today, such as downloading and installing software and streaming video movies, that many people can do without a DVD drive. Check out Chapter 18 for more about working with online services and programs.

Understand Processor Speed and Memory

Your laptop contains a processor stored on a computer chip. The speed at which your laptop runs programs or completes tasks is determined in great measure by your computer processor speed. Processor speed is measured in *gigahertz* (GHz). The higher this measurement, the faster the processor. I won't quote the speed you should look for because these chips are constantly getting smaller and more powerful. However, when you shop, you probably shouldn't consider anything lower than 2 GHz. Higher numbers give the best performance. Factor that into your decision, depending on your needs.

In addition, computers have a certain amount of storage capacity for running programs and storing data. You'll see specifications for RAM and hard-drive data storage capacity when you go laptop shopping. Again, the specific numbers will change, so the rule of thumb is to look for a laptop with higher RAM numbers if you feel you need more storage capacity.

⟶ **RAM is the memory needed to simply access and run programs.** RAM chips come in different types, including DRAM, SDRAM, and the latest version, DDR2. Look for a minimum of 1 gigabyte (GB) of RAM for everyday computing.

⟶ **RAM chips are rated by *access speed*, which relates to how quickly a request for data from your system can be completed.** You might see RAM speed measured in megahertz (MHz). Today, 800 MHz could be considered an acceptable access speed. Note that there are two common RAM types — SRAM and DRAM, with DRAM being the more efficient.

⟶ **Your hard drive has a certain capacity for data storage measured in gigabytes (GB).** These days, you should probably look for a minimum of a 250GB hard drive, but hard drives can come with a range of huge capacities, with the largest being measured in *terabytes* (TB, measured in thousands of gigabytes).

⟶ **Your laptop requires some RAM to run the operating system.** Windows 8.1 requires 1GB of main memory for a 32-bit system and 2GB for a 64-bit system. It also requires 16GB of hard drive space for a 32-bit system and 20GB for a 64-bit system. Check your computer user guide to find out which system you have.

⟶ **Your processor has multiple cores.** Most processors today are multiple-core processors, such as the i3, i5, and i7 processor lines from Intel. *Multiple core* means that two or more processors are involved in reading and executing software instructions as you use your laptop. Those with two processors are called *dual-core*, those with four processors are called *quad-core*, and processors with six cores are referred to as *hexa-core*. The bottom line with cores is that the more you have, the faster your laptop can process instructions because all the cores can be working at once, making multitasking possible. (*Multitasking* is when you're running several programs at once, for example, playing music, downloading files from the Internet, running an antivirus scan, and working in a word processor — all at the same time.)

Determine How You'll Connect to the Internet

You have to decide how you'll connect to the Internet. You can use a dial-up connection over a standard phone line or pay a fee to get a broadband connection such as DSL. (Check with AARP to find out if they offer discounted connections in your area.) However, if you want a wireless connection that picks up a signal in range of a wireless home network, or have a laptop and want to access certain public networks called hotspots, you have to be sure to buy a laptop with wireless capabilities (and luckily, most new model laptops have these). Here's how these connections work:

→ **Dial-up:** If you intend to use a dial-up connection (that is, connect over your phone line), your laptop has to have a dial-up modem either built in or in an external model. Dial-up connections can be very slow, and while you're using them you can't use your phone to make or receive calls. I discourage using dial-up unless you absolutely have to.

→ **Wireless:** These connections require that you have a laptop equipped with wireless capability. You can access the Internet wirelessly through a wireless network set up in your home, or when you're near a wireless *hotspot* (a place that offers wireless service), and many hotspots are available at public places such as hotels, airports, and restaurants. You can also subscribe to a Wireless Wide Area Network (WWAN) service from a mobile phone provider to tap into its connection, or use a technology called *tethering* to connect via your smartphone's 3G or 4G connection. Check laptop models to be sure they are wireless-enabled. There are various techy standards for wireless, such as 802.11a, b, or g. The very latest standard to look for is 802.11n, which delivers better wireless performance.

➡ **Broadband:** These connections typically come through a DSL (digital subscriber line) or cable modem in your home. In both cases, you pay a fee to a provider, which might be your phone company or cable company. DSL works over your phone line but doesn't prohibit you from using the phone when you're online. Cable runs over your cable TV line and is a bit faster than DSL, although connections can be less dependable. Both are considered *always-on* connections, meaning that you don't have to wait to dial up to a phone connection or connect to a wireless network — you're always connected.

 See Chapter 16 for more about setting up your Internet connection.

Buy a Customized Laptop

You can buy prepackaged laptops online or in an electronics store. An alternative is to buy a customized laptop. Companies such as Toshiba (see **Figure 2-3**) and Gateway offer customized laptops. When you buy the laptop, you can pick and choose various features, and the provider will build the system for you.

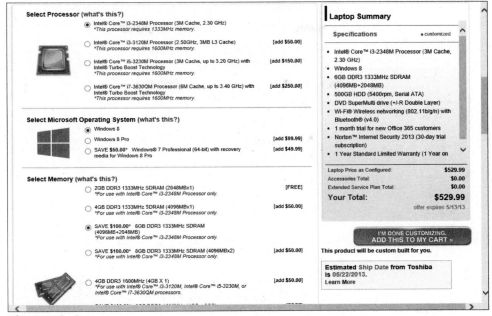

Figure 2-3

Here are some of the variables you'll be asked about when you purchase a customized system, many of which are discussed in this chapter:

➥ Type and speed of processor

➥ Amount of RAM or hard drive capacity

➥ Installed software, such as a productivity suite like Microsoft Office or Microsoft Works, or a premium version of an operating system

➥ More sophisticated graphics or sound cards

➥ Peripherals such as a printer or the addition of a wireless mouse

➥ Larger or higher-end monitor

➥ Wireless capability

➥ Warranty and technical support

These choices can add to your final price, so be sure you need an option before you select it. Most of these companies provide explanations of each item to help you decide.

Setting Up Your Laptop

After you unpack your new laptop, you may need help getting it set up. Here I cover the basics: installing and charging your laptop battery; turning the computer on and off; setting up and logging on to Windows 8.1; mastering the basic use of your touchpad, becoming familiar with some basic keystroke shortcuts, and, if you have a touchscreen, learning to use it.

Next, you can set up the date and time in your computer's internal clock so they match your time zone, and you can apply daylight saving time settings. Finally, you get to work with your user accounts. Windows allows you to create multiple user accounts; each account saves certain settings and allows you to control each user's files and folders separately. When a user logs on with a particular user account, it's like accessing a unique personal computer.

Here, then, are the procedures that you can follow to get going with your laptop and Windows 8.1.

Install and Charge the Battery

Your laptop comes with a battery that you should insert and charge when you first take the laptop out of the box. The battery is a rectangular affair (similar to the one shown in **Figure 3-1)** that slips into the bottom of your laptop.

 Note that tablet models are typically sealed so that your battery is not accessible; if yours is one of those, you don't have to insert a battery; just plug the tablet in to charge the battery.

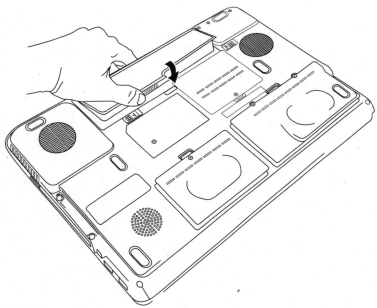

Figure 3-1

It's a good idea to charge your battery completely when you first plug it in, which could take several hours. Follow these instructions to do that:

1. Locate the plug in your laptop packaging. (It's usually a two-piece cable; one half of the cable has a large, boxy transformer on one end that plugs in to the other half.)

2. Plug one end of the cable into a wall outlet and the other into the round power connection port on your laptop. Your user's manual should indicate where this connection is located (usually on the back or near the back of the right or left side of the laptop).

3. When you turn your laptop on (see the next task), you'll find a small icon on the Windows Desktop screen in the taskbar (usually called the Battery Meter icon) that looks like a standard battery with a plug next to it. Click this Battery Meter icon to see whether the battery is charged to 100 percent of its capacity. (If you aren't yet sure how to move around the screen and click, see the upcoming task, "Use the Mouse".)

This icon changes to just a battery (no plug) when the computer isn't plugged in; this battery icon indicates visually how much charge your battery has left before it drains.

Log on to Windows 8.1

When you turn on your laptop, it takes a few moments to load the files it needs to run your operating system. If this is the first time you've started up a brand-new Windows 8.1 computer, you might be asked to make certain simple choices to set it up. If the computer has been used before (perhaps you bought it used, or the person in the store showed you how to start it up and make some settings), you won't see the setup screens; instead, you'll be taken to a user sign-in screen. At that point, if a password has been set for your account, you'll have to type it in; if not, you'll just click a user icon to sign on and go to the Windows Start screen. Here are the steps to turn on your laptop and log on to Windows:

1. With your laptop set up, next time you want to use it start by pressing the power button on your computer to begin the Windows 8.1 start-up sequence.

2. In the resulting Windows 8.1 Welcome screen, click the screen to reveal the sign-in screen.

Enter your password or PIN, if you've set one. (If you haven't set up the password-protection feature for more than one user, you're taken directly to the Windows 8.1 Start screen when you turn on your computer unless you've set your computer up to login directly to the Desktop. (The Start screen and Desktop are two alternate views of your computer's contents. If you have more than one user, you have to choose the one you want to login as.) Windows 8.1 verifies your password and displays the Windows 8.1 Start screen, as shown in **Figure 3-2**.

 For more on adding and changing user passwords, see Chapter 23. After you set up more than one user, before you get to the password screen, you have to click the icon for the user you wish to log on as.

Figure 3-2

Login to the Desktop

By default, when you login to a Windows 8.1 computer, the Start screen appears. If you prefer to use the Desktop interface of Windows 8.1, which is more familiar to users of Windows 7 and earlier versions, you might want to set up your laptop to log in to the Desktop.

1. Log in to Windows 8.1 and click the Desktop tile to go to the Desktop interface.

2. Right-click the taskbar and click Properties on the pop-up menu that appears.

3. Click the Navigation tab (see **Figure 3-3**).

4. Click the check box labeled Go to the Desktop Instead of Start When I Sign In.

5. Click OK.

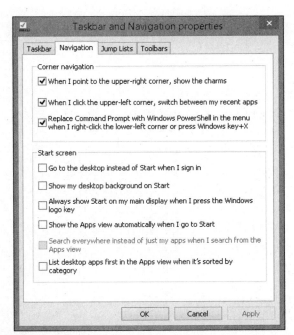

Figure 3-3

Use the Mouse

Unlike using a typewriter, which uses only a keyboard to enter text into documents, with a non-touchscreen computer, you use both a keyboard and a mouse to enter text and give commands to the computer. On a laptop, the mouse device is in the form of a touchpad, a flat rectangle beneath the keyboard which you maneuver by tapping or sliding your forefinger on the pad. On a very few models, the mouse comes in the form of a touch button located somewhere near the center of the keyboard; if you have such a model, check your owner's manual for more about using a touch button.

Though you might have used a keyboard before, a mouse might be new to you, and frankly, it takes a little getting used to. In effect, when you move your finger on the touchpad, a corresponding mouse pointer (a small arrow symbol) moves around your computer screen. You control the actions of that pointer by using the right and left side of the touchpad.

Here are the main functions of a mouse and how to control them:

→ **Click:** When people say "click," they mean that you should press and release the left side of the touchpad.

Clicking has a variety of uses. You can click while you're in a document to move the *insertion point,* a little line that indicates where your next action will take place. For example, in a letter you're writing, you might click in front of a word you already typed and then type another word to insert it. Clicking is also used in various windows to select check boxes or radio buttons (also called *option buttons*) to turn features on or off or to select an object such as a picture or table in your document.

→ **Right-click:** If you click the right side of the touchpad, Windows displays a shortcut menu that's specific to the item you clicked. For example, if you right-click a picture, the menu that appears gives you

options for working with the picture. If you right-
click the Windows Desktop, the menu that appears
lets you choose commands that display a different
view or change Desktop properties.

➡ **Click and drag:** To click and drag, you press and
continue to hold down the left side of the touchpad
and then move your finger to another location (this
is the dragging motion). For instance, you can click
in a document and drag your finger up, down, right,
or left to highlight contents of your document. This
highlighted text is *selected*, meaning that any action
you perform, such as pressing the Delete key on your
keyboard or clicking a button for bold formatting, is
performed on the selected text.

➡ **Scroll:** Many touchpads allow you to swipe down
the right side with your finger to scroll through a
document or website on your screen. Just swipe
down to move through pages going forward, or
swipe up to move backward in your document.

Note that many users of laptops like to use a wireless mouse instead
of the touchpad to provide input to their computers. With a wireless
mouse, you move the physical mouse around your desktop with your
hand and click the right or left side to perform actions described
above. There is typically a scroll wheel in the middle of a wireless
mouse you can use to scroll through a document. You can buy a wireless mouse at any office supply store, plug the small transmitter into a
USB port of your laptop, and then use the mouse instead of the touchpad. Throughout this book, when I say mouse, you can assume that
either your built-in touchpad or a wireless mouse will work with the
steps provided.

Work with a Touchscreen

Although most people don't have touchscreen computers today,
Windows 8.1 was designed to work with this form of input, so I want

to give you an overview of how to use a touchscreen laptop with Windows 8.1.

With a touchscreen laptop, touching the screen with your finger replaces a mouse click. You can tap the screen to select something, to activate features with buttons, and to make a field active so you can type content. Windows 8.1 also offers an onscreen keyboard that touchscreen users can work with to enter text with the tap of a finger.

You can also use your finger to swipe to the right, left, up, or down to move from one page to another (for example, from one web page to another or from one photo to the next in the Gallery app) or to move up or down on a page. Table 3-1 provides some common gestures and what they're used for.

Table 3-1	Touchscreen Gestures for Windows 8.1
Gesture	*Result*
Swipe up or down.	Move up or down on a web page or swipe down from the top edge to close an app.
Swipe left or right.	Move to the right or left; for example, you can swipe left or right on the Start screen to display more app tiles.
Swipe the right edge of the screen.	Display the Charms bar.
Pinch to zoom in or out.	Zoom in or out on a page or the Start screen.
Tap.	Select an item.
Right-click, which involves pressing and holding down the screen.	Hold screen until a small pop-up appears and then lift your finger to reveal the context-specific menu.
Double-tap near the bottom of the screen.	Display the Desktop taskbar.

Windows 8.1 also offers some gestures you can make with your fingers, such as moving your fingers apart and then pinching them

together to minimize elements on your screen, or swiping down from the top of the screen to close an app. If you do own a touchscreen and want to learn more, visit `http://windows.microsoft.com/en-US/windows-8/touch-swipe-tap-beyond` for more information.

Use the Function Keys

On a laptop computer, you might find that in order to save space, some shortcut functions, such as muting sound or brightening your screen, are accessible by using function keys. Here are the basics of function keys:

➡ Function keys run across the top of your laptop keyboard, labeled F1, F2, and so on.

➡ You'll find a key labeled Fn (for Function) near the bottom of your keyboard.

➡ By pressing and holding down the Function key (Fn) and a numbered function key (F1, for example), you can perform actions such as controlling your built-in speaker's volume.

➡ The functions assigned to your laptop's keys vary depending on the model and manufacturer. Check your user's manual to find out the specific functions assigned to your keyboard.

 You'll typically find small icons on your function keys that give you a clue about what the keys do. For example, pressing both the function key that has a little light bulb icon and the up arrow key will probably brighten your screen. Pressing a function key with double, right-pointing arrows (like those you see on a music player) may move you to the next track on an audio DVD.

Use Keyboard Shortcuts

A *keyboard shortcut* refers to a key or combination of keys that you press and hold to perform an action. Many shortcuts involve the Windows key (it's the one near the left bottom corner of your keyboard that sports the Windows logo). For example, you can press and hold the Windows key plus C (Win+C) to display the Charms in Windows 8.1.

In Windows 8.1, keyboard shortcuts can be very helpful to those who don't have a touchscreen computer. Table 3-2 lists some handy shortcuts to know.

Table 3-2	Common Windows 8.1 Keyboard Shortcuts
Key(s)	**Result**
Windows key	Displays the Start screen.
Win+B	Displays the Desktop.
Win+C	Displays the Charms bar.
Win+E	Displays Windows Explorer.
Win+F	Displays the Files search field.
Win+I	Displays the Settings panel.
Win+L	Displays the Lock screen.
Alt+D	Displays the Address field in Internet Explorer 11.
Win+Tab	Displays recently used apps.

Set the Date and Time

1. The calendar and clock on your computer keep good time, but you might have to provide the correct date and time for your location. Press Win+I to display the Settings panel of the Charms bar.

2. In the Settings panel, click Change PC Settings.

3. In the PC Settings panel, click Time & Language (see **Figure 3-4**).

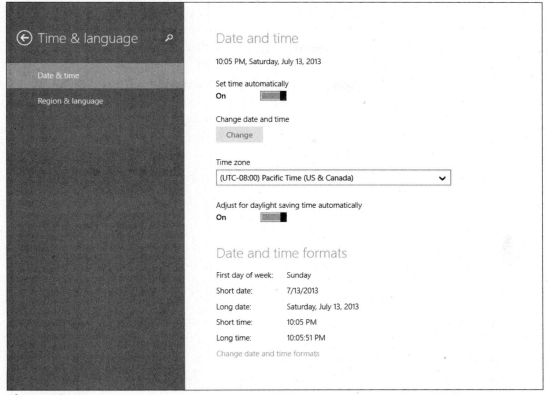

Figure 3-4

4. Click the Time Zone field in the right panel and then choose a time zone from the drop-down list.

5. If you want to, click the Adjust for Daylight Saving Time Automatically On/Off button to turn this feature on or off.

Press the Windows key on your keyboard to return to the Start screen.

 Another way to display the Charms is to move your cursor to the bottom right or top right corner of the Start screen or Desktop.

If you want to set the date and time manually, you can use the Windows 8.1 Desktop Control Panel. This panel is similar to the Control Panel you may have used in previous versions of Windows. On the

Start screen, click the All Apps button and begin typing the words **Control Panel.** Click the Control Panel app that appears in the search results. Click Clock, Language, and Region, and then click the Set the Time and Date link to open the Date and Time dialog box and make settings.

Create a New User Account

1. You must have administrator status to create new users. Press Win+I to display the Settings panel.

2. Click Change PC Settings.

3. In the PC Settings screen shown in **Figure 3-5,** click Accounts and then click Other Accounts.

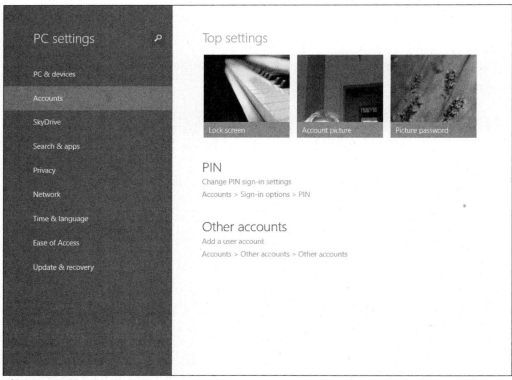

Figure 3-5

4. Click the Add a User button. In the next screen, shown in **Figure 3-6,** enter the user's Microsoft e-mail address (such as a Microsoft Hotmail account ending in @msn. com, @live.com, @hotmail.com, and accounts in the most recent version of Microsoft mail, Outlook.com). By providing this account information, you make it easy to sync settings, files, and apps (programs such as the Weather or Calendar app) among different devices.

If the person doesn't have such an account, click the Sign Up For A New Email Address link under the Email address field and follow instructions to create an account; or if the person doesn't want to use such an account, click the Sign In Without A Microsoft Account link at the bottom of the page and then click the Local Account button on the screen that appears and fill in the user information.

Enter the e-mail address here

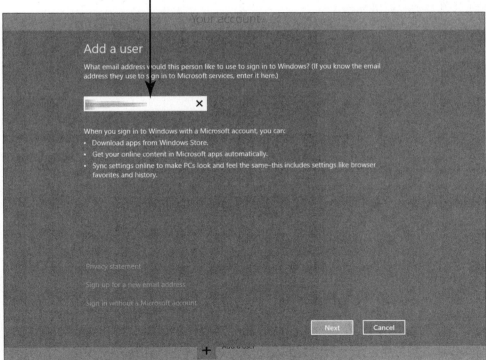

Figure 3-6

5. After you've entered account information in Step 4, click Next.

6. On the next screen, click Finish.

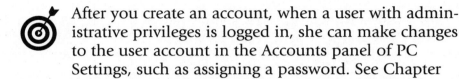 After you create an account, when a user with administrative privileges is logged in, she can make changes to the user account in the Accounts panel of PC Settings, such as assigning a password. See Chapter 23 for information about setting and changing user passwords.

7. If you prefer, you can log in with a four-digit PIN in place of a traditional password. This makes it quicker to sign in. When you've logged in as the user for whom you want to set a PIN, follow the first two steps of the previous task. In the Accounts section of PC Settings, click Sign-in Options in the left panel, and then, under PIN, click the Change button, enter the current password, enter a four-digit PIN and verify it, and then click OK.

 You can set up several user accounts for your computer, which helps you save and access specific user settings and provides privacy for each user's files with passwords.

Switch User Accounts

1. To change to another user account after you've logged in, you can click the logged in user's name in the upper right corner of the Start screen and choose Sign Out.

Alternatively, you can click the Power button in the Settings screen and then click Sleep (see **Figure 3-7**). Windows 8.1 logs off.

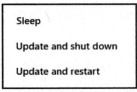

Sleep

Update and shut down

Update and restart

Figure 3-7

2. Drag the welcome screen that appears upward.

3. Click the username you want to log in with, type the password, and press Enter to go to the Windows Start screen.

Change the User Account Type

1. Only users with administrator status can create and make changes to user accounts. You set the type of account (administrator or standard user) for the logged-in user in the Desktop Control Panel. From the Desktop, press Win+I and then click Control Panel.

2. Click User Accounts and Family Safety.

3. Click User Accounts (see **Figure 3-8**).

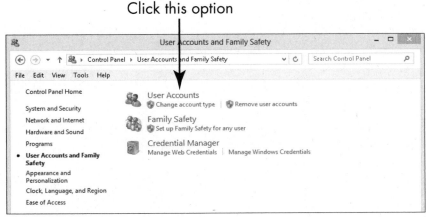

Click this option

Figure 3-8

4. Click Change Your Account Type and enter an administrator password if requested.

5. Select the type of account you want to create in the screen shown in **Figure 3-9**:

- **Standard:** A standard user can access his own account, but can't make the changes to user account settings that an administrator can.

- **Administrator:** An administrator can do things such as creating and changing accounts and installing programs.

Select the account type here

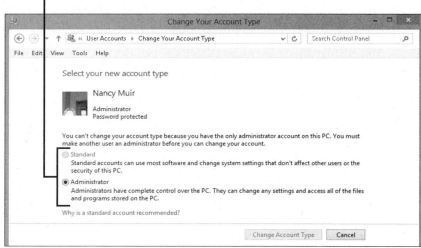

Figure 3-9

6. Click the Change Account Type button and then close the Control Panel.

Shut Down Your Laptop

1. With a Windows 8.1 laptop, you can simply close the lid to put the computer to sleep, saving power and returning you to where you left off when you open the lid and sign in again. To turn off your laptop completely, you need to initiate a shutdown sequence in your operating system instead of simply turning off the power. Press Win+I to open the Settings panel.

2. Click the Power button (refer to **Figure** 3-7). If you prefer to stop your computer running but not turn the power off, click Sleep (or simply close the lid of your laptop). If you want to reboot (turn off and turn back on) your computer, choose Update and Restart. To shut the power off, click Shut Down.

 If your laptop freezes up for some reason, you can turn it off in a couple of ways. Press Ctrl+Alt+Delete twice in a row, or press the power button on your CPU and hold it until the computer shuts down.

 Don't simply turn off your laptop at the power source by pressing the power button. Some processes could be running and Windows might not start up properly the next time you turn it on if you don't follow the proper shutdown procedure by pressing Win+I, clicking the Power button, and choosing Shut Down from the menu that appears.

Managing Power

One of the big differences between a desktop computer and your laptop is that your laptop can run off of a battery. *Battery life,* or the length of time it takes your laptop battery to run out of juice, is getting better all the time — some recent laptop batteries get as many as 9 hours on one charge. A recent comparison by *Laptop Magazine* found very few models that stayed the course for as many as 20 hours. Consider avoiding laptops that get as little as a couple of hours of battery life.

For that reason, it's important that you understand some tools that Windows 8.1 provides to help you manage your laptop power, including these:

➠ Choosing a *power plan,* which has preset timings for actions such as dimming your screen or putting your computer to sleep.

➠ Creating a customized power plan by choosing settings you want.

➠ Adjusting settings for your display that deal with the screen brightness (a brighter screen uses more power), how frequently your screen automatically dims to save battery charge, and so on.

➡ Changing how much time lapses before your laptop automatically goes to sleep — a state that uses minimal power but keeps the currently open documents and programs active (and quickly available to you).

➡ Defining power button functionality gives you some control over what happens when you press the laptop's power button or close the lid.

Choose a Power Plan

1. From the Desktop, press Win+I to open the Settings panel of the Charm bar and then click Control Panel.

2. In the Control Panel window that appears, click Hardware and Sound⇨Power Options.

3. In the Power Options window that appears (see **Figure 4-1**), click the radio button next to a plan to select it. Note that there might be a laptop manufacturer's power plan among your selections; for a High Performance plan, you can click the arrow to the right of Show Additional Plans. The Power Saver plan (in **Figure 4-1,** this is listed in the Plans Shown on the Battery Meter section) causes your computer to go to sleep more frequently and dims the screen brightness. A higher-performance setting will never put the computer to sleep and will have a brighter screen setting. If you run your laptop on a battery frequently, the Power Saver plan is your best bet.

4. Click the Close button to close the window.

There are several options you can use for shutting down or putting your laptop to sleep. See Chapter 3 for more about these.

The recommended plan

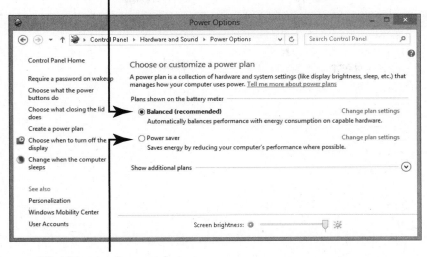

The Power Saver plan

Figure 4-1

Create a Customized Power Plan

1. If the preset power plans don't appeal to you, you can modify one and save it as your own customized power plan. From the Control Panel, click Hardware and Sound⇨Power Options.

2. In the Power Options window that appears, click the Create a Power Plan link on the left side.

3. In the Create a Power Plan window that appears (shown in **Figure** 4-2), select the preset plan that is closest to what you want to create.

4. Enter a name for the plan in the Plan Name text box and click Next.

Select a power plan to customize

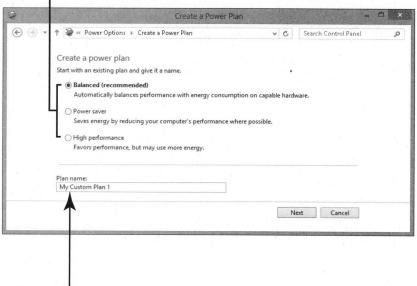

Enter a name for the customized plan

Figure 4-2

5. In the Edit Plan Settings window that appears (see **Figure 4-3**), make settings for how the laptop power functions when plugged in or running off the battery. (See the next two tasks in this chapter for information about changing display settings and changing how quickly the computer goes to sleep.)

6. Click Create to create your new plan. Windows returns you to the Power Options window with your new plan added to the list of power plans.

 If you choose to run your laptop with the power cord plugged in, your laptop could get warm to the touch, even though it has an internal fan. Consider unplugging your laptop occasionally to run off of battery power, or buying a *laptop cooler*, a pad with a fan inside that dispels heat from your laptop when you place it on the pad.

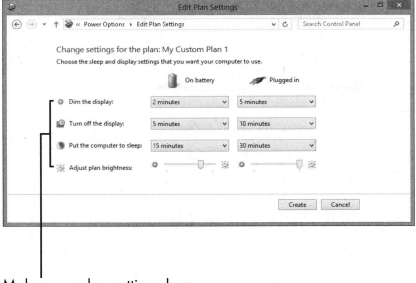

Make your plan settings here
Figure 4-3

Adjust Display Settings

1. From the Control Panel, choose Hardware and Sound. The Hardware and Sound window appears.

2. Click the Power Options link.

3. Find the selected power plan. (There's a dot in the radio button to the left of it.) To the right of the selected power plan, click the Change Plan Settings link.

4. In the Edit Plan Settings window that appears (shown in **Figure** 4-4), modify any of the following display settings to control the laptop when it's running on the battery and you haven't used it for a time — keeping in mind that the longer your screen stays on, the more power it uses:

  • **Turn Off the Display:** Sets the time interval after which the screen goes black.

- **Put the Computer to Sleep:** Indicates the time interval after which the computer sleeps. See the next task for more on this option.

- **Adjust Plan Brightness:** Adjusts the preset screen brightness; a less-bright screen saves power.

5. Click the Save Changes button to close the Edit Plan Settings window and save your new settings.

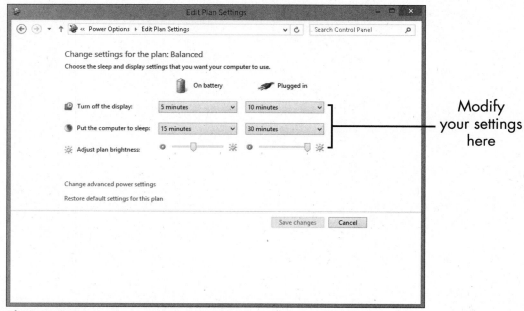

Modify your settings here

Figure 4-4

 You can adjust many settings for screen brightness and modify your power plan in the Mobility Center, a kind of control panel for many common settings such as brightness, volume, and your power plan. From the Control Panel, choose Hardware and Sound, and then click the Windows Mobility Center link.

 You can also use the Brightness setting in the Settings panel that you access from the Charm bar to quickly adjust brightness. Just press Win+I, and then click

Brightness. Use the slider to make the screen brighter or dimmer.

Change How Quickly the Computer Goes to Sleep

1. The third option in the Edit Plan Settings window you saw in the previous task deals with putting your computer to sleep. After a certain period of inactivity, your computer goes to sleep, which can save battery power. To change this setting, from the Control Panel, choose Hardware and Sound. The window shown in **Figure** 4-5 appears.

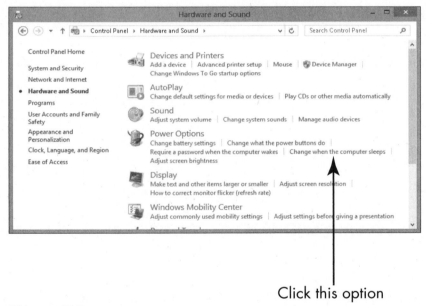

Click this option

Figure 4-5

2. In the Power Options section, click the Change When the Computer Sleeps link.

3. In the Edit Plan Settings window that appears (see **Figure** 4-6), find the Put the Computer to Sleep field and click the arrow in the field in the On Battery column.

4. From the drop-down list, select another setting for when the computer automatically puts itself to sleep. A smaller interval saves battery power, but it might disrupt your work. So choose a setting according to your preferences.

Click to change settings

Figure 4-6

5. Click the Save Changes button to save the new setting.

 You can adjust the Brightness, Screen off, and Sleep settings for your computer through PC Settings if you prefer. Press Win+I from either the Desktop or Start screen and click Change PC Settings⇨PC & Devices⇨ Power & Sleep. Use the Brightness, Screen, and Sleep settings there to control whether to have your device automatically adjust screen brightness, and how long to delay before turning the screen off or putting the PC to sleep.

Define Power Button Functions

1. You can control what happens when you press the Power button, close the computer lid, or press the Sleep button (if your laptop offers one). From the Control Panel, choose Hardware and Sound. The Hardware and Sound window appears.

2. In the Power Options section, click the Choose What the Power Button Does link.

3. In the System Settings window that appears (see **Figure 4-7**), click the When I Press the Power Button or When I Close the Lid fields in the On Battery column. The options that appear include

- **Do Nothing:** Does nothing. You guessed that, right?

- **Sleep:** Essentially pauses your computer, leaving your open programs and documents intact, held in your computer memory. When you awaken your computer, it comes back almost immediately, ready for you to work. Sleep draws a small amount of power.

- **Hibernate:** Saves open programs and documents on your computer hard drive and then turns off your computer so you're not using any power. If you'll be away from your computer for a while but want to return to the items you had opened before quickly, Hibernate is a good choice. Hibernate is usually the default action when you close a laptop lid. Hibernate requires you to log on again when you revive your computer by pressing Enter, clicking the power button, or using your mouse.

- **Shut Down:** Closes any open programs and powers down your computer. You have to turn the power on again to use it — no programs or documents are open when you turn the laptop on again.

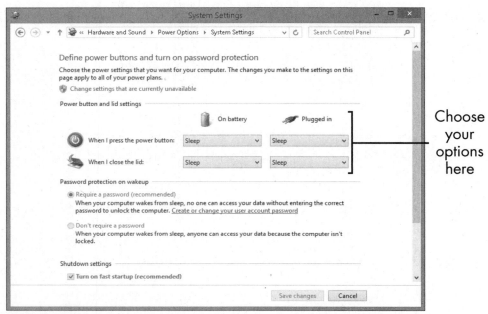

Choose your options here

Figure 4-7

 For security, consider using the Require a Password setting in the System Settings window (scroll down to find this setting in the window shown in **Figure 4-7)** to require that a password be entered to access your computer.

 You can also use the System Settings window to define the power button functions that apply when you have your laptop plugged in to a power source. These are listed in the column to the right of the battery power settings.

Part II

Exploring Windows

Visit www.dummies.com/extras/laptopsforseniors for a list of useful accessories for your laptop.

Getting Around Windows 8.1

Chapter

5

Windows has always used a desktop metaphor for the main Windows screen, a place where you can access all the tools you use to get your work done. However, starting with Windows 8, Microsoft delivered both a Desktop and a Start screen interface (the *interface* is simply what you see on the screen), and you can use either one to complete most of the tasks you need to do. This dual interface, which also exists in Windows 8.1, helps users of earlier versions of Windows to fall back on the more familiar Desktop as they learn their way around the Start screen.

This chapter is an introduction to the things you can do from the Desktop and Start screen and how these two interfaces differ. Along the way, you discover the Charms bar, accessible from either interface and used for accessing various settings, and how to view open apps. You discover how to work with the new integrated Search feature from the Start screen and what the Desktop Start button allows you to do. You also encounter the Recycle Bin accessed through the Desktop; this is where you place deleted files and folders. Finally, you find out how to work with Desktop Windows, create a Desktop shortcut, and close a Desktop program window.

Understand Changes in Windows 8 and 8.1

Beginning with Windows 8 and continuing with Windows 8.1, Microsoft reinvented its operating system. Though these versions share many features that may be new to you, 8.1 brought along its own changes, which I review here.

Beginning with features common to both versions of the operating system, the Start screen (see **Figure 5-1**) is made up of small boxes called *tiles* that represent apps such as Weather, Music, and Mail. The Start screen is a command center for organizing your computer work. You can add or remove tiles to access the apps you use most often.

Figure 5-1

The Start screen is also designed to work well with touchscreen devices, such as touchscreen laptops, because it's graphical in nature. You tap a tile with your finger, and an app opens without you having to select from a menu or list. But you can also easily use a mouse and keyboard to get things done on the Start screen.

You can toggle back and forth from the Start screen to the Desktop (see **Figure** 5-2). On the Desktop, a taskbar offers settings for items such as your computer's date and time, as well as shortcuts to Internet Explorer and File Explorer. If you've used previous versions of Windows, you're familiar with the Desktop. Windows 8.1 added a Start button to the Desktop. Clicking it takes you to the Start screen; right-clicking it produces a menu of commands that allow you to go to Control Panel, Task Manager, or to manage devices and network connections, and much more. Although it's not like the Windows 7 Start button, it does provide access to some functions that were harder to find in Windows 8.

The taskbar

Figure 5-2

In addition to pressing the Start button on the Desktop to go to the Start screen, you can move back and forth between the Start screen and Desktop at any time by pressing the Windows key on your keyboard. If you press this key from within an app, you go to the Start screen.

Work with the Start Screen

1. If the Start screen isn't displayed, press the Windows key on your keyboard to display it.

2. Click the Weather tile (see **Figure 5-3**); the Weather app opens.

Figure 5-3

3. Press the Windows key to return to the Start screen.

4. Hover your mouse over the bottom of the screen and on the scroll bar that appears, click the right arrow to scroll to the right and view more apps (see **Figure 5-4**).

5. Click the left arrow at the bottom of the screen to scroll to the left. You can also simply click on the bar within the scrollbar and drag it right or left to move from side to side of the screen.

6. Move your mouse over the top-left corner of the screen to see thumbnails of open apps (see **Figure 5-5**).

Scroll left

Scroll right

Figure 5-4

Thumbnails of open apps

Figure 5-5

Display the Charms Bar

1. The Charms bar provides another way to go to the Start screen, the integrated Search feature, and various settings for your computer. Move your mouse to the top- or bottom-right corner of the screen to display the Charms bar or press Win+C (see **Figure 5-6**).

Figure 5-6

2. Click the Settings charm to display some of the most commonly accessed settings, such as Volume and Power (see **Figure 5-7**).

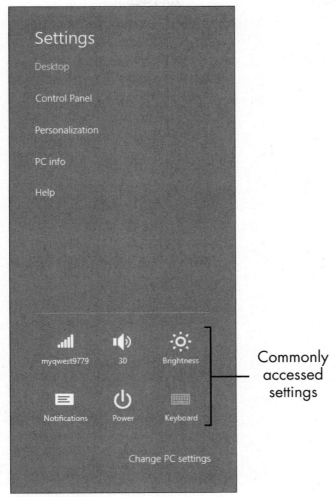

Figure 5-7

3. Move your mouse to the top- or bottom-right corner of the screen again and click the Start charm to display the Start screen.

Search for Files, Settings, and Apps

1. Windows 8.1 has an integrated search feature that you access by simply typing on the Start screen. Typing part of the name of any file, setting, or app brings up the Search screen and any search results. This is the easiest way to open an app that doesn't have a dedicated tile on the Start screen. If you type a topic such as **Winter Olympics** and click it in the results, you get a full search of articles, images, websites, apps, and more that you can browse to your heart's content. With the Start screen displayed, begin to type **air**.

2. On the Search screen that appears (see **Figure 5-8**), click Air France and scroll through the results, which may range from a Wikipedia entry about Air France to articles from the Air France Magazine and travel discount offers.

3. Press the Windows key to go to the Start screen and type **firewall**. This time, click Windows Firewall in the results (see **Figure 5-9**) to go to the Windows Firewall settings in the Control Panel.

4. Press the Windows key on your keyboard to return to the Start screen.

 Desktop apps open in the Desktop, and Windows 8.1 apps (those designed to be accessed through tiles on the Start screen) open full-screen. To test this out, type **taskbar** from the Start screen and then click Taskbar and Navigation. The Taskbar and Navigation Properties dialog box appears on the Desktop.

Figure 5-8

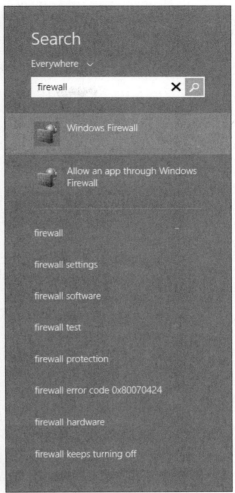

Figure 5-9

View All Apps

1. On the Start screen, click the downward arrow shaped All Apps button in the lower left corner (you may need to move your mouse on the screen for it to appear).

2. Click on the horizontal scrollbar and drag to the right to view more apps (see Figure 5-10).

3. Enter an app name in the Search field to narrow down to a smaller list of apps.

4. Click the app to open it.

Enter an app name here to search

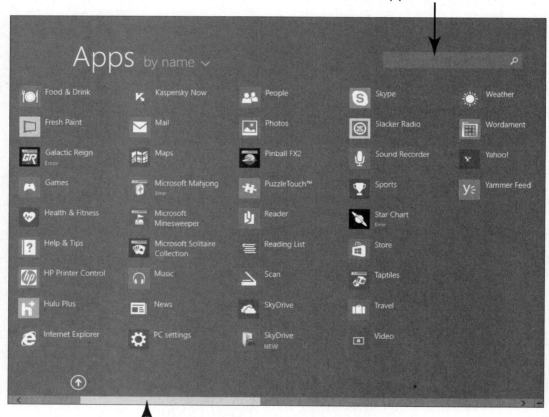

Click and drag to view more apps

Figure 5-10

View Open Apps

1. Move your mouse to the upper-left corner of the Start screen till a thumbnail of an app appears.

2. Drag your mouse down the left edge of the screen to see all open apps (see **Figure 5-11**).

Figure 5-11

3. Click to open the item whose thumbnail appears to the right of the mouse cursor. The app opens.

 The Open Apps feature also works from the Desktop. When you display recently opened apps from the Desktop or Start screen, you see a Start Screen thumbnail at the bottom of the display that you can click to go to the Start screen and hide the open apps display. You can also right-click this Start button to access more commands.

 With open apps displayed, you can also right-click an app and then click the Close command on the menu that appears to close the app.

Pin Items to the Desktop Taskbar

1. If you use certain programs often, you might want to pin them to the jump list area, which is on the left end of the taskbar (see **Figure 5-12**), for easy access. To open any of these items, click its icon. The window for that program opens.

Click any icon to open its item

Figure 5-12

2. To close the window, click the Close button in the top-right corner (with an X on it).

3. To pin additional items to the taskbar, right-click an application on the Desktop and then choose Pin to Taskbar. You can also drag a Desktop icon to the taskbar.

 If you want help creating a Desktop shortcut, see the task, "Create a Desktop Shortcut," later in this chapter.

You can add other functions to the taskbar. Right-click a blank area of the taskbar and choose Properties. Click the Toolbars tab to display it. Click the check box for any of the additional items listed there, such as a browser address bar or links.

Explore the Desktop

You can use various elements of the Desktop to open or manage files, access Windows settings, go online, and more. **Figure 5-13** shows the Desktop and some of the elements on it, including the following:

➡ The **taskbar** displays frequently used programs such as Internet Explorer and File Explorer. It also shows currently open programs; you can click an icon to switch programs.

The Recycle Bin

The taskbar

The notification area

Figure 5-13

➠ The right end of the taskbar, which is called the **noti-fication area,** contains many commonly used functions such as the computer date and time settings, the network connections icon, and the icon to control system volume.

➠ The **Recycle Bin** holds recently deleted items. It will empty itself when it reaches its maximum size (which you can modify by right-clicking the Recycle Bin and choosing Properties), or you empty it manually. Check out the task "Empty the Recycle Bin" later in this chapter for more about this.

➠ **Desktop shortcuts** are icons that reside on the Desktop and provide a shortcut to opening a software program or file, much like tiles on the Start screen. Your computer usually comes with some shortcuts, such as the Recycle Bin and a browser shortcut, but you can also add or delete shortcuts. Double-click a Desktop shortcut to launch the associated program. See the "Create a Desktop Shortcut" task later in this chapter.

 You might be familiar with a set of apps called Gadgets (available in versions of Windows earlier than Windows 8) that you can access from the Desktop. Unfortunately Gadgets are gone, giving way to the brave new world of apps.

The Desktop is always there as you open Desktop program windows to get your work done. If you make a program window as big as it can be (maximize it by clicking the Maximize button in the top-right corner, to the left of the Close button), you won't see the Desktop, but you can go back to the Desktop at any time by shrinking a window (minimizing it by clicking the Minimize button in the top-right corner) or closing the window (clicking the X button in the top-right corner). You can also press Alt+Tab simultaneously and choose the Desktop from the open program icons in the window that appears.

Use the Start Button

The Start button in versions of Windows prior to Windows 8 displayed a panel with recently used applications, commonly used items such as the Control Panel, and shortcuts to folders such as Documents. In Windows 8.1 the Start button returned, but with different functionality and options.

1. From the Desktop, move your mouse towards the bottom of the screen and, on the taskbar that appears, click the Start button in the lower-left corner to go to the Start screen.

2. Click the Desktop tile to return to the Desktop.

3. Drag your mouse towards the bottom of the screen to display the taskbar and right-click the Start button.

4. From the menu that appears (see **Figure** 5-14), click a command to open an app such as Task Manager or Control Panel, to go directly to settings such as device Manager or Network Connections, to run a search or a program, or to access commands to shut down your computer.

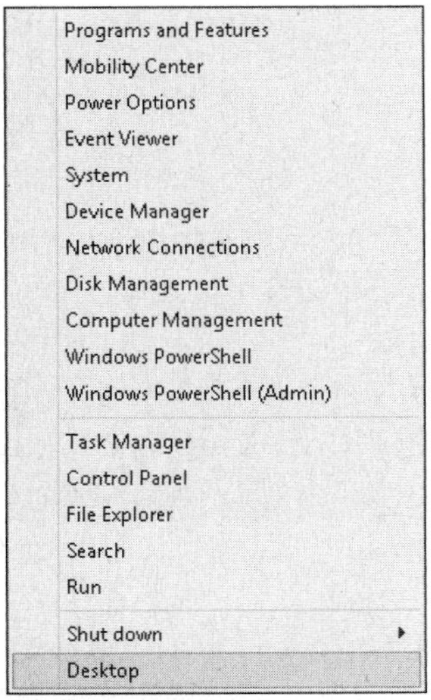

```
Programs and Features
Mobility Center
Power Options
Event Viewer
System
Device Manager
Network Connections
Disk Management
Computer Management
Windows PowerShell
Windows PowerShell (Admin)

Task Manager
Control Panel
File Explorer
Search
Run

Shut down              ▶
Desktop
```

Figure 5-14

Arrange Icons on the Desktop

1. Right-click the Desktop and choose View from the resulting shortcut menu; be sure that Auto Arrange Icons isn't
selected, as shown in **Figure 5-15.** If it is selected, deselect it before proceeding to the next step.

2. Right-click the Windows Desktop. From the resulting
shortcut menu, choose Sort By, and then click the criteria
for sorting your Desktop shortcuts (see **Figure 5-16**).

3. You can also click any icon and drag it to another location
on the Desktop — for example, to separate your favorite
game from other Desktop icons so you can find it easily.

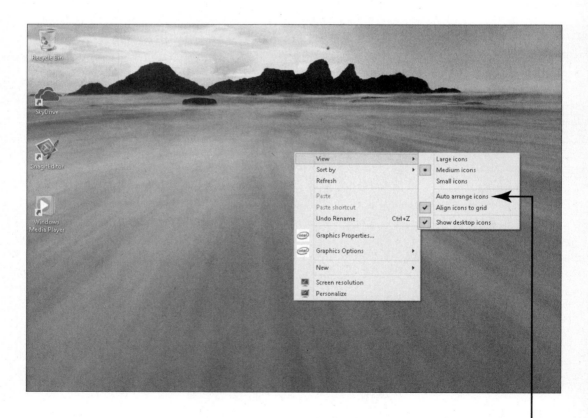

Make sure this isn't selected

Figure 5-15

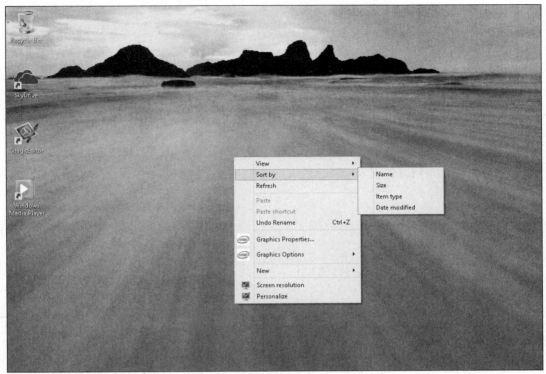

Figure 5-16

If you've rearranged your Desktop by moving items hither, thither, and yon and you want your icons in orderly rows along the left side of your Desktop, snap them into place with the Auto Arrange feature. Right-click the Desktop and then choose View⇨Auto Arrange Icons.

Use the shortcut menu in Step 1 and choose Large Icons, Medium Icons, or Small Icons in the View submenu to change the size of Desktop icons.

Empty the Recycle Bin

When you throw away junk mail, it's still in the house — it's just in the wastebasket instead of on your desk. That's the idea behind the Windows Recycle Bin. Your old files sit there, and you can retrieve

them until you empty it — or until it reaches its size limit and
Windows dumps a few files.

1. Right-click the Recycle Bin icon on the Windows Desktop
and choose Empty Recycle Bin from the menu that
appears (see **Figure 5-17**).

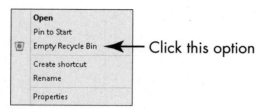 —— Click this option

Figure 5-17

2. In the confirmation dialog box that appears (see **Figure
5-18**), click Yes. A progress dialog box appears, indicating
the contents are being deleted. *Remember:* After you empty
the Recycle Bin, all files that were in it are unavailable to
you.

 Up until the moment you permanently delete items
by performing the preceding steps, you can retrieve
them from the Recycle Bin by double-clicking the
Recycle Bin Desktop icon. Select the item you want
to retrieve and then click the Restore the Selected
Items link on the Manage tab of the Recycle Bin
ribbon.

Figure 5-18

 You can modify the Recycle Bin properties by right-
clicking it and choosing Properties. In the dialog box
that appears, you can change the maximum size for
the Recycle Bin and whether to immediately delete

files you move to the Recycle Bin. You can also deselect the option of having a confirmation dialog box
appear when you delete Recycle Bin contents.

Resize Windows

1. When you open a Desktop application window, it can be
maximized to fill the whole screen, restored down to a
smaller window, or minimized to an icon on the taskbar.
With a Desktop application such as Word or WordPad
open and maximized, click the Restore Down button (the
icon showing two overlapping windows) in the top-right
corner of the program window (see **Figure 5-19**). The
window reduces in size.

 The Restore Down button

Figure 5-19

2. To enlarge a window that has been restored down, to
again fill the screen, click the Maximize button. (***Note:***
This button is in the same location as the Restore Down
button; this button changes its name to one or the other,
depending on whether you have the screen reduced in
size or maximized. A ScreenTip identifies the button
when you rest your mouse pointer on it.)

3. Click the Minimize button (it's to the left of the Restore
Down/Maximize button and looks like a dash or under-
line) to minimize the window to an icon on the taskbar.
To open the window again, just click the taskbar icon.

 With a window maximized, you can't move the window. If you reduce a window in size, you can then
click and hold the title bar to drag the window
around the Desktop, which is one way to view more
than one window on your laptop screen at the same
time. You can also click and drag the corners of a
reduced window to resize it to any size you want.

Find a File or Open an Application with File Explorer

1. File Explorer is a program you can use to find a file or folder by navigating through an outline of folders and subfolders. It's a great way to look for files on your computer. From the Desktop, click the File Explorer button on the taskbar (it looks like a set of folders).

2. In the resulting File Explorer window (shown in **Figure 5-20)**, double-click a folder in the main window or in the list along the left side to open the folder.

Double-click a folder to open it

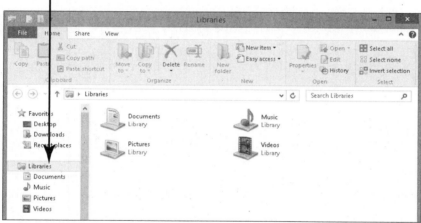

Figure 5-20

3. The folder's contents are displayed. If necessary, open a series of folders in this manner until you locate the file you want.

4. When you find the file you want, double-click it to open it.

 To see different perspectives and information about files in File Explorer, click the View tab and choose one of the following options: Extra Large Icons, Large Icons, Medium Icons, or Small Icons for graphical displays, or choose Details to show details such as the last date files were modified.

Switch between Programs

1. Open two or more programs. The last program that you open is the active program.

2. Press Alt+Tab to reveal all open programs and press Tab to cycle from one open application window to another, as shown in **Figure 5-21**.

Press the Tab key to select another open application in this list

Figure 5-21

3. Release the Alt key, and Windows 8 switches to whichever program is selected. To switch back to the last program that was active, simply press Alt+Tab, and that program becomes the active program once again.

 All open programs also appear as items on the Windows 8.1 Desktop taskbar. Just click any running program on the taskbar to display that window and make it the active program. If the taskbar isn't visible, move your mouse towards the bottom of the Desktop to display it.

Create a Desktop Shortcut

1. Shortcuts are handy little icons you can put on the Desktop for quick access to items you use on a frequent basis. (See the earlier task, "Explore the Desktop," for an introduction to shortcuts.) To create a new shortcut, first click the File Explorer icon on the taskbar.

2. Locate a file or folder and then right-click and choose Create Shortcut, as shown in **Figure 5-22**. A corresponding item labelled "shortcut" appears in the list of files and folders.

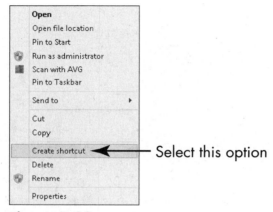

Select this option

Figure 5-22

3. Click and drag the shortcut that appears to the Desktop (see **Figure 5-23**). Double-click the icon to open the file or folder.

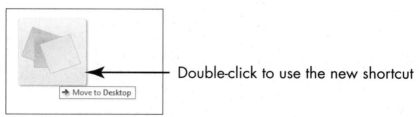

Double-click to use the new shortcut

Figure 5-23

 Another method for sending a shortcut to the Desktop is to select the file or folder in File Explorer, and then with the Home tab displayed, click the Copy to item in the Organize tools and choose Desktop.

To restore your Desktop to its original shortcuts, right-click the Desktop and choose Personalize. Click the Change Desktop Icons link to the left. In the Desktop Icon Setting dialog box that appears, click the Restore Default button, which returns to the original Desktop shortcuts set up on your computer when you bought it.

 You can create a shortcut for a brand-new item by right-clicking the Desktop, choosing New, and then choosing an item to place there, such as a text document, bitmap image, or contact. Then double-click the shortcut that appears and begin working on the new file in the associated application.

Snap Apps

You can use a feature called *snapping* to display an open application reduced in size, which is useful for showing two windows, such as a browser and word processor, side by side. You can also snap an open but reduced in size app upward to restore it to full-screen view.

You can snap windows using either your touchscreen or a mouse. Open an app by clicking the All Apps button on the Start screen and clicking the app in the search results. To snap an open app using your touchscreen, simply do one of two things:

➡ Press your finger on the top of an app displayed full screen and swipe it to the right or left side of your screen; it reduces in size and moves to that side.

➡ Or, press your finger on a reduced app window at the top and snap it upward; it is restored to a full-screen display.

To snap using your mouse, follow the same procedures, but use your mouse cursor rather than your finger. Press your left mouse button on the top of an app window and quickly drag to the right, left, or upward, depending on what result you want to achieve.

Setting Up Your Display

You chose your designer Day Planner, paper clip holder, and solid maple inbox for your real-world desktop, right? Why shouldn't the Windows Desktop and Start screen give you the same flexibility to make things look the way you like? After all, these are the main work areas of Windows, spaces that you traverse many, many times in a typical day. Take it from somebody who spends many hours in front of a computer: Customizing your laptop interface can pay off in increased productivity as well as decreased eyestrain.

The Desktop and Start screen each offer their own customization options. To customize their appearance, you can do the following:

➡ Set up the Desktop, Start screen, and lock screen to display background images and colors.

➡ Set up the Start screen to use the Desktop background, providing a more cohesive look to your computing environment.

➡ Use screen saver settings to switch from the tasks you work on every day to a pretty animation when you've stopped working for a time.

Get ready to . . .

➡ You can modify your *screen resolution* setting, which controls the visual crispness of the images your screen displays. (See Chapter 7 for more about resolution settings that help those with visual challenges.)

➡ Resize and rearrange tiles on the Start screen, and name groups of tiles to organize them in a way that makes sense to you.

Customize Windows' Appearance

When you take your computer out of the box, Windows comes with certain preset, or default, settings such as the appearance of the Desktop and a color scheme for items you see on your screen. During the setup process, you have an opportunity to choose a color scheme for your computer. After setup, here are some of the things you can change about the Windows environment and why you might want to change them:

➡ **Desktop and Start screen backgrounds:** As you work with your computer, you might find that changing the appearance of various elements on your screen not only makes it more pleasant to look at, but also helps you see the text and images more easily. You can change the graphic that's shown as the Desktop background, even displaying your own picture there, or choose from several preset background patterns for the Start screen. You can also set up the Start screen to automatically use the Desktop pattern you choose.

➡ **Screen resolution:** You can adjust your screen resolution to not only affect the crispness of images on your screen but also cause the items on your screen to appear larger, which could help you if you have visual challenges. (See Chapter 7 for more about

Windows features that help people with visual, hearing, or dexterity challenges.)

➡ **Themes:** Windows has built-in Desktop *themes* that you can apply quickly. Themes save sets of elements that include menu appearance, background colors or patterns, screen savers, and even mouse cursors and system sounds. If you choose a theme and then modify the way your computer looks in some way — for example, by changing the color scheme — that change overrides the setting in the theme you last applied.

➡ **Screen savers:** These animations appear after your computer has remained inactive for a specified time. In the early days of personal computers, screen savers helped to keep your monitor from burning out from constant use. Today, people use screen savers to automatically conceal what they're doing from passersby or just to enjoy the pretty picture when they take a break.

Set Your Screen's Resolution

1. Changing screen resolution can make items onscreen easier to see. From the Desktop, right-click the Start button and then click Control Panel in the menu that appears.

2. Click the Adjust Screen Resolution link under Appearance and Personalization.

3. In the resulting Screen Resolution window, click the arrow to the right of the Resolution field.

4. Use the slider (as shown in **Figure 6-1**) to select a higher or lower resolution. You can also change the orientation of your display by making a choice in the Orientation drop-down list (located just below the Resolution option).

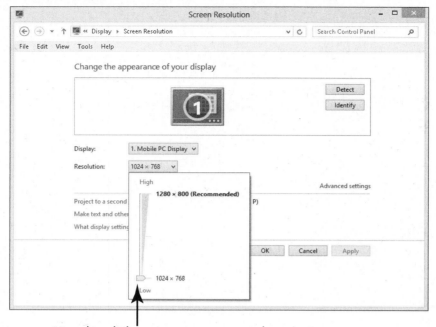

Use the slider to set screen resolution

Figure 6-1

5. Click OK to accept the new screen resolution and then click the Close button to close the window.

Higher resolutions, such as 1400 x 1250, produce smaller, crisper images. Lower resolutions, such as 800 x 600, produce larger, somewhat jagged images. The upside of higher resolution is that more fits on your screen; the downside is that words and graphics are smaller and so can be harder to see.

The Advanced Settings link in the Screen Resolution window displays another dialog box where you can work with color management and monitor settings.

Remember that you can also use your View settings in most software programs to get a larger or smaller view of your documents without having to change your screen's resolution.

Change the Start Screen Background and Color

1. Windows 8.1 offers several preset background patterns and color sets you can choose from the PC Settings. Press Win+I and then click Personalize.

2. Click on a background (see **Figure 6-2**).

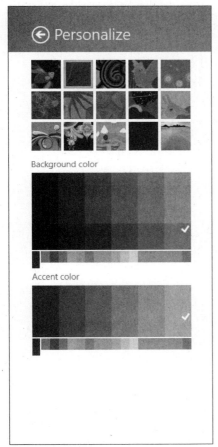

Figure 6-2

3. Click to modify the background color or accent color. Click a background.

4. Click anywhere on the Start screen to close the Personalize panel.

Staring at a screen, especially smaller laptop screens, can be hard on the eyes. Some colors are easier on the eyes than others. For example, green is more restful to look at than purple. Choose a color scheme that's pleasant to look at and easy on the eyes!

Use the Desktop Background on the Start Screen

1. If you want a more cohesive look in your computing environment, consider using the Desktop background on the Start screen. Once you make this setting, if you change the Desktop background it will be reflected on the Start screen. From the Desktop, right-click on the taskbar and choose Properties.

2. Click the Navigation tab (see **Figure 6-3**).

3. Select the Show My Desktop Background on Start check box.

4. Click OK.

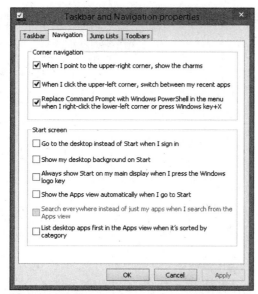

Figure 6-3

Change the Lock Screen Picture

1. You can choose a Windows 8.1 picture for your lock screen (the screen that appears when your computer goes to sleep) or use one of your own pictures for the lock screen background. Press Win+I and then click the Change PC Settings link.

2. Click Lock Screen (see **Figure 6-4**).

3. Click one of the pictures displayed, or click Browse to choose another picture.

4. If you chose to browse for one of your own pictures, from the Pictures folder that's displayed, click a picture to use. If the picture is located in another folder, click the Go Up link to browse other folders.

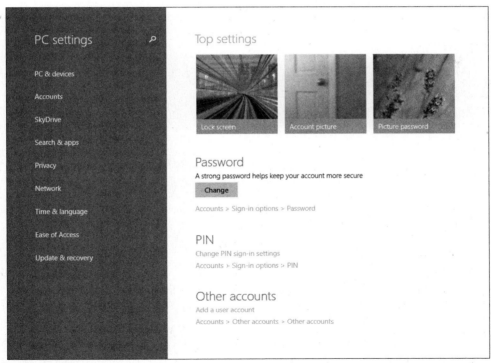

Figure 6-4

5. Click the Choose Image button.

 You can also choose a few apps that you want to keep running when your lock screen appears. On the Lock Screen tab, scroll down and click one of the plus signs to display the apps that are available to display, such as Weather or Mail.

Change Your Account Picture

1. Windows 8.1 allows you to assign a unique picture to each user account you create. When you perform these steps, you should be logged in as the user for whom you want to change the account picture; see Chapter 3 for more about this procedure. Press Win+I and then click the Change PC Settings link.

2. Click Accounts (see **Figure 6-5**).

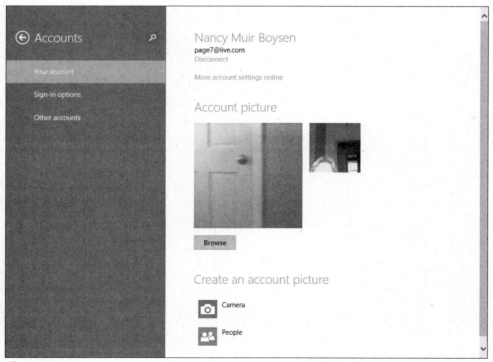

Figure 6-5

3. At this point, you can do one of two things:

- **Click the Browse button** and choose a picture from the files that appear (see **Figure 6-6**); click the Go Up link to explore other folders on your computer. Click the picture and then click the Choose Image button to apply it to the active account.

- **Click the Camera button** and, in the Camera app that opens (see **Figure 6-7**), snap a picture of a person or object near your computer's *webcam* (a built-in camera device). Click the screen to take the picture, and then click the OK button to apply it to the active account.

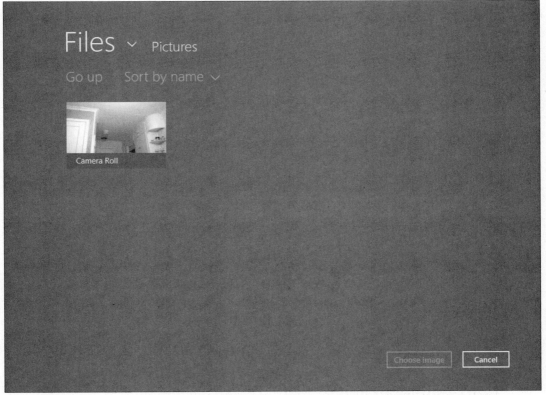

Figure 6-6

Figure 6-7

 Many computers allow you to switch between a front- and a rear-facing camera to give you more options for taking pictures of objects around you. While in the Camera app, just click the Change Camera button to do this, if your computer has two cameras.

Change the Desktop Background

1. You can display a picture or color that appeals to you on your Desktop. Right-click the Desktop and choose Personalize from the shortcut menu.

2. In the resulting Personalization window, click the Desktop Background link to display the Desktop Background dialog box, shown in **Figure 6-8.**

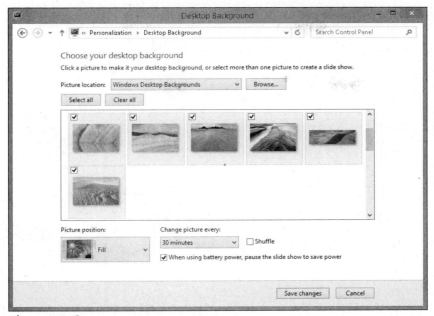

Figure 6-8

3. Select a category of Desktop background options from the Picture Location drop-down menu (see **Figure 6-9**) and then click the image from the background preview list that you want to use. The background is previewed on your Desktop.

4. Click the arrow on the Picture Position list and choose a position for the picture from the thumbnails displayed there. For example, you can have the image fill the entire screen or tile multiple copies of the image across the screen.

5. Click the Change Picture Every setting to have the Desktop background change at a regular interval of your choosing.

6. Click Save Changes to apply the settings and close the dialog box, and then close the Personalization window.

If you apply a Desktop theme (see the next task), you overwrite whatever Desktop settings you've made in this task. If you apply a Desktop theme and then go back and make Desktop settings, you replace the

theme's settings. However, making changes is easy
and keeps your Desktop interesting, so play around
with themes and Desktop backgrounds all you like!

Select a category of background options

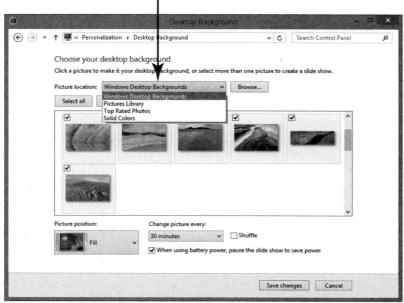

Figure 6-9

Choose a Desktop Theme

1. Themes apply several color and image settings at once.
Right-click the Desktop and choose Personalize. The
Personalization window opens.

2. In the resulting Personalization window, shown in
Figure 6-10, click to select a theme. Theme categories
include the following:

- **My Themes:** Uses whatever settings you have and
saves them with that name.

- **Windows Default Themes:** Offers you the default
Windows theme and themes related to Nature,

Landscapes, Light Auras, and your country of residence.

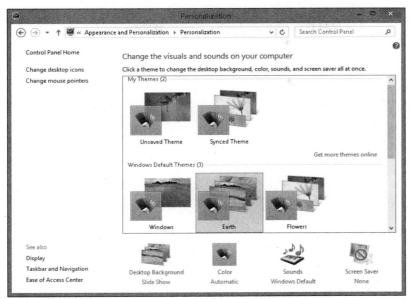

Figure 6-10

3. Click the Close button to close the dialog box.

 Themes save sets of elements that include menu appearance, background colors or patterns, screen savers, and even mouse cursors and sounds. If you modify any of these individually — for example, by changing the screen saver to another one — that change overrides the setting in the theme you last applied.

 You can save custom themes. Simply apply a theme, make any changes to it you like using the various Appearance and Personalization settings options, and then in the Personalization dialog box, right-click the Unsaved Theme and then select Save Theme from the menu that appears. In the resulting dialog box, give your new theme a name and click Save. It will now appear on the My Themes list with that name.

Set Up a Screen Saver

1. If you want an animated sequence to appear when your computer isn't in use for a period of time to protect your data from prying eyes, set up a screen saver. Right-click the Desktop and choose Personalize. In the resulting Personalization window, click the Screen Saver button to display the Screen Saver Settings dialog box, as shown in **Figure 6-11**.

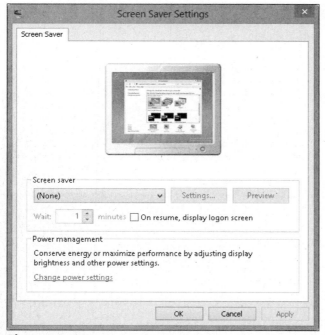

Figure 6-11

2. From the Screen Saver drop-down list, choose a screen saver.

3. Use the arrows in the Wait *xx* Minutes text box to set the number of inactivity minutes that Windows 8.1 waits before displaying the screen saver.

4. Click the Preview button to take a peek at your screen saver of choice (see **Figure 6-12**). When you're happy with your settings, click to stop the preview, and then click OK.

5. Click the Close button in the Personalization window to close it.

 A screen saver can be particularly useful to laptop users because they take their computers into public places. To avoid having the people at the next table in a café or the next seat in an airplane from seeing your personal information, set a screen saver to come on after a brief time of inactivity.

Figure 6-12

Set Lock Screen Apps

1. If you like, you can put some apps on your Lock screen so that you can see, for example, the date and time or weather without having to log on to Windows first.

2. Press Win+I and then click Change PC Settings.

3. Click PC & Devices, and then click Lock Screen on the left (see **Figure 6-13**).

4. The available Lock Screen apps are Alarms, Mail, or Calendar. You can click a plus sign (+) button and add Facebook Touch, which isn't displayed by default.

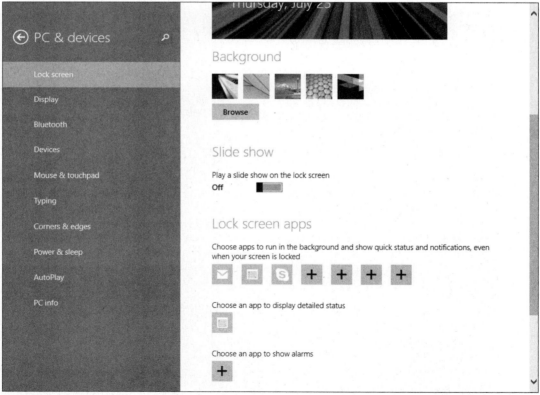

Figure 6-13

To remove an app from display on the Lock screen, click it in the Personalize settings and choose Don't Show Quick Status Here.

Rearrange Tiles

1. If you pin your favorite app to the Start screen and always have to scroll to find it, you might want to move it nearer to the left side of the Start screen. Conversely, if there's an app you only use occasionally, you might want to shift it to the right. To move a tile on the Start screen, right-click the Start screen and then click Customize in the toolbar that appears.

2. Click on a tile and drag it to another location on the screen (see **Figure 6-14**).

3. When the tile is at the location you want, release the mouse.

Figure 6-14

Name Tile Groups

1. If you like, you can name groups of tiles to help you find the tiles you need more easily. Right-click the Start screen and then click Customize in the toolbar that appears.

2. Click on any bar labeled Name Group.

3. Type a name for the group (see **Figure 6-15**) and then click anywhere outside the name bar to save the name. You can also click in a bar to which you've assigned a name and type a new one to change it.

4. Press Escape on your keyboard to return to the Start screen.

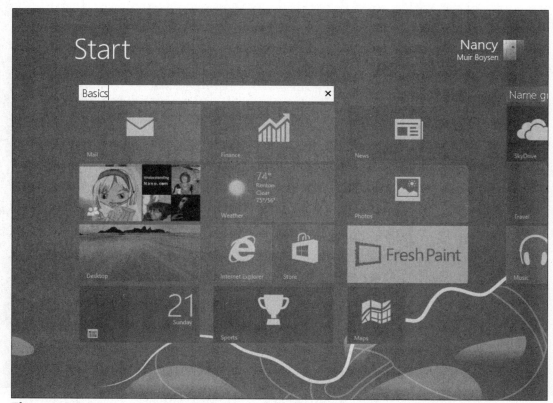

Figure 6-15

Resize Tiles

1. Most tiles allow you to display them in a larger or smaller size; some even offer small, medium, wide, and large settings. This can be especially handy with laptops that have smaller screens when you want to fit more on the Start screen. To show you how this works, right-click the Weather tile.

2. In the settings that appear along the bottom of the screen (see **Figure 6-16**), click Resize, and then click Small from the list that appears. If you had clicked on a smaller tile whose size can be customized, you would click the Larger setting to change it.

Click to resize

Figure 6-16

If there are tiles on your Start screen that you seldom use, you can remove them. Right-click a tile and then click the Unpin from Start button from the tools that appear.

 You can also right-click the Start screen and then click the Customize button. Click any tile and commands appear that you can use to make changes to any number of tiles. To exit the Customize screen so that clicking on tiles opens individual apps, press the Escape button on your keyboard.

Getting Help with Vision, Hearing, and Dexterity Challenges

Although Windows knows how to do a lot of things right out of the box, when it comes to being more accessible to each person using it, it has to be taught how to behave. For example, if you have a vision challenge that requires special help or a larger cursor, or you have difficulty using a keyboard, Windows depends on you to make settings that customize its behavior. This is good news for you because the ability to customize Windows gives you a lot of flexibility in how you interact with it.

Here's what you can do to customize Windows accessibility:

➡ Control features that help visually challenged users work with a laptop, such as setting a higher screen contrast, using the Narrator feature to read the onscreen text aloud, or increasing the size of text onscreen.

➠ Work with the Speech Recognition feature, which allows you to input data into a document using speech rather than a keyboard or mouse.

➠ Modify the touchpad functionality, change the mouse cursor to sport a certain look, or make your cursor easier to view as it moves around your screen.

➠ Work with keyboard settings that make input easier for those who are challenged by physical conditions such as carpal tunnel syndrome or arthritis.

Although this chapter uses mostly settings in the Control Panel, many Ease of Access settings can also be made using the PC Settings accessed from the Start screen Charm bar.

Use Tools for the Visually Challenged

1. You can set up Windows to use higher screen contrast to make things easier to see, read descriptions to you rather than make you read text, and more. From the Desktop, press Win+I and then click **Control Panel**.

2. In the Control Panel window, click the Optimize Visual Display link under the Ease of Access tools.

3. In the resulting Make the Computer Easier to See dialog box (as shown in **Figure 7-1**), select the check boxes for features you want to use:

• **High Contrast:** Turn on the Higher Contrast When Alt+Left Shift+Print Screen Is Pressed setting. High contrast is a color scheme that increases the darkness of darker elements and the lightness of lighter elements so it's easier for your eyes to distinguish one from the other. You can also choose to have a warning message appear when you turn this setting on, or play a sound when it's turned off or on.

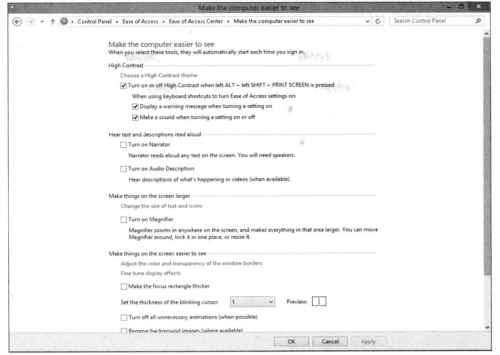

Figure 7-1

You can also go to the PC Settings from the Start Screen Charm bar (Win+I⇨Change PC Settings) and click Ease of Access. In the Ease of Access panel, you can click the Highlight the Cursor setting to turn on this feature that helps you see the cursor on your screen.

- **Hear Text and Descriptions Read Aloud:** You can turn on a Narrator feature that reads onscreen text or an Audio Description feature to describe what's happening in video programs.

You can also go to the PC Settings from the Charm bar to access a setting that allows you to turn the Narrator on or off, or set Narrator to start automatically when you start your computer. You can also choose a voice style, speed, and pitch in these settings.

- **Make Things on the Screen Larger:** If you click Turn on Magnifier, there will be two cursors displayed onscreen. One cursor appears in the Magnifier window, where everything is shown enlarged, and one appears in whatever is showing on your laptop (for example, your Desktop or an open application). You can maneuver either cursor to work in your document. (They're both active, so it does take some getting used to.)

- **Make Things On the Screen Easier to See:** Here's where you make settings that adjust onscreen contrast to make things easier to see, enlarge the size of the blinking cursor (see **Figure 7-2**), and get rid of distracting animations and backgrounds.

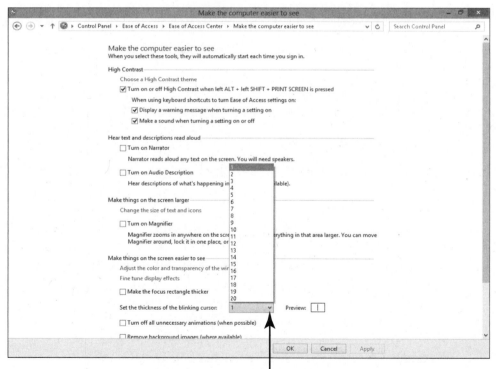

Set the size of the mouse cursor

Figure 7-2

4. When you finish making your settings, click OK to apply them and then click the Close button to close the dialog box.

 If you bought a laptop with a smaller screen and find text is hard to read, don't run out and buy a new laptop. It's possible to connect your laptop to a standalone monitor using a port on the side of the computer (called a VGA port). If you mainly use your laptop at home, this may be a less expensive way to upgrade your screen to a larger size. Consult your laptop manual for instructions on how to hook up to a separate monitor.

Replace Sounds with Visual Cues

1. Sometimes Windows alerts you to events with sounds. If you have hearing challenges, you might prefer to get visual cues. From the Control Panel, choose Ease of Access and then click the Replace Sounds with Visual Cues link.

2. In the resulting Use Text or Visual Alternatives for Sounds window (see **Figure 7-3**), adjust any of the following settings:

- Select the Turn on Visual Notifications for Sounds (Sound Sentry) option so that Windows gives you a visual alert when a sound plays.

- Choose a warning setting for visual notifications. These warnings allow you to choose which portion of your screen flashes to alert you to an event.

- To control text captions for any spoken words, select Turn on Text Captions for Spoken Dialog (When Available). *Note:* This isn't available with some applications.

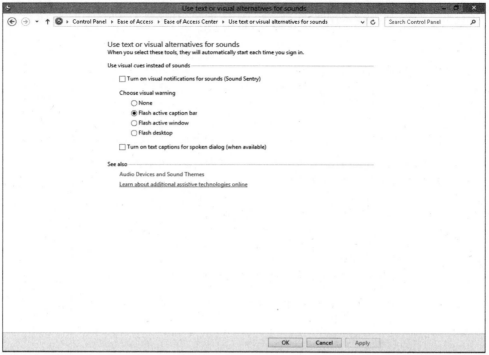

Figure 7-3

3. To save the new settings, click OK, and then click the Close button to close the window.

Visual cues are useful if you're hard of hearing and don't always pick up system sounds that play to alert you to error messages or a device disconnect, but the setting may annoy other users of your laptop. After the setting is turned on, it is active until you go back to the Use Text or Visual Alternatives for Sounds window and turn it off.

This may seem obvious, but if you're hard of hearing, you may want to simply increase the volume of the sound coming out of your speakers. You can modify your system volume by pressing Win+I from the Start screen, and then clicking the Volume button and using the slider that appears to adjust volume up or down. Most laptop keyboards also offer special

volume keys you can click to quickly adjust system sounds.

Make Text Larger or Smaller

1. You can change the size of items and/or text on the Desktop. From the Control Panel, choose Appearance and Personalization. In the resulting window under the Display options, click Make Text and Other Items Larger or Smaller.

2. In the resulting Display window (see **Figure** 7-4), under the Change the Size of All Items heading, click and drag the slider to set the size of text you prefer. Smaller is the default, but you can expand text size to 125 percent with the Medium setting and 200 percent using the Larger setting.

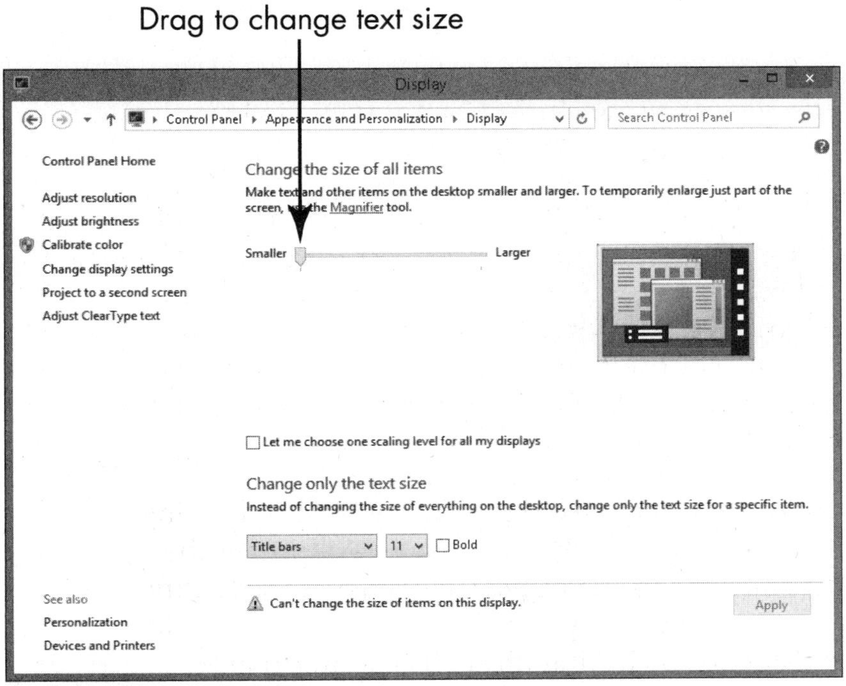

Drag to change text size

Figure 7-4

3. If you only want to change the size of text on your screen, in the Change Only the Text Size section, click the box on the left to choose where the text size should be changed (for example Title Bars, Menus, or Tooltips) and then use the Font Size drop-down menu to choose the size your prefer.

4. Click Apply and then click the Close button to close the window. You'll see the results (see **Figure 7-5,** which shows the Larger setting for all items applied) next time you log on to Windows.

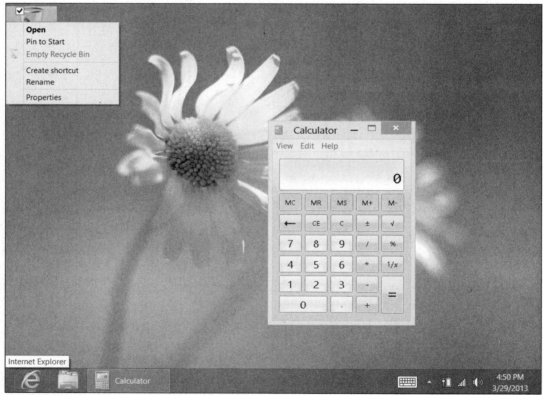

Figure 7-5

Set Up Speech Recognition

1. If you have dexterity challenges from a condition such as arthritis, you might prefer to speak commands using a technology called *speech recognition* rather than type them. If your laptop doesn't have a built-in microphone (most do), plug a headset with a microphone into your laptop headset ports (see your owner's manual if you're not sure where they're located).

2. From the Control Panel, choose Ease of Access⇨Start Speech Recognition.

3. The Welcome to Speech Recognition message appears; click Next to continue. (*Note:* If you've used Speech Recognition before, this message does not appear.)

4. In the resulting Set Up Speech Recognition dialog box (as shown in **Figure 7-6**), select the type of microphone that you're using and then click Next. The next screen tells you how to place and use the microphone for optimum results. Read the message and click Next.

5. In the dialog box that appears (see **Figure 7-7**), read the sample sentence aloud to help train Speech Recognition to your voice. When you're done, click Next. A dialog box appears, telling you that your microphone is now set up. Click Next.

 During the Speech Recognition setup procedure, you are given the option of printing out commonly used commands. It's a good idea to do this, as speech commands aren't always second nature!

Figure 7-6

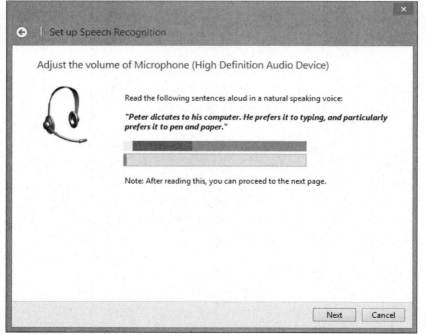

Figure 7-7

6. In the resulting dialog box, choose whether to enable or disable *document review*, which allows Windows to review your documents and e-mail to help it recognize the way you typically phrase things. Click Next.

7. In the next dialog box, choose either Manual Activation mode, where you can use a mouse, pen, or keyboard to turn the feature on; or Voice Activation mode, which is useful if you have difficulty manipulating devices because of conditions such as arthritis or a hand injury. Click Next.

8. In the resulting screen, if you wish to view and/or print a list of speech recognition commands, click the View Reference Sheet button and read about or print reference information, and then click the Close button to close that window. Click Next to proceed.

9. In the resulting dialog box, either leave the default setting of running speech recognition selected when you start up, or click the Run Speech Recognition at Startup check box to disable this feature. Click Next.

10. The final dialog box informs you that you can now control the laptop by voice, and it offers you a Start Tutorial button to help you practice voice commands. Click that button, or click Skip Tutorial to skip the tutorial and leave the Speech Recognition setup.

11. The Speech Recognition control panel appears. (See **Figure** 7-8.) Say "Start listening" to activate the feature if you used voice activation in Step 7, or click the Start Speech Recognition button (it looks like a microphone) if you chose manual activation in Step 7. You can now begin using spoken commands to work with your laptop.

 To stop Speech Recognition, click the Close button on the Speech Recognition Control Panel. To start the Speech Recognition feature again, from the Control Panel choose Ease of Access and then click the Start Speech Recognition link. To learn more about Speech Recognition commands, click Speech Recognition from the Ease of Access panel and then click the Take Speech Tutorial link in the Speech Recognition Options window.

The Speech Recognition control panel

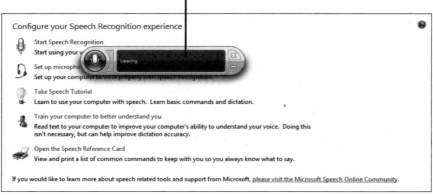

Configure your Speech Recognition experience

Start Speech Recognition
Start using your v...

Set up microph...
Set up your computer to work properly with Speech Recognition.

Take Speech Tutorial
Learn to use your computer with speech. Learn basic commands and dictation.

Train your computer to better understand you
Read text to your computer to improve your computer's ability to understand your voice. Doing this isn't necessary, but can help improve dictation accuracy.

Open the Speech Reference Card
View and print a list of common commands to keep with you so you always know what to say.

If you would like to learn more about speech related tools and support from Microsoft, please visit the Microsoft Speech Online Community.

Figure 7-8

Modify How Your Keyboard Works

1. If your hands are a bit stiff with age or you have carpal tunnel problems, you might look into changing how your keyboard works. From the Control Panel, choose Ease of Access and then click the Change How Your Keyboard Works link.

2. In the resulting Make the Keyboard Easier to Use dialog box (see **Figure 7-9**), make any of these settings:

- **Turn on Mouse Keys:** Select this option to control your cursor by entering keyboard commands. If you turn on this setting, click the Set Up Mouse Keys link to specify settings for this feature.

- **Turn on Sticky Keys:** Select this option to enable keystroke combinations (such as Ctrl+Alt+Delete) to be pressed one at a time, rather than simultaneously.

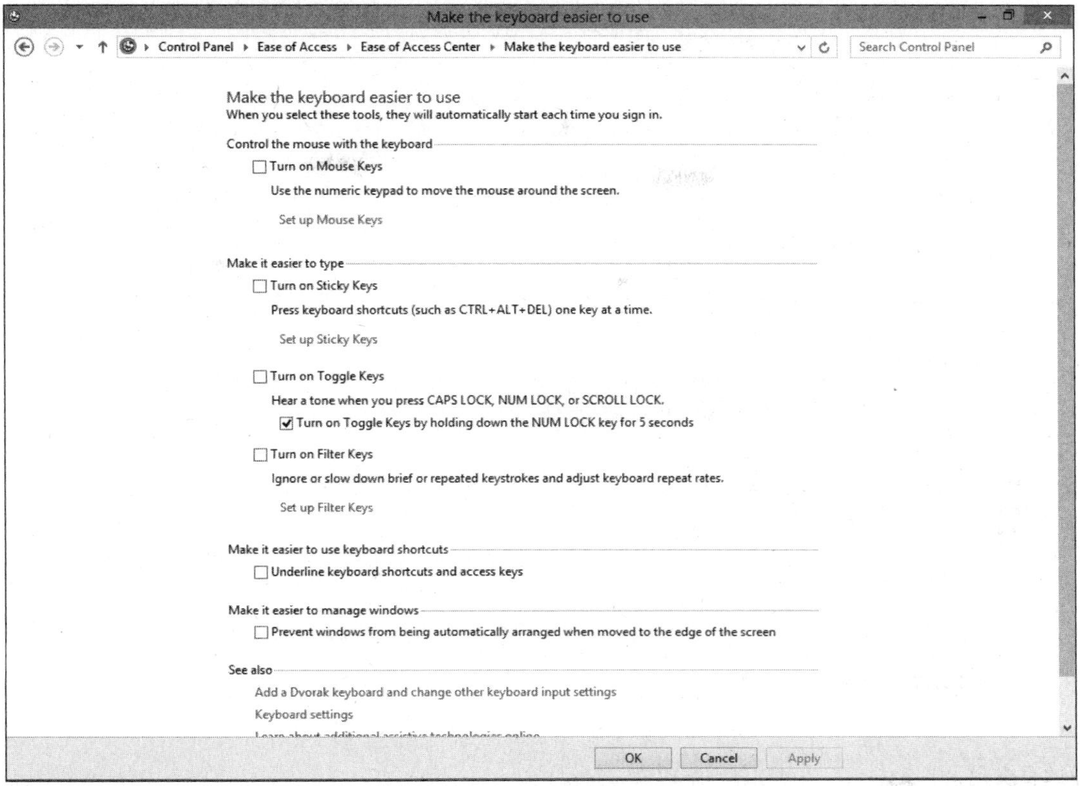

Figure 7-9

- **Turn on Toggle Keys:** You can set up Windows to play a sound when you press Caps Lock, Num Lock, or Scroll Lock (which I do all the time by mistake!).

- **Turn on Filter Keys:** If you sometimes press a key very lightly or press it so hard that it activates twice, you can use this setting to adjust repeat rates to adjust for that. Use the Set Up Filter Keys link to fine-tune settings if you make this choice.

- **Make It Easier to Use Keyboard Shortcuts:** To have Windows underline keyboard shortcuts and access keys wherever these shortcuts appear, click this setting.

- **Make It Easier to Manage Windows:** If you want to avoid windows shifting automatically when you move them to the edge of your screen, use this setting.

3. To save the new settings, click OK, and then click the Close button to close the Ease of Access Center.

You can click the Learn about Additional Assistive Technologies Online link at the bottom of the keyboard settings window to go to the Microsoft website and discover add-on and third-party programs that might help you if you have a visual, hearing, or input-related challenge.

Keyboards all have their own unique feel. When you buy a laptop, it's important to try different keyboards to see whether one works better for you than another. See Chapter 2 for more about selecting the right laptop.

Use the Onscreen Keyboard Feature

1. Some people have problems pressing the keys on a regular keyboard. If you have a touchscreen laptop, there's often a handy onscreen keyboard feature that appears when you tap in a text entry area that you can tap with your fingers. If you have a non-touchscreen laptop, Windows offers its own onscreen keyboard you can use by clicking its (virtual) keys with your mouse. To use the onscreen keyboard, from the Control Panel, choose Ease of Access.

2. In the resulting window, click the Ease of Access Center link to open the Ease of Access Center window. (See **Figure 7-10.**)

Click this link

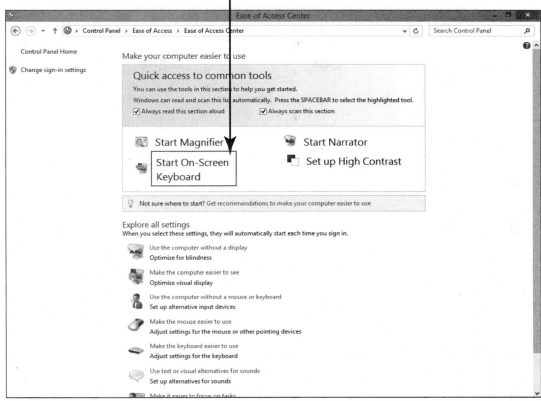

Figure 7-10

3. Click Start On-Screen Keyboard. The onscreen keyboard appears. (See **Figure 7-11**.)

Figure 7-11

4. Open a document in any application where you can enter text, and then click the keys on the onscreen keyboard with your mouse to make entries. (If you have a tablet with a touchscreen and Windows 8.1 operating system, tap the keyboard with your finger.)

 To use keystroke combinations (such as Ctrl+Z), click the first key (in this case, Ctrl), and then click the second key (Z). You don't have to hold down the first key as you do with a regular keyboard.

5. To change settings, such as how you select keys (Typing Mode) or the font used to label keys (Font), click the Options key on the onscreen keyboard. Choose any one of the options shown in the Options dialog box and click OK.

6. Click the Close button on the onscreen keyboard to remove it from your screen.

 You can set up the Hover typing mode to activate a key after you hover your pointer over it for a pre-defined period of time (*x* number of seconds). If you have arthritis or some other condition that makes clicking difficult, this option can help you enter text. Click the Hover over Keys item in the Options dialog box and use the slider to set how long you have to hover before a key is activated.

 The Ease of Access settings in the PC Settings screen offer a setting that has Windows activate keys on a touchscreen keyboard whenever you remove your fingers from the physical keyboard. Press Win+I⇨Change PC Settings⇨Ease of Access to reach this setting.

Set Up Keyboard Repeat Rates

1. Adjusting your keyboard settings might make it easier for you to type, and it can be helpful to people with dexterity challenges. To see your options, in the Control Panel, begin to type **keyboard** in the Search field. In the resulting window, click the Keyboard category link.

2. In the Keyboard Properties dialog box that appears, click the Speed tab (see **Figure 7-12**) and drag the sliders to adjust the two Character Repeat settings, which do the following:

- **Repeat Delay:** Affects the amount of time it takes before a typed character is typed again when you hold down a key.

- **Repeat Rate:** Adjusts how quickly a character repeats when you hold down a key after the first repeat character appears.

 If you want to see how the Character Repeat rate settings work in action, click in the text box below the two settings and hold down a key to see a demonstration.

Figure 7-12

3. Drag the slider in the Cursor Blink Rate section. This affects how fast cursors, such as the insertion line that appears in text, blinks.

4. Click OK to save and apply changes and close the dialog box. Click the Close button to close the Control Panel window.

 If you have trouble with motion (for example, because of arthritis or a hand injury), you might find that you can adjust these settings to make it easier for you to get your work done. For example, if you can't pick up your finger quickly from a key, a slower repeat rate might save you from typing more instances of a character than you'd intended. This is especially helpful for laptops with smaller keyboards, such as netbooks.

Customize Touchpad Behavior

1. To avoid having to click your touchpad too often, you can use your keyboard to move the cursor instead of moving your mouse with your hand, or you can activate a window by hovering your mouse over it rather than clicking. From the Control Panel, choose Ease of Access and then click the Change How Your Mouse Works link. The Make the Mouse Easier to Use dialog box opens (as shown in **Figure 7-13**).

2. To use the numeric keypad to move your cursor on your screen, choose the Turn on Mouse Keys setting. If you turn this feature on, click Set Up Mouse Keys to fine-tune its behavior.

3. Select the Activate a Window by Hovering Over It with the Mouse check box to enable this (pretty self-explanatory!) feature.

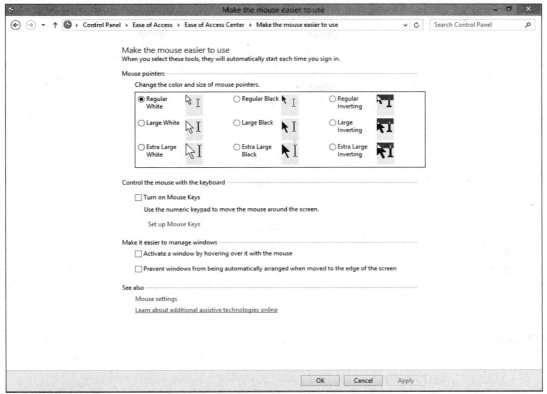

Figure 7-13

4. Click OK to save the new settings and then click the Close button to close the Ease of Access Center.

 If you're left-handed, click the Mouse Settings link in the Make the Mouse Easier to Use window; then, on the Buttons tab, use the Left-handed button to make the right mouse button handle all the usual left-button functions, such as clicking and dragging, and the left button handle the typical right-button functions, such as displaying shortcut menus. This helps left-handed people use the mouse more easily. If you use your computer a lot, it's also recommend that you swap these settings occasionally to avoid carpal tunnel issues.

If you want to modify the behavior of the pointer, from the Control Panel, choose Hardware and Sound➪Mouse (under Devices and Printers). In the Mouse Properties dialog box that appears, click the Pointer Options tab to set the pointer speed (how quickly you can drag the pointer around your screen), activate the Snap To feature that automatically moves the cursor to the default choice in a dialog box, or modify the little trails that appear when you drag the pointer.

 Although some laptop keyboards have separate number pads, many have them embedded in the regular keyboard to save space. Using these embedded keys requires that you press the Fn key on the keyboard and then the letter key where the number you want is embedded. (The numbers are usually included on the key in a different color, such as red or blue.)

 If your touchpad isn't working well for you, consider buying a wireless mouse, similar to the one you use with your desktop computer. You simply plug a transmitter into a USB port on your laptop, and the mouse is active. When using a standard mouse you might want to invest in a mouse pad with a wrist rest to reduce strain that can lead to carpal tunnel syndrome.

Change the Cursor

1. Having trouble finding the mouse cursor on your screen? You might want to enlarge it or change its shape. From the Control Panel, choose Ease of Access and then click Change How Your Mouse Works. In the resulting Make the Mouse Easier to Use dialog box, click the Mouse Settings link.

2. In the resulting Mouse Properties dialog box, on the Pointers tab, as shown in **Figure 7-14,** click to select a pointer, such as Normal Select, and then click the Browse button. (*Note:* This dialog box may have slightly different tabs depending on your mouse model features.) In the Browse dialog box that appears, click an alternate cursor and then click Open.

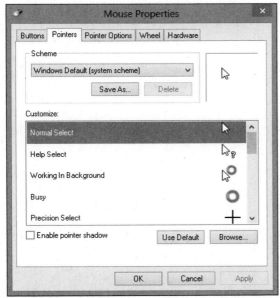

Figure 7-14

3. Click Apply to use the new pointer setting and then click the Close button to close the Mouse Properties dialog box.

 Be careful not to change the cursor to another standard cursor (for example, changing the Normal Select cursor to the Busy hourglass cursor). This could prove slightly confusing for you and completely baffling to anybody else who works on your laptop. If you make a choice and decide it was a mistake, click the Use Default button on the Pointers tab in the Mouse Properties dialog box to return a selected cursor to its default choice.

 You can also choose the color and size of mouse pointers in the Make the Mouse Easier to Use dialog box. A large white or extra large black cursor might be more visible to you, depending on the color scheme you've applied to Windows 8.1.

Setting Up Printers and Scanners

A laptop is a great place to store data, images, and other digital information. Often you need to print that data in the form of documents or change printed text into electronic files you can work with on your laptop. Here are a few key ways to do just that, as discussed in this chapter:

➠ **Printers** allow you to create *hard copies* (a fancy term for printouts) of your files on paper, transparencies, or whatever stock your printer can accommodate. To use a printer, you have to install software — called a *printer driver* — and use certain settings to tell your laptop how to find the printer and what to print.

➠ You use a **scanner** to create electronic files from hard copies of newspaper clippings, your birth certificate, driver's license, pictures, or whatever will fit into/ onto your scanner. You can then work with the electronic files, send them to others as e-mail attachments, or print them. Scanners also require that you install a driver that comes with your scanning machine.

Install a Printer

Read the instructions that came with your printer. Some printers require that you manually install software before connecting them, but others install the needed software automatically and can be connected right away. After reading the instructions, turn on your laptop and then follow the option that fits your needs:

➠ If your printer is a Plug and Play device, connect it and power it on; Windows installs what it needs automatically.

➠ Insert the disc that came with the device and follow the onscreen instructions.

➠ If you have a wireless printer, connect it to your laptop and then open the Control Panel (from the Desktop, press Win+I and then click Control Panel on the Settings panel). Click the Add a Device link in the Hardware and Sound category in the Control Panel window. Windows searches for any newly connected devices; when it finds one, follow the instructions to install it.

Note: In the step that follows the one where you name the printer, you can indicate whether you want to share the printer on your network. You can select the Do Not Share This Printer option to prevent others from using the printer, or you can select the Share Name option and enter a printer name to share the printer on your network. This means that others who belong to your network can see and select this printer to print their documents.

If none of those options is suitable, follow these steps:

1. From the Control Panel, choose Hardware and Sound.

2. In the Hardware and Sound window that appears, click the Advanced Printer Setup under Devices and Printers.

3. Click the link The Printer That I Want Isn't Listed. In the resulting Add Printer window (the first of a series of windows that will guide you through a task) shown in **Figure 8-1**, click the Add a Local Printer or Network Printer with Manual Settings radio button and click Next.

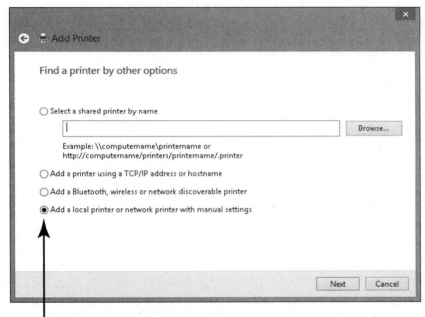

Select this option and click Next
Figure 8-1

4. In the Choose a Printer Port dialog box shown in **Figure 8-2,** click the down arrow on the Use an Existing Port field and select a port, or just use the recommended port setting that Windows selects for you. Click Next.

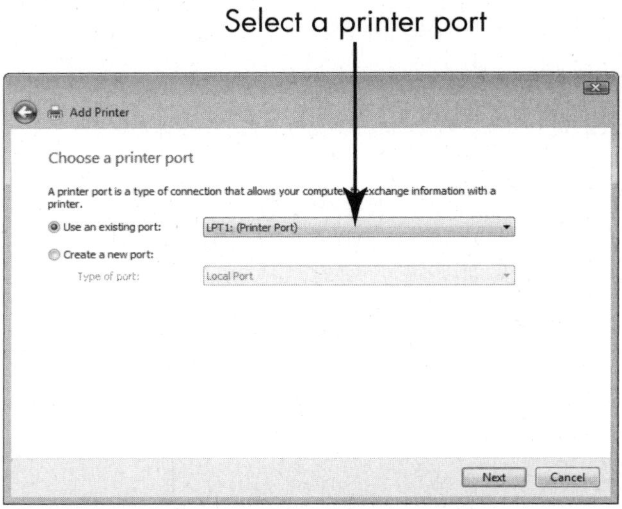

Select a printer port

Choose a printer port

A printer port is a type of connection that allows your computer to exchange information with a printer.

Add Printer

Use an existing port: LPT1: (Printer Port)

Create a new port:

Type of port: Local Port

Next   Cancel

Figure 8-2

5. In the Install the Printer Driver dialog box, shown in **Figure 8-3,** choose a manufacturer and then choose a printer. You then have two options:

    - If you have the manufacturer's disc, insert it in the appropriate CD or DVD drive now and click the Have Disk button. Click Next.

    - If you don't have the manufacturer's disc, click the Windows Update button to see a list of printer drivers that you can download from the Microsoft website. Click Next.

6. In the resulting Type a Printer Name dialog box (see **Figure 8-4**), enter a printer name. Click Next.

7. In the resulting dialog box, click Finish to complete the Add Printer Wizard.

 If you need to print on the go, consider a portable printer. These lightweight (five pounds or less) units don't offer the best print quality, but for quick, on-the-fly printing, they can be useful. See Chapter 2 for more about buying laptop accessories.

Choose a manufacturer   Then choose a printer

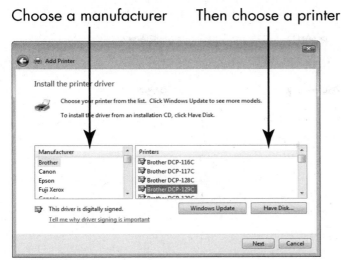

Figure 8-3

Enter a name for your printer

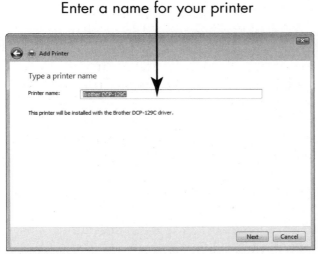

Figure 8-4

Set Up a Wireless Printer

A wireless printer connects to your laptop either through a technology called Bluetooth, which requires devices to be next to each other or, if you have access to a wireless network, using Wi-Fi (available to devices within 50 to 100 feet or so). Here's a rundown of things you should be aware of when setting up your laptop to connect to a wireless printer:

➡ Bluetooth and Wi-Fi are short-range wireless connections (meaning you have to be near the printer to connect to it).

➡ To use a Bluetooth-based wireless printer, you may have to connect a Bluetooth transmitter to a USB port on your laptop. This transmitter is a small device about the size of a stick of gum that transmits a signal to your printer. If you have a Wi-Fi–enabled laptop, you can skip this step.

➡ You should run through the procedure in the previous task to set up the printer in Windows Control Panel and install any required drivers. After you click Advanced Printer Setup in the Hardware and Sound window, click the The Printer That I Want Isn't Listed link, and then choose Add a Bluetooth, Wireless, or Network Printer in the first dialog box that appears and follow the instructions.

➡ The Add a Printer wizard walks you through the process of pairing your laptop and printer; you may need a passcode (provided with your printer) for this.

➡ After you've installed the printer, you should be able to print just as you would with any other kind of printer, but without the hassle of extra wires littering your desk.

If you run into a problem, check your wireless printer's instructions for help.

If you own a printer with Air-Print capability, you can print directly from your iPhone, iPad, or iPod touch device. See your printer's user manual to find out whether your model has this capability and how to use it.

Set a Default Printer

1. You can set up a default printer that will be used every time you print so that you don't have to select a printer each time. From the Control Panel, choose Hardware and Sound.

2. Click Devices and Printers. In the resulting Devices and Printers window, the current default printer is indicated by a check mark (as shown in **Figure 8-5**).

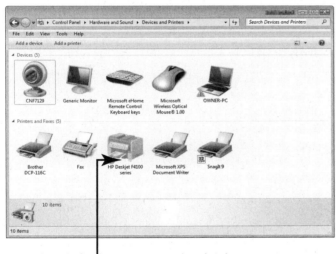

The default printer is checked

Figure 8-5

3. Right-click any printer that isn't set as the default and choose Set as Default Printer from the shortcut menu, as shown in **Figure 8-6**.

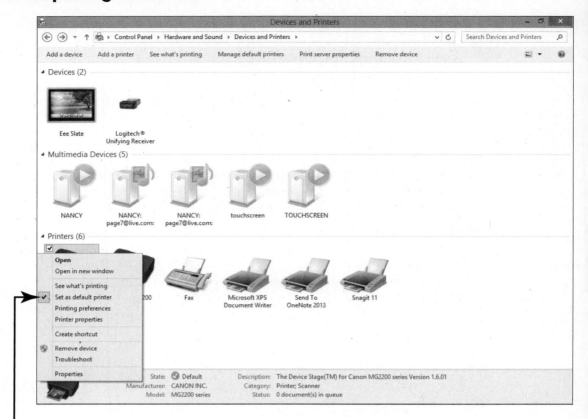

── Choose Set As Default Printer

Figure 8-6

4. Click the Close button in the Devices and Printers window to save the new settings.

To modify printing properties that are available for your particular printer model (for example, whether the printer prints in draft or high-quality mode, or whether it uses color or only black and white), right-click a printer in the Devices and Printers window (refer to **Figure 8-6**) and choose Printing Preferences. This same dialog box is available from most common Windows-based software programs, such as Microsoft Word or Excel, by selecting the Print command and then clicking the Properties button in the Print dialog box.

If you right-click the printer that is already set as the default, you'll find that the Set as Default Printer command will not be available on the shortcut menu mentioned in Step 3.

Set Printer Preferences

1. Your printer might offer you a choice of capabilities — such as printing in color or black and white, printing in draft quality (which uses less ink), or high quality (which produces a darker, crisper image). To modify these settings for all documents you print, from the Control Panel choose View Devices and Printers (in the Hardware and Sound group).

2. In the resulting Devices and Printers window, any printers you have installed are listed. Right-click a printer and then choose Printing Preferences.

3. In the Printing Preferences dialog box that appears (as shown in **Figure 8-7**), click any of the tabs to display various settings, such as Color or Paper. (See **Figure 8-8.**) Note that different printers might display different choices and different tabs in this dialog box, but common settings include the following:

- **Color/Grayscale:** If you have a color printer, you have the option of printing in color or not. The grayscale option uses only black ink. When printing a draft of a color document, you can extend the life of your color ink cartridge (which is more expensive to replace or refill than the black one) by printing in grayscale.

- **Quality:** If you want, you can print in fast or draft quality (these settings might have different names depending on your manufacturer) to save ink, or you can print in a higher or best quality for your finished documents. Some printers offer a dpi (dots per inch) setting for quality — the higher the dpi setting, the better the quality.

- **Paper Source:** If you have a printer with more than one paper tray, you can select which tray to use for printing. For example, you might have 8 ½ x 11 paper (letter sized) in one tray and 8 ½ x 14 (legal sized) in another.

- **Paper Size:** Choose the size of paper or envelope you're printing to. In many cases, this option displays a preview that shows you which way to insert the paper. A preview can be especially handy if you're printing to envelopes or label sheets and need help figuring out how to insert them in your printer.

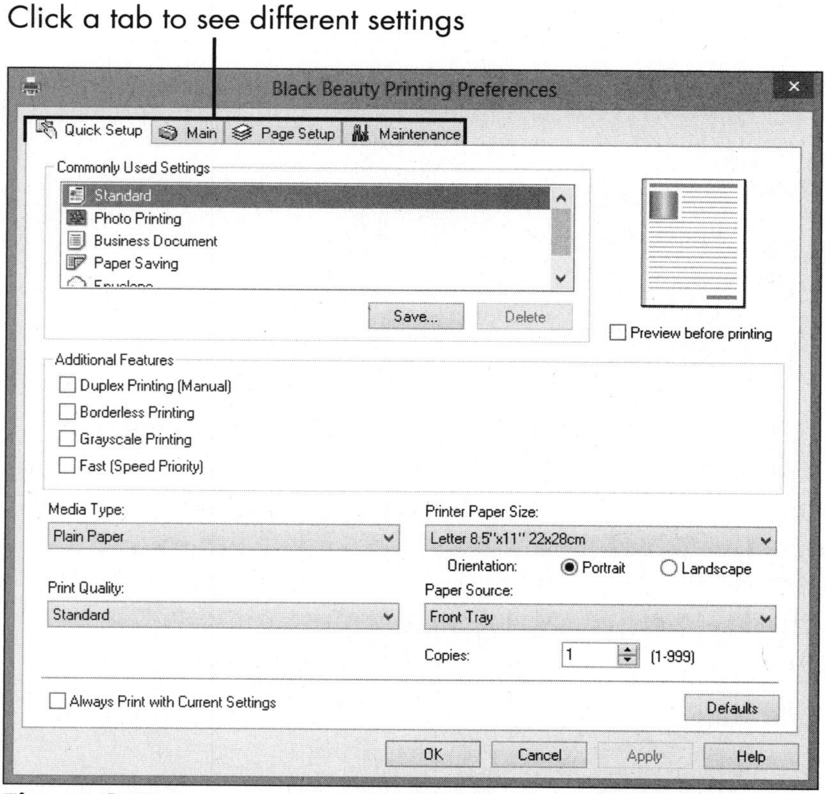

Click a tab to see different settings

Figure 8-7

Click OK to save settings

Figure 8-8

4. Click the OK button to close the dialog box and save settings and then click the Close button to close other open Control Panel windows.

The settings in the Printing Preferences dialog box might differ slightly depending on your printer model; color printers offer different options from black and white ones, for example.

The settings you make using the procedure in this task will become your default settings for all the printing you do. However, when you're printing a document from within a program, such as Microsoft Word, the Print dialog box you display gives you the opportunity to change the printer settings for that document only. See Chapter 11 for information about printing a document.

View Currently Installed Printers

1. Over time, you might install multiple printers; in which case, you might want to remind yourself of the capabilities of each or view the documents you have sent to be printed. To view the printers you have installed and view any documents currently in line for printing, from the Control Panel, choose View Devices and Printers under Hardware and Sound.

2. In the resulting Devices and Printers window (see **Figure 8-9**), a list of installed printers and fax machines appears.

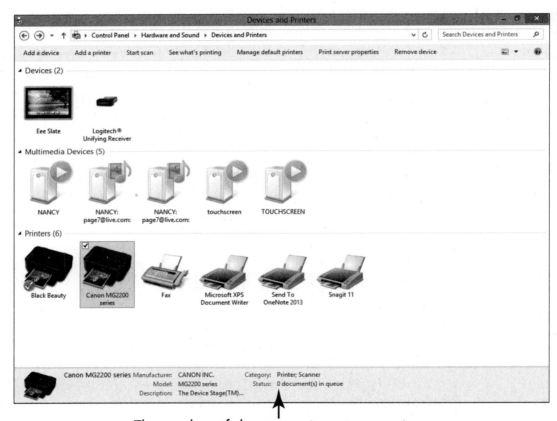

The number of documents in queue to print

Figure 8-9

If a printer has documents in its print queue, the number of documents is listed at the bottom of the window. If you want more detail about the documents or want to cancel a print job, select the printer and click the See What's Printing button at the top of the window. In the window that appears, click a document and choose Document⇨Cancel to stop the printing, if you want. Click the Close button to return to the Devices and Printers window.

3. You can right-click any printer to display a list of options and then choose Properties to see details about that printer, such as which port it's plugged into or whether it can print color copies (see **Figure 8-10**).

Figure 8-10

4. Click the Close button (the red X in the upper-right corner) to close the Devices and Printers window.

Remove a Printer

1. Over time, you might upgrade to a new printer and toss the old one (recycling it appropriately, of course). When you do, you might want to also remove the older printer driver from your laptop so that your Printers window isn't cluttered with printers that you don't use anymore. To remove a printer, from the Control Panel, click View Devices and Printers (in the Hardware and Sound group).

2. In the resulting Devices and Printers window, right-click a printer and choose Remove Device (as shown in **Figure** 8-11). (Or you can select the printer and click the Remove Device button at the top of the window.)

3. In the Remove Device dialog box that appears, click Yes; the Devices and Printers window closes, and your printer is removed from the printer list.

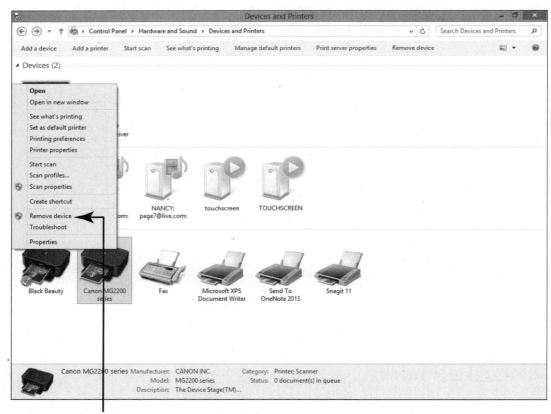

Click Remove Device
Figure 8-11

If you remove a printer, it's removed from the list of installed printers; if it was the default printer, Windows makes another printer you have installed the default printer. You can no longer print to the removed printer, unless you install it again. See the task, "Install a Printer," if you decide you want to print to that printer again.

Install a Scanner

1. Before you can scan documents into your laptop creating electronic versions of them, you need to install the scanner driver so that your scanner and laptop can communicate. Start by connecting the scanner to your laptop's USB port. (See your scanner manual for information about how it connects to your laptop.)

2. Turn the scanner on. Some scanners use Plug and Play, a technology that Windows uses to recognize equipment, install it automatically, and set it up.

If your scanner is Plug and Play–enabled, Windows 8.1 shows a Found New Hardware message on the taskbar notification area (in the lower-right corner of the Desktop) or near the top of the Start screen. Most Plug and Play devices will install automatically; then the message changes to indicate that the installation is complete, and that's all you have to do.

If that doesn't happen, either you're not using a Plug and Play device or Windows doesn't have the driver for that device. Click the Found New Hardware message to proceed.

3. In the resulting Found New Hardware Wizard (this starts only if you don't permit Windows 8.1 to connect automatically to Windows Update), click Yes, This Time Only and then click Next.

4. If you have a DVD for the scanner, insert it in your CD/ DVD drive and click Next. Windows 8.1 searches for your scanner driver software and installs it.

5. Display the Control Panel. In the Search box, type **scanners.** Windows returns a set of links. Click the View Scanners and Cameras link. In the resulting Scanners and Cameras window, click the Add Device button.

6. In the resulting Scanner and Camera Installation Wizard window, click Next. In the next screen of the wizard (see **Figure 8-12**), click your scanner's manufacturer in the list on the left and then click the model in the list on the right.

Select a manufacturer   Then select a model

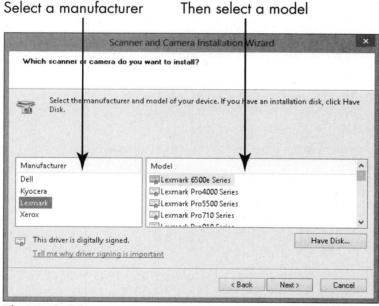

Figure 8-12

7. Follow the wizard directions for the model of scanner you chose in Step 6. Note whether you have a manufacturer's disc (a CD- or DVD-ROM) for your scanner; if you don't have a disc, Windows will help you download software from the Internet. When you reach the end of the wizard, click Finish to complete the installation.

Modify Scanner Settings

1. After you install a scanner, you might want to take a look at or change its default settings — for example, whether you usually want to scan in color or grayscale. To do so, from the Control Panel, click View Devices and Printers under Hardware and Sound.

2. In the resulting Control Panel window, right-click your scanner and choose Properties (see **Figure 8-13**).

3. In the resulting dialog box, review the settings, which might include (depending on your scanner model) color management for fine-tuning the way colors are scanned and resolution settings that control how detailed a scan is performed. (The higher the resolution, the crisper and cleaner your electronic document, but the more time it might take to scan.)

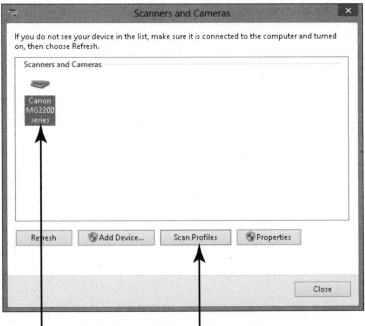

Click a scanner   Then click Scan Profiles
Figure 8-13

4. Click OK to save any changed settings and then click the Close button twice to close the Devices and Printers window.

 When you're ready to run a scan, you place the item to be scanned in your scanner. Depending on your model, the item may be placed on a flat "bed" with a hinged cover or fed through a tray. Check your scanner manual for the specific procedure to initiate a scan (for example, clicking a Scan or Start button). After you begin the scan, your laptop automatically detects it and displays a dialog box that shows you the scan progress and allows you to view and save the scanned item.

Getting Help

*W*ith so many Windows features, you're bound to run into something that doesn't work right or isn't easy to figure out (or that this book doesn't cover). That's when you need to call on the resources that Microsoft provides to help you out.

Through the Help and Support Center, you can get help in various ways, including the following:

➡ **Access information that's stored in the Help and Support database.** You can access this information whether you're online or not. Logically enough, a database contains data; in this case, it contains information about Windows 8.1, organized by topic. You can search for or browse through topics using a powerful search mechanism to find articles by keywords such as *printer* or *e-mail*.

➡ **Read helpful articles.** You can take advantage of several articles that provide insight into working with the Start screen and useful Help & How-To articles on the Windows website.

➡ **Search Microsoft Answers.** Microsoft offers a way to search answers in the Windows Forum to see if somebody else has had a similar problem. You can also ask a question yourself. A Microsoft employee responds and gives you advice when you post a question.

Get ready to . . .

➡ **Invite someone to help you through Remote Assistance.** Get help from another person by using the Windows 8.1 Remote Assistance feature.

Search Windows Help and Support

1. The Help and Support window provides access to a variety of topics. Begin to type **help** from the Start screen and then click Help and Support in the results to display it (see **Figure 9-1**).

2. Click in the Search field, enter a search term, and click the Search button (the button with a drawing that looks like a magnifying glass).

Type "help" here

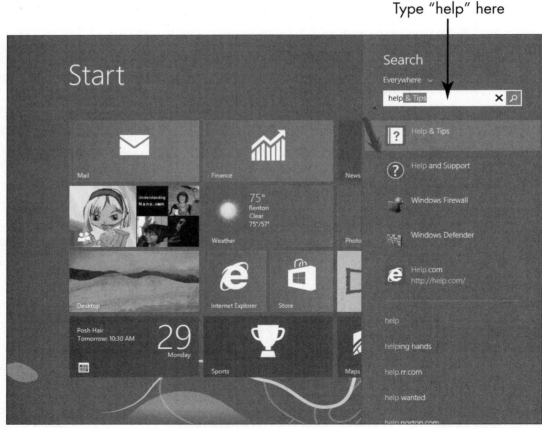

Figure 9-1

3. In the resulting screen shown in **Figure** 9-2, click an article to narrow your search or open an article, depending on the topic.

4. Click the Close button to close the Windows Help and Support window.

 If your search contains one, click a Troubleshoot item (as shown in Figure 9-2) to get a step-by-step walkthrough of possible solutions to common problems. Some troubleshooting topics will even run a check on your laptop to attempt to find a solution specific to your computer. In addition, you may encounter some video links that take you to step-by-step video instruction.

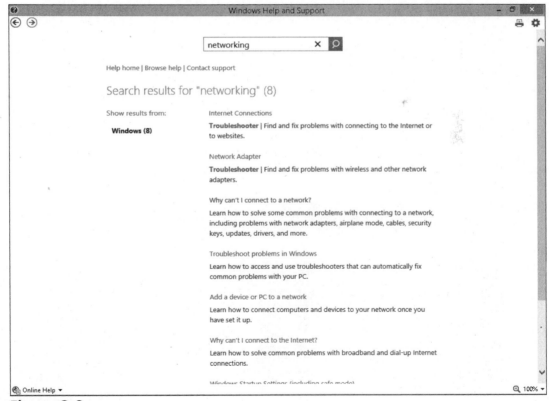

Figure 9-2

If you don't find what you need with Search, consider clicking the Browse Help link in the Windows Help and Support window to display a list of major topics. Those topics may also give you some ideas for good search terms to continue your search.

Get Help Getting Started with Windows 8.1

If you need a basic tutorial on how to use Windows 8.1, consider using the Getting Started section of the Windows website. Here you can find videos, blogs, and articles to help you get started. Press the Windows key to display the Start screen.

1. Begin to type **help** from the Start screen and then click Help and Support in the results to display it.

2. Click the Get Started link (see **Figure 9-3**).

Click to get started

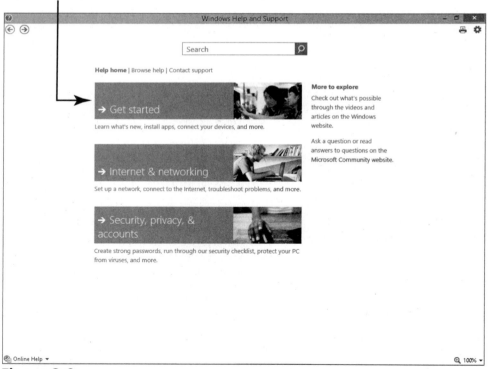

Figure 9-3

3. Click the Get to Know Windows link (see **Figure** 9-4) to read the introductory tutorial.

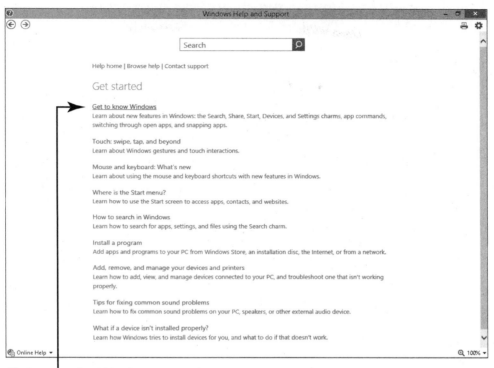

Click to read a Windows tutorial
Figure 9-4

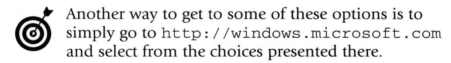
Another way to get to some of these options is to simply go to `http://windows.microsoft.com` and select from the choices presented there.

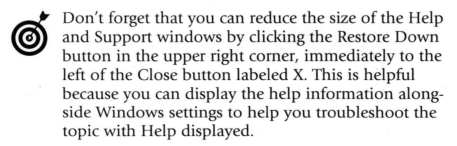
Don't forget that you can reduce the size of the Help and Support windows by clicking the Restore Down button in the upper right corner, immediately to the left of the Close button labeled X. This is helpful because you can display the help information along-side Windows settings to help you troubleshoot the topic with Help displayed.

When you first arrive at the Get Started page shown in **Figure** 9-4, take a moment to explore other links to read blogs or get more information on specific issues such as How to Search in Windows 8.1 and Touch: Swipe, Tap, and Beyond.

Find Help on Featured Topics in Help and Support

1. Because the Start screen offers an entirely new dynamic for Windows users, Microsoft built in three help topics to get you going. Begin to type **help** from the Start screen and then click Help and Support in the results to display it.

2. Click Help.

3. Click the second or third topic link in the Help panel (see **Figure** 9-5) after the Get Started topic (in this example Internet & Networking or Security, Privacy, & Accounts).

Figure 9-5

4. Scroll through the articles that appear (see **Figure** 9-6). If you want to, click any links in the article to display related information.

Figure 9-6

Get Answers from the Windows Community

1. If you want to see how other Windows users have solved a problem, you can visit the Windows Forum and read posted messages and the solutions suggested by Microsoft and others. You can also post your own questions. Begin typing **help** on the Start screen and then click Help and Support to open the Windows Help and Support window; then click the Microsoft Community Website link.

2. On the web page shown in **Figure** 9-7, click in the Search field and enter a search term. Click the Search button to search for all answers.

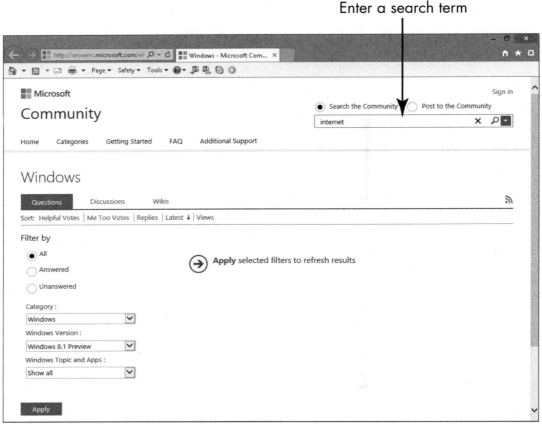

Enter a search term

Figure 9-7

3. Click the title of a question that relates to your question and read the answers (see **Figure** 9-8).

4. To ask your own question, click the Post to the Community radio button above the Search field (refer to **Figure** 9-7).

5. Enter a question and then press Enter.

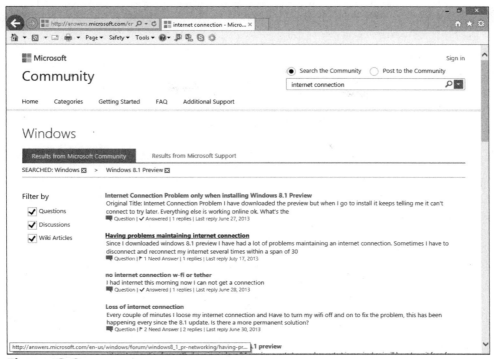

Figure 9-8

6. On the following page, scroll through to see if somebody else has posted a similar question; if not, click the Create button (see **Figure 9-9**) at the bottom of the page and enter a more detailed description of your problem or question. You may have to sign up if you haven't used this site before, accepting the rules of conduct.

7. Change the title for your question if you wish. Click the Category field to choose an appropriate forum (the appropriate area of the Community for your question), the Windows Version field to choose Windows 8.1, and the Windows Topic and Apps field and choose the appropriate topic for your question from the drop-down list.

8. If you want to get an e-mail when somebody responds to your question, be sure the Notify Me When Someone Responds to This Post check box is selected. If this isn't selected, you'll have to return to the forum and check to see if any answers have been posted.

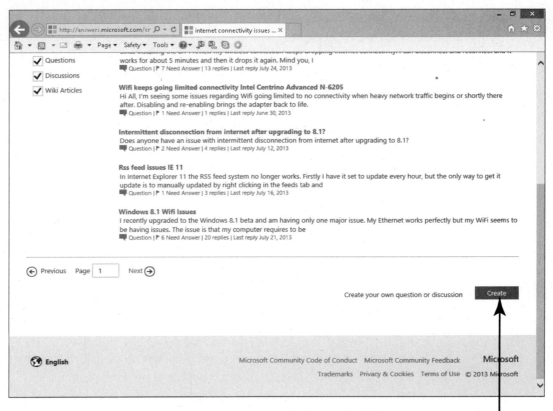

Click to post a new question

Figure 9-9

9. Click the Submit button.

 It's a good idea to roam around the forum for a bit before you post a question to see if it's been addressed before. If you post a question that's been answered several times before, you not only waste your time and the time of others, but you may find yourself the recipient of a bit of razzing by regulars to the forum.

Switch between Online and Offline Help

1. Much of the help and support you get from Microsoft for Windows these days is driven by their online content. If you don't have an Internet connection but you need help, you do have an option. If you switch to Offline Help, you can work with the help system database built into Windows 8.1, though it may not be as up to date as the online help. Begin to type **help** from the Start screen and then click Help & Support in the results.

2. In the Windows Help and Support window shown in **Figure 9-10**, click Online Help in the lower-left corner.

Figure 9-10

3. Click Get Offline Help.

4. Enter a term in the Search field and click the Search button.

5. Click a topic to read more about it.

 Online search engines are also a good way to get help from sources outside of Microsoft. Just open your browser (begin typing your browser name such as Mozilla Firefox from the Start screen and click on it in the results or click the Internet Explorer tile on the Start screen), go to a search engine such as Google (www.google.com) or Bing (www.bing. com), and enter your question. Results may range from advertisements for products or services to informational sites, blogs, or discussion forums where other users offer suggestions.

Connect to Remote Assistance

Remote Assistance can be a wonderful feature for new computer users because it allows you to permit somebody else to view or take control of your laptop from her own computer no matter where she is. You can contact that person by phone or e-mail, for example, and ask for help. Then, you can send an invitation using Windows 8.1 Help.

When that person accepts the invitation, you can give her permission to access your system. Be aware that by doing so you give the person access to all your files, so be sure this is somebody you trust. When that person is connected, she can either advise you about your problem or actually make changes to your laptop to fix the problem for you. To use Remote Assistance, you and the other person first have to have Windows 8.1 and an Internet connection.

1. From the Desktop, press Win+I and click Control Panel.

2. Click System and Security and then under the heading System, click Allow Remote Access.

3. On the Remote tab of the System Properties dialog box that's displayed (see **Figure 9-11**), select the Allow Remote Assistance Connections to This Computer check box, and then click OK.

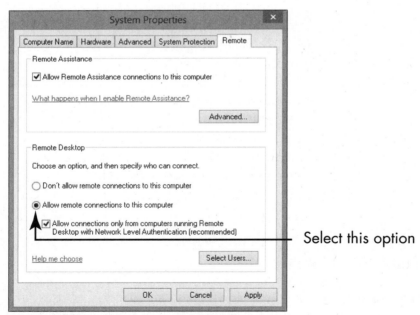

Figure 9-11

4. Enter the search term **remote assistance** in the Control Panel Search field.

5. Click the Invite Someone to Connect to Your PC and Help You, or Offer to Help Someone Else link.

6. On the window that appears, shown in **Figure** 9-12, click the Invite Someone You Trust to Help You link. If Windows Firewall or a third-party firewall is active, you may have to disable that feature to allow remote access to your laptop.

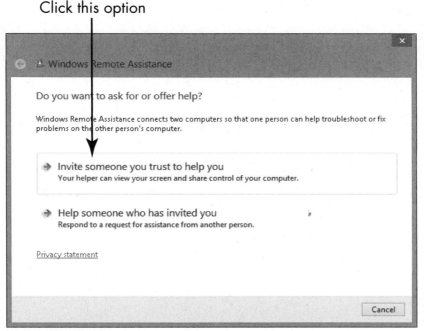

Click this option

Figure 9-12

7. On the page that appears, shown in **Figure** 9-13, you can choose to use your e-mail to invite somebody to help you. You have three options:

- Click the Save This Invitation as a File option and follow the instructions to save it as a file; then you can attach the file to a message using your web-based e-mail program.

- Click the Use E-mail to Send an Invitation option to use a pre-configured e-mail program to send an e-mail. In the e-mail form that appears, enter an address and additional message content, if you like, and send the e-mail.

- Click Use Easy Connect to get a step-by-step wizard to help you with the remote assistance process.

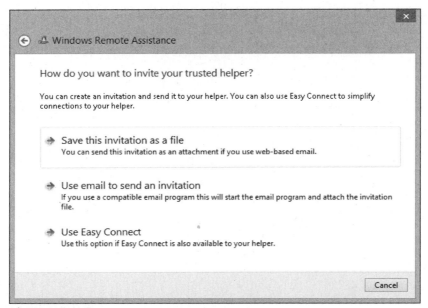

Windows Remote Assistance

How do you want to invite your trusted helper?

You can create an invitation and send it to your helper. You can also use Easy Connect to simplify connections to your helper.

➡ Save this invitation as a file
   You can send this invitation as an attachment if you use web-based email.

➡ Use email to send an invitation
   If you use a compatible email program this will start the email program and attach the invitation file.

➡ Use Easy Connect
   Use this option if Easy Connect is also available to your helper.

Cancel

Figure 9-13

8. In the Windows Remote Assistance window, as shown in **Figure** 9-14, note the provided password and provide it to your remote helper. When that person makes an incoming connection, use the tools there to adjust settings, chat, send a file, or pause, cancel, or stop sharing.

9. When you're finished, click the Close button to close the Windows Remote Assistance window.

 Remember that it's up to you to let the recipient know the password — it isn't included in your e-mail unless you add it in the e-mail message.

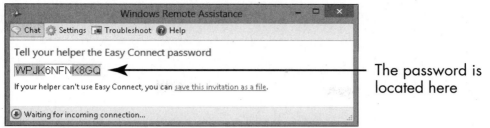

The password is
located here

Figure 9-14

 If you no longer want to use Remote Assistance, it's a good idea to return to the System window of Control Panel and, in the Allow Remote Access dialog box, uncheck Allow Remote Assistance Connection to This Computer on the Remote tab.

Part III

Having Fun and Getting Things Done

Visit www.dummies.com/extras/laptopsforseniors for tips on how to customize the Internet Explorer toolbar.

Working with Software Programs and Apps

You may think of Windows 8.1 as a set of useful accessories, such as a music player and a weather app to keep you out of the rain, but Windows 8.1 is first and foremost an operating system. Windows 8.1's main purpose is to enable you to run and manage other software programs and apps, from programs that manage your finances to a great animated bingo app. By using the best methods for accessing and running programs and apps with Windows 8.1, you save time; setting up Windows 8.1 in the way that works best for you can make your life easier.

In this chapter, you explore several simple and very handy techniques for launching and moving information between applications. You go through step-by-step procedures ranging from setting program defaults to removing programs when you no longer need them.

Install a Program

Your laptop came with Windows 8.1 or another operating system installed, as well as several other programs. For example, Windows computers usually have the Microsoft browser, Internet Explorer, pre-installed, as well as apps for accessing e-mail, weather, news, and more.

These pre-installed programs get you started, but you're likely to want to install other programs such as games or a financial management program such as Quicken.

Today you buy software in a couple of ways: You can buy a packaged product, which includes a CD or DVD disc, or you can buy software online and download it directly to your laptop. There are also apps you can use in the cloud (that is, you use them from an online source without ever installing them on your computer).

Assuming you either buy a CD/DVD or download and install the program, here's how the installation process varies, based on which option you choose:

If you buy a boxed product, you simply take out the disc, insert it into the CD/DVD drive of your laptop (or an external DVD drive), and then follow the onscreen instructions. If no instructions appear, you should open File Explorer (click the **File Explorer** icon on the Desktop), locate your CD/DVD drive on the computer, and double-click the program name. This should launch a wizard (a set of instructions that walk you through the steps) for the installation. If your laptop doesn't have a CD/DVD drive, as many smaller, lighter ones don't, you can plug in an external CD/DVD drive using a USB port; these are not that expensive and will come in very handy.

If you purchase software online at a store such as Amazon (www.amazon.com) or Newegg (www.newegg.com/), or from a software manufacturer's site, you simply click the appropriate button to buy the product, follow directions to pay for it, and then download the product. Typically during this process you will see a dialog box that asks if you want to save or run the program. Running it should start the installation. If you want to buy an app through the Windows Store, simply click the Store tile on the Start screen. In the page that appears, enter an app name in the Search For Apps field and click the Search button. Click on an app and buy it (see Chapters 14 and 15 for more about buying items from the Windows Store).

Launch a Program

1. Launch a program by using any of the following methods:

- Click a tile on the Start screen. (For more about pinning apps to the Start screen, see Chapter 5.)

- Click the All Apps button on the Start screen. This displays a list of apps arranged in categories such as Windows Accessories and Windows Ease of Access (as shown in **Figure 10-1**). Click an app to open it.

Figure 10-1

- Double-click a program shortcut icon on the Desktop (see **Figure 10-2**).

- Click an item on the Desktop taskbar. The taskbar should display by default; if it doesn't, move your mouse cursor to the bottom of the screen to display it, and then click an icon on the taskbar (as shown in **Figure 10-2**). See Chapter 5 for more about working with the taskbar.

2. When the application opens, if it's a game, play it; if it's a spreadsheet, enter numbers into it; if it's your e-mail program, start deleting junk mail . . . you get the idea.

See Chapter 12 for more about working with pre-installed apps in Windows 8.1.

Program shortcut icons

Items on the taskbar

Figure 10-2

Access Settings Specific to a Program or App

When you have an app open and use the Settings selection on the Charm bar (press Win+I to display the Settings), the settings that you see are typically specific to that app. For example, if you open SkyDrive, display the Settings panel, and then click Options, you get settings for your SkyDrive account and storage options (see **Figure 10-3**).

Figure 10-3

If, on the other hand, you open the Weather app and go to Settings through the Charm bar, the Options choice allows you to clear Weather search history.

These app specific settings only relate to Start Screen apps, not Desktop apps such as Word or Excel.

Move Information between Programs

1. Click the Desktop tile on the Start screen.

2. Click the File Explorer icon in the taskbar to open it.

3. Browse and open documents in two programs (see the previous section "Launch a Program" for more about opening applications). Right-click the taskbar on the Windows Desktop (see **Figure 10-4**) and choose Show Windows Side by Side.

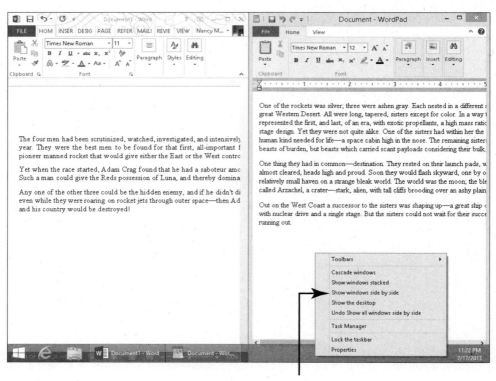

Select Show Windows Side by Side

Figure 10-4

4. If you don't need one of the active programs displayed, click the Minimize button in the program window so that just the program you're working with appears.

5. Select the information that you want to move (for example click and drag your mouse to highlight text or numbers, or click on a graphical object in a document), and then click the selected content and, using your mouse, drag it to the other document window (see **Figure** 10-5).

6. Release your mouse, and the information is copied to the document in the destination window.

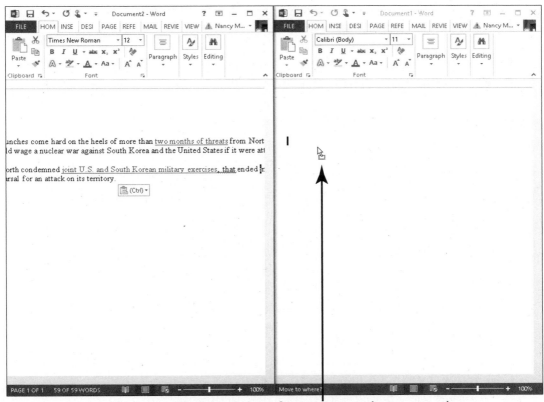

Click and drag from one window to another

Figure 10-5

You can also use simple cut-and-paste or copy-and-paste keystroke shortcuts to take information from one application and move it or place a copy of it into a document in another application. To do this, first click and drag over the information in a document, and then press Ctrl+X to cut or Ctrl+C to copy the item. Click in the destination document where you want to place the item and press Ctrl+V. Alternately, you can right-click content and choose Cut, Copy, or Paste commands from the menu that appears.

 Remember, dragging content won't work between every type of program. For example, you can't click and drag an open picture in Paint into the Windows Calendar. It will most dependably work when dragging text or objects from one Office or other standard word-processing, presentation, database, or spreadsheet program to another.

Set Program Defaults

1. To make working with files easier, you may want to control which programs are used to open files of different types. From the Desktop, press Win+I and click Control Panel in the Settings panel that appears.

2. Click Programs and, in the resulting Programs window shown in **Figure 10-6,** click the Set Your Default Programs link in the Default Programs section to see specifics about the programs that are set as defaults.

3. In the resulting Set Default Programs window, click a program in the list on the left (see **Figure 10-7**) and then click the Set This Program as Default option. You can also click Choose Defaults for this Program and select specific file types (such as the JPEG graphics file format or DOCX Word 2013 file format) to open in this program; click OK after you've made these selections.

Click here

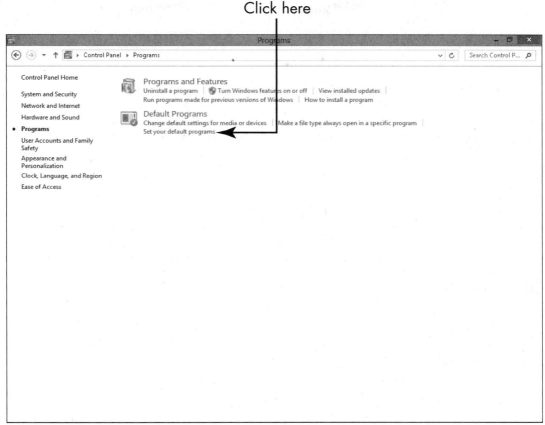

Figure 10-6

4. Click OK to save your settings.

 You can also choose which devices to use by default to play media such as movies or audio files by selecting Change Default Settings for Media or Devices in the Programs window you opened in Step 2 earlier.

Select a program

Figure 10-7

Remove a Program

1. If you don't need a program, removing it may help your laptop's performance, which can get bogged down when your hard drive is too cluttered. From the Control Panel, click Uninstall a Program (under the Programs category).

2. In the resulting Programs and Features window, shown in **Figure 10-8,** click a program and then click the Uninstall (or sometimes this is labeled Uninstall/ Change) button that appears. Although some programs will display their own uninstall screen, in most cases, a confirmation dialog box appears (see **Figure 10-9**).

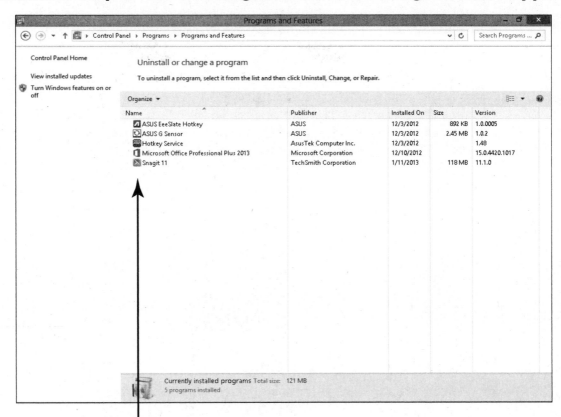

Select a program

Figure 10-8

Figure 10-9

3. If you're sure that you want to remove the program, click Yes in the confirmation dialog box. A progress bar shows the status of the procedure; it disappears when the program has been removed.

4. Click the Close button to close the Program and Features window.

 With some programs that include multiple applications, such as Microsoft Office, you get both an Uninstall and a Change option in Step 2. That's because you might want to remove only one program, not the whole shooting match. For example, you might decide that you have no earthly use for Access but can't let a day go by without using Excel and Word — so why not free up some hard drive space and send Access packing? If you want to modify a program in this way, click the Change button rather than the Uninstall button in Step 2 of this task. The dialog box that appears allows you to select the programs that you want to install or uninstall or even open the original installation screen from your software program.

 If you click the Change or Uninstall button, some programs will simply be removed with no further input from you. Be sure that you don't need a program before you remove it, that you have the original software on disc, or that you have a product key for software you downloaded from the Internet so you can reinstall it should you need it again.

Working with Files and Folders

*1*f you've ever worked in an office, even the supposedly "paperless" office of today, you remember the metal filing cabinets and manila file folders holding paper documents.

With a computer, you still organize the work you do every day in files and folders, but with a computer, the metal and cardboard have been dropped in favor of electronic bits and bytes. *Files* are the individual documents that you save from within applications, such as Word and Excel, and you use folders and sub-folders to organize several files into groups or categories, such as by project or by year.

In this chapter, you find out how to organize and work with files and folders, including

➡ **Finding your way around files and fold-ers:** This includes tasks such as locating and opening files and folders.

➡ **Manipulating files and folders:** These tasks cover moving, renaming, deleting, and printing a file.

➡ **Squeezing a file's contents:** This involves creating a compressed folder to reduce a large file to a more manageable size.

➡️ **Sharing files**: You can easily print a hard copy or share a file as an e-mail attachment.

➡️ **Backing up files and folders:** To avoid losing valuable data, you should know how to make backup copies of your files and folders on a recordable CD/DVD or USB stick (also called a *flash drive*, this is a small, stick-shaped storage device that slots right into a USB port on your laptop). DVDs are a newer technology than CDs and allow you to save more data on a single disc. The USB stick is small and more portable, and for those who have laptops with no CD/DVD drive, are the ideal way to store data.

Understand How Windows Organizes Data

When you work in a software program, such as a word processor, you save your document as a file. Files can be saved to your laptop hard drive, removable storage media such as USB flash drives (which are small plastic "sticks" that you slot into your laptop), or to recordable CDs or DVDs (small, flat discs you insert into a disc drive on your laptop).

You can organize files by placing them in folders. The Windows operating system helps you to organize files and folders in the following ways:

➡️ **Take advantage of predefined folders.** Windows sets up some folders for you. For example, the first time you start Windows 8, you find folder libraries for Documents, Pictures, Videos, and Music already set up on your laptop. You can see them listed in File Explorer (click the File Explorer button in the Desktop taskbar), as shown in **Figure 11-1**.

The Documents folder is a good place to store letters, presentations for your community group, household budgets, and so on. The Pictures folder is where you store picture files, which you may transfer from a digital camera or scanner, receive in an e-mail message from a friend or family member, or download from the Internet. Similarly, the Videos folder is a good place to put files from your camcorder or video files shared with you, and the Music folder is where you place tunes you download, rip from a DVD, or transfer from a music player.

Click to open File Explorer

Figure 11-1

➠ **Create your own folders.** You can create any number of folders and give each one a name that identifies the types of files you'll store in it. For example, you might create a folder called *Digital Scrapbook* if you use your laptop to create scrapbooks, or a folder called *Taxes* where you save e-mailed receipts for purchases and electronic tax-filing information. The task "Create a Desktop Shortcut" in Chapter 5 explains how to create a shortcut to a folder that you place on your Desktop, or pin a tile shortcut to the Start screen.

➡ **Place folders within folders to further organize files.** A folder you place within another folder is called a *subfolder*. For example, in your Documents folder, you might have a subfolder called *Holiday Card List* that contains your yearly holiday newsletter and address lists. In my Pictures folder, I organize the picture files by creating subfolders that begin with the year and then a description of the event or subject, such as *Home Garden Project, 2013 Christmas, 2011 San Francisco Trip, Family Reunion, Pet Photos,* and so on. In **Figure 11-2,** you can see subfolders and files stored within the Pictures folder.

Folder   Files in Picture folder

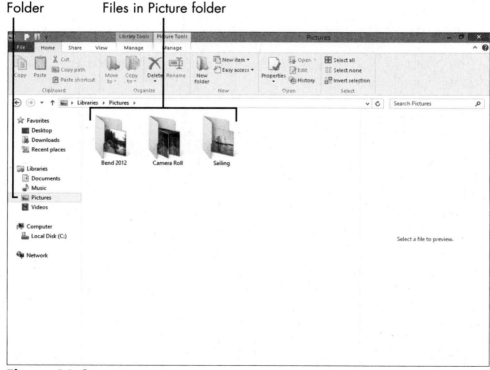

Figure 11-2

➡ **Move files and folders from one place to another.**
Being able to move files and folders is helpful if you
decide it's time to reorganize information on your
laptop. For example, when you start using your laptop, you might save all your documents to your
Documents folder. That's okay for a while, but in
time, you might have dozens of documents saved in
that one folder. To make your files easier to locate,
you can create subfolders by topic and move files
into them.

Access Open Files

1. You may often have several files open at one time. If
you're working on several files, Windows offers a shortcut
to viewing what's open and going to the file you want to
work on. From the Start screen, move your mouse cursor
to the top left corner of the screen. Currently open files
and active apps appear.

2. Slide your mouse down the left side to reveal other open
files or apps (see **Figure 11-3**).

3. When you find the item you want, click on it to make it
the active file.

 When you are working in an application such as
Excel, you can open the most recently used files by
choosing File⇨Open and choosing the file you want
to work with from a list of recent files.

Currently open files and apps

Figure 11-3

Locate Files and Folders Using Start Screen Search

1. Can't remember what you named a folder or where on your laptop or storage media you saved it? You can use the great Start Screen Search feature. Open the Start screen (press the Win key on your keyboard if you have the Desktop displayed).

2. Begin to type the file name and a Search window appears (see **Figure 11-4**).

3. Click the file in the results to open it.

Begin typing your search

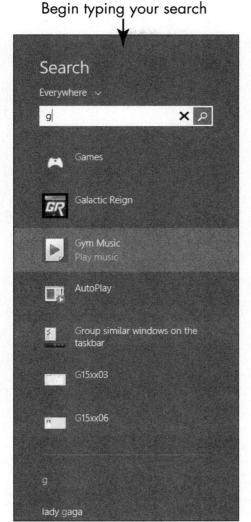

Figure 11-4

Search for a File with File Explorer

1. You can also use File Explorer to locate files and folders in a hierarchical listing. From the Desktop, click the File Explorer icon in the taskbar (see **Figure 11-5**).

Click the File Explorer icon

Figure 11-5

2. In the File Explorer window, click on Favorites, Libraries, or Computer; the item to be searched changes in the Search field based on what you've selected. (See Figure 11-6.)

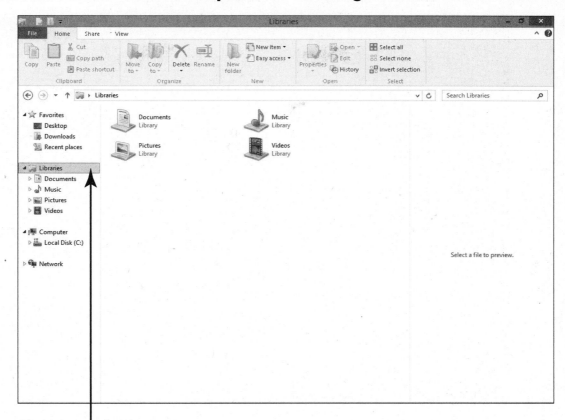

Click to search Libraries

Figure 11-6

3. Enter a term in the Search field.

4. In the results that appear (see **Figure 11-7**), double-click an item to view it.

 To view recent searches you've performed, click the Recent Searches button on the Search tab of File Explorer's toolbar that appears when you perform a search. To save search results so you can view them later, click the Save Search button, enter a name for the search in the dialog box that appears, and then click Save.

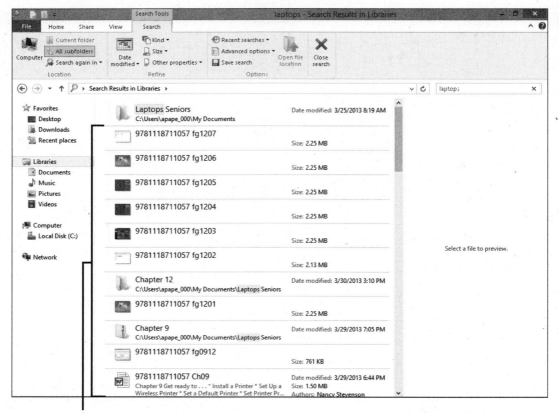

Double-click an item to view it
Figure 11-7

 Use the settings in the Refine area of the Search tab of the toolbar to set criteria on which your searches will be based such as the kind or size of file, or the date the file was last modified.

Move a File or Folder

1. Sometimes you save a file or folder in one place but, in reorganizing your work, decide you want to move the item to another location. To do so, from the Desktop, click the File Explorer icon.

2. In File Explorer, double-click a folder or series of folders to locate the file that you want to move. (See **Figure 11-8.**)

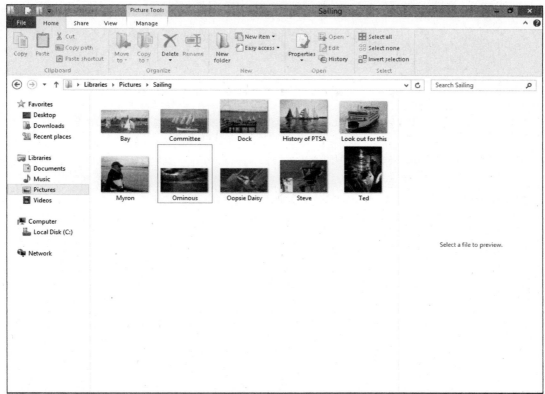

Figure 11-8

3. Take one of the following actions:

- Click and drag the file or folder to another folder in the Navigation pane on the left side of the window. If you have more than one item to move, click on the first item and then, pressing the Shift key on your keyboard, click on an adjacent item, or, pressing the Ctrl key, click on non-adjacent items in a list of files or folders. If you right-click and drag, you are offered the options of moving, copying, or creating a shortcut to the item when you place it via the shortcut menu that appears.

- Right-click the file(s) and choose Send To. Then choose from the options shown in the submenu that appears (as shown in **Figure 11-9**); these options may vary slightly depending on the type of file you choose and what software you have installed.

- With a file or files selected, Click the Move to button in the Organize group of tools on the Home tab, and then either choose a location from the list that appears or click Choose Location and then choose any location, such as your Desktop or a USB drive.

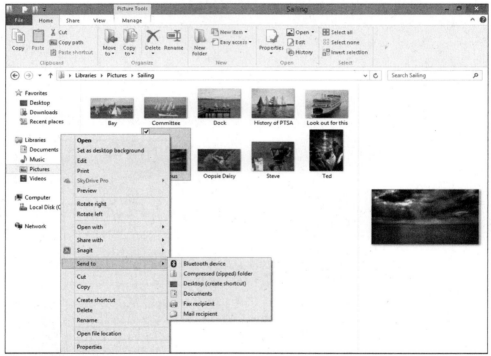

Figure 11-9

4. Click the Close button in the upper-right corner of File Explorer to close it.

If you change your mind about moving an item using the right-click-and-drag method, you can click Cancel on the shortcut menu that appears.

If you want to create a copy of a file or folder in another location on your laptop, right-click the item and choose Copy. Use File Explorer to navigate to the location where you want to place a copy, right-click, and choose Paste or press Ctrl+V.

Rename a File or Folder

1. You may want to change the name of a file or folder to update it or make it more easily identifiable from other files or folders. Locate the file that you want to rename by using File Explorer. (On the Desktop, click the File Explorer icon on the taskbar, and then browse to find the file you want to rename.)

2. Right-click the file and choose Rename. (See **Figure 11-10**.)

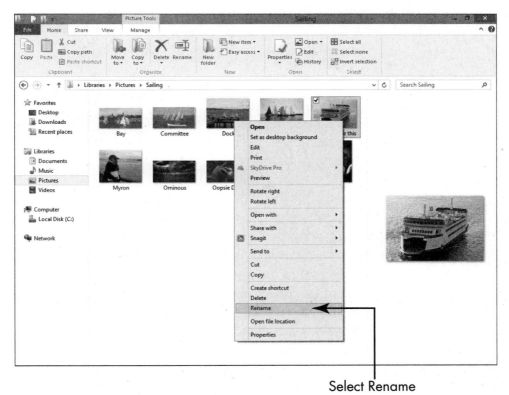

Select Rename

Figure 11-10

3. The filename is now available for editing. Type a new name, and then click anywhere outside the filename to save the file with its new name.

 You can't rename a file to have the same name as another file located in the same folder. To give a file the same name as another, cut it from its current location, paste it into another folder, and then follow the procedure in this task. Or open the file and save it to a new location with the same name, which creates a copy. Be careful, though: Two files with the same name can cause confusion when you search for files. If at all possible, use unique filenames.

Delete a File or Folder

1. If you don't need a file or folder anymore, you can clear up clutter on your laptop by deleting it. Locate the file or folder by using File Explorer. (Click the File Explorer icon on the Desktop, and then browse or search to locate the file you want to delete.)

2. In File Explorer, right-click the file or folder that you want to delete and then choose Delete from the shortcut menu, as shown in **Figure 11-11.** (Or you can simply click the file to select it and then press the Delete key.)

 When you delete a file or folder in Windows, it's not really gone. It's removed to the Recycle Bin. Windows periodically purges older files from this folder, but you might still be able to retrieve recently deleted files and folders from it. To try to restore a deleted file or folder, double-click the Recycle Bin icon on the Desktop. Right-click the file or folder and choose Restore. Windows restores the file to wherever it was when you deleted it.

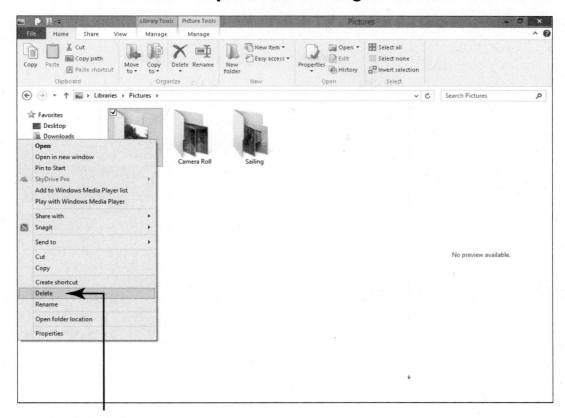

Select Delete

Figure 11-11

Compress a File or Folder

1. To shrink the storage size of a file, or of all the files in a folder, you can compress the file(s). This is often helpful when you're sending an item as an attachment to an e-mail message. Locate the files or folders that you want to compress by using File Explorer.

2. (Optional) In File Explorer, you can do the following (as shown in **Figure 11-12**) to select multiple items:

- **Select a series of files or folders.** Click a file or folder, press and hold Shift to select a series of items listed consecutively in the folder, and click the final item.

- **Select nonconsecutive items.** Press the Ctrl key and click the items.

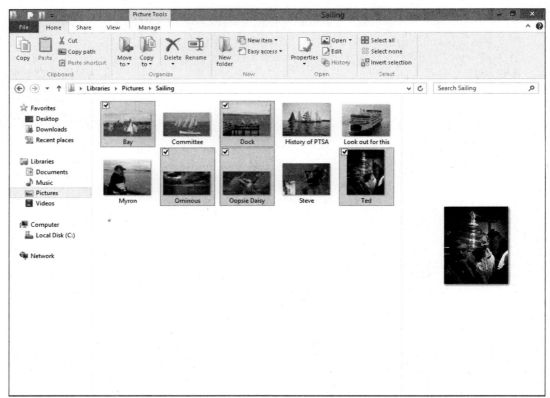

Figure 11-12

3. Right-click the selected item(s). In the resulting shortcut menu (see **Figure 11-13**), choose Send To⇨Compressed (Zipped) Folder. A new compressed folder appears below the last selected file in the File Explorer list. The folder icon is named after the last file you selected in the series, but it's open for editing. Type a new name or click outside the item to accept the default name.

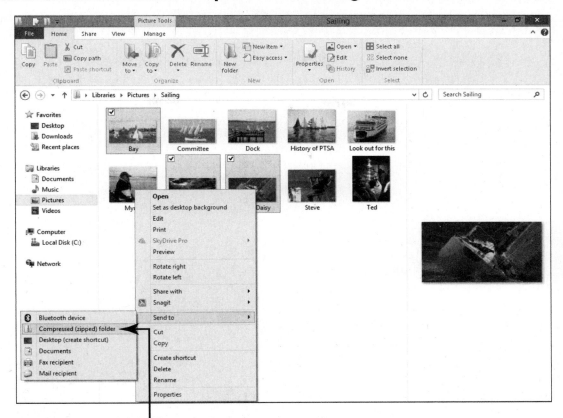

Select Compressed (Zipped) Folder

Figure 11-13

 Another method for creating a zipped folder containing multiple files is to select the files in File Explorer, click the Share tab, and then click the Zip icon in the ribbon of tools.

 You might want to subsequently rename a compressed folder with a name other than the one that Windows automatically assigns to it. See the task "Rename a File or Folder," earlier in this chapter to find out just how to do that.

Add a File to Your Favorites List

1. The Favorites feature in the Start menu offers another quick way to access frequently used items. Locate the files or folders that you want to add to the Favorites list by using File Explorer. (Click the File Explorer icon in the taskbar of the Desktop.)

2. In File Explorer, click a file or folder and drag it to any of the Favorites folders in the Navigation pane on the left. (See **Figure 11-14**.) The file or folder is added to your Favorites.

Adding a file to the Favorites list

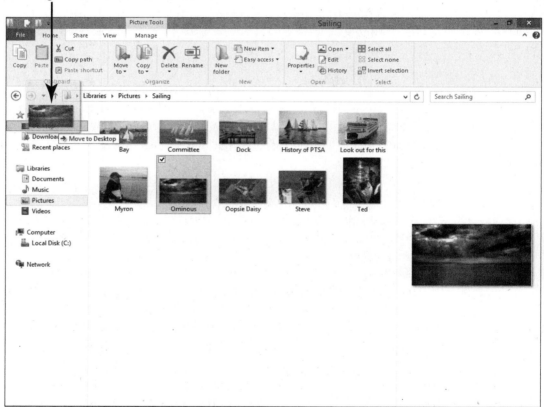

Figure 11-14

Understand File Storage Options

You may want to save copies of your files somewhere other than your laptop's hard drive. You might, for example, want to keep a copy of your work just in case you lose your laptop or the hard drive fails. Or, you may want to copy a file onto a DVD so you can hand it on to a friend to read or work on.

You have four main options for storing your files:

➡ **Utilize a USB stick:** You can purchase a USB stick (also called a *flash drive*) to store your files on. These are about the dimensions of a couple of sticks of gum (though designs vary — some are very tiny). You insert the stick into a USB port on your laptop (most laptops have three or four of these). Then you can use File Explorer (or the Finder on a Mac) to copy files from your computer onto the USB stick.

➡ **Use a CD or DVD to store files, if your laptop has a CD/DVD slot:** Some laptops, especially smaller ones like ultrabooks, don't have a CD/DVD drive, but many laptops do. Slip a disc into your laptop just as you would a music CD or DVD, and copy files to it (see the next task for detailed steps).

➡ **Attach an external hard drive to your laptop:** You can buy what amounts to a second hard drive and attach it to your laptop to store and retrieve files. This will run you around $50–$100, depending on the model and storage capacity.

➡ **Store files online:** Today you can use an online service such as Windows SkyDrive (www.skydrive.com) or Dropbox (www.dropbox.com) to store your files online, usually for free. The handy thing about this option is that you can then easily access your files from anywhere without carrying a storage device. It's also a great way to share files (for example, photos or a set of meeting minutes) with others.

Back Up Files to a Read/Writable CD/DVD or USB Stick

1. In the event that your laptop is damaged or loses data, you'd be fortunate to have a copy safely tucked away. Storing data on a USB stick or CD or DVD disk is a popular choice. If your laptop doesn't have a CD/DVD drive built in, you'll have to use a USB stick or purchase an external CD/DVD drive and connect it to your laptop to perform these steps. Place a USB stick in a USB port, or place a blank writable CD-R/RW (read/writable) or DVD-R/RW in your CD-RW or DVD-RW drive and then choose click the File Explorer icon on the Desktop and click to select a folder such as Documents or Pictures.

2. In the resulting Documents or Pictures window, select all the files that you want to copy to disc.

3. Right-click the files that you want and then choose Copy (see **Figure 11-15**).

4. Click the USB, CD-R/RW, or DVD-RW drive in the Computer category in the left pane, right-click, and then click Paste.

5. Click the Close button to close the File Explorer window.

An alternate method to send files to a disc is to click the Burn to Disc button in the Send group on the Share tab.

If you want to back up the entire contents of a folder, such as the Document folder, you can just click the Documents folder itself in Step 2 and follow the rest of the steps.

You can also back up to a specified drive by using the Save Backup Copies of Your Files with File History link in the Control Panel. Using File History, you can set up Windows to regularly back up to any drive.

Remember that in addition specifying a drive to back up to, you have to turn File History on.

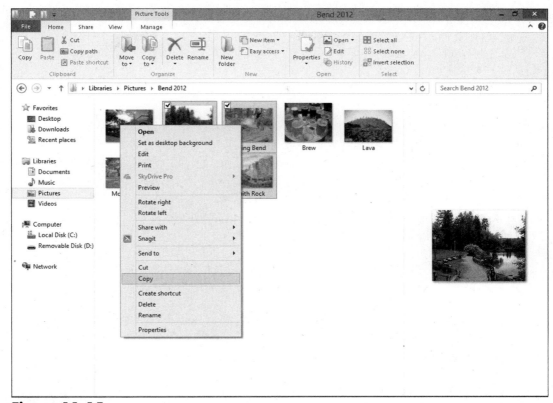

Figure 11-15

Using Windows 8.1 Built-in Apps

Several preinstalled apps in Windows 8.1 let you tap into the power of the Internet right from your Start screen. All provide tools as well as information that is current when you are connected to the Internet. Also, all are represented by a tile on the Start screen whenever you log into Windows.

Note that several apps such as Music, Video, Maps, and SkyDrive are covered in other chapters in this book. In this chapter you get a quick tour of the rest of the preinstalled apps including News, Finance, Weather, Sports, People, and Calendar.

Get up to Speed with the News App

The News app tile typically previews a heading or photo from a current story, but you can recognize it by the word News in the lower left corner of the tile, as shown in **Figure 12-1**. Although the last displayed story may appear if you click the tile while not connected to the Internet, you won't get much further. This app needs an Internet connection to be of value.

Chapter 12

Figure 12-1

1. After you click the News tile on the Start screen, you see the hottest story. Scroll to the right and you see the Get Started tools (see **Figure 12-2**) that help you learn how to follow stories to keep current, how to customize what news you want to get on the Start screen, and how to add a section dedicated to a topic or source on your home screen.

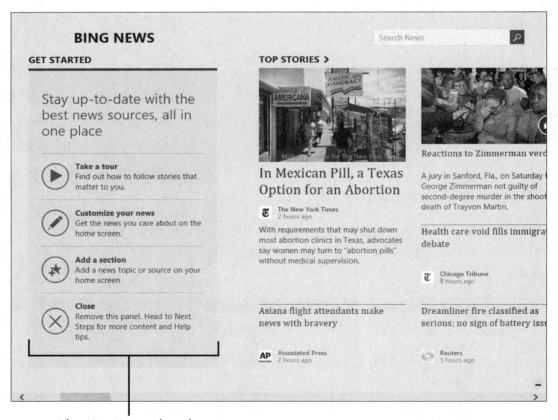

The Get Started tools

Figure 12-2

2. Scroll further to the right using the horizontal scroll bar and you get Top Stories, a list of Sources (such as Reuters and *The Wall Street Journal*) that you can click to go to those websites, and news categories such as World News, Technology and Science, and Entertainment.

3. Click any story that sounds of interest and it's displayed (see **Figure 12-3**).

4. Use the arrows on the middle of the right and left sides to move to the next or previous page or story, and click the arrow in a circle in the top left corner to go back to the News app home screen.

Click to go to the News home screen

LISA LEFF
Associated Press - Saturday, July 13, 2013

Asiana flight attendants make news with bravery

SAN FRANCISCO — Before Asiana Flight 214 crash-landed in San Francisco, the last time the Korean airlines' flight attendants made news it was over an effort by their union earlier this year to get the dress code updated so female attendants could wear trousers.

Now, with half of the 12-person cabin crew having suffered injuries in the accident and the remaining attendants receiving praise for displaying heroism

AP ASSOCIATED PRESS

Page 1 of 5

Figure 12-3

If you right-click the News app screen, you can click the Customize button to get tools for customizing the app by featuring the sources, topics, or categories of news that you use most.

Manage Your Money with the Finance app

1. If you're connected to the Internet the Finance app tile typically shows the current stock market values and sometimes just an optimistic logo of graph lines topped by an ascending arrow plus the word Finance in the lower left corner (see **Figure 12-4**).

Figure 12-4

2. Click the Finance tile and you see a current article from Bing Finance as well as the latest Dow, NASDAQ, and S&P numbers from services such as TheStreet.com.

3. Scroll to the right and click a Get Started tool that offers a tour of Finance features and a tool to set up your stock watch list so you can quickly check items of interest from the Finance home screen.

4. Scroll further right and you can view charts (see **Figure 12-5**) and articles about the world of finance. At the far right is a set of Tools including a Mortgage Calculator, Currency Converter, and Retirement Planner.

BING FINANCE

MARKET >

DOW NASDAQ S&P 500

▲ 15,464.30 +3.38
+0.02%

	Day Range	Open	1 Year Return %
	15,410.27 - 15,498.39	15,460.69	22.99
	52-Week Range	Previous Close	No. of Constituents
	12,471.49 - 15,542.40	15,460.92	30

7/12/2013 4:34 PM EDT

| Day | Week | Month | 1 Year |

Index Details

Last Updated 11:05 PM. BATS real time data – Disclaimer. Market data by Morningstar.

Figure 12-5

Get the Weather Report

The Weather app allows you to set one or more cities for quick access to local weather information. This includes information on wind, visibility, humidity, and barometer readings. You get this information from several services such as Bing Weather, AccuWeather, and Foreca.

1. Click the Weather tile on the Start screen (it sports the word *Weather* in the lower left corner and information about today's weather from your default location, as shown in **Figure 12-6**).

Figure 12-6

2. If the small arrow button in the lower right corner points up, click it to display more information from other weather services, as shown in **Figure 12-7**. Click this button again to hide information from services other than Bing Weather.

3. Scroll to the right to see information such as maps, historical weather patterns, and an hourly forecast.

Figure 12-7

4. Right-click to display the tools shown in **Figure 12-8**. You can use the Change Home button on the bottom left to set the current location as your Weather home page. On the bottom right, tools allow you to display weather for your current location (if you're connected to the Internet so the Weather app can find you), or change readings to Celsius.

5. The buttons on the top shown in Figure 12-8 allow you to add and display other locations for weather, display weather at locations around the globe, or return to your default location at the Weather Home page.

Set current location as
your Weather home page

See weather of current location

Figure 12-8

 To switch between locations, right-click the Weather screen, click Places, and then click another saved location on the page that appears.

Follow Your Team with the Sports App

You can spot the Sports app tile on the Start screen by the winner's cup icon, as shown in **Figure 12-9**. Clicking this displays Bing Sports, which includes a tool for tracking your favorite sports, top sports stories, a list of headlines, favorite sports, and a constantly updated scoreboard. In addition, there are videos and slide shows for your sporting pleasure.

Figure 12-9

1. Click the Sports app tile on the Start screen. A top story appears with Get Started tools to the right (see **Figure 12-10**).

BING SPORTS

Enter a team or player name

GET STARTED

Follow the teams and sports you care about with Bing Sports

Take a tour
Learn all about our rich content, schedules and scores

Add your favorite sports
Get easy access to the sports you follow

Close
Remove this panel. Head to Next Steps for more sports and help content

LINCECUM NO-HITS PADRES

ASSOCIATED PRESS

Tim Lincecum throws his first career no-hitter, a 13-strikout gem saved by Hunter Pence's diving catch in the eighth inning of San Francisco's 9-0 win over San Diego.

Figure 12-10

2. Right-click anywhere on the screen to display a set of tools for various sports associations such as the NFL and NBA. Click the arrow next to one of these to display a list of options including schedule, leading players, and standings (see **Figure 12-11**).

Click arrows to see options ⸻

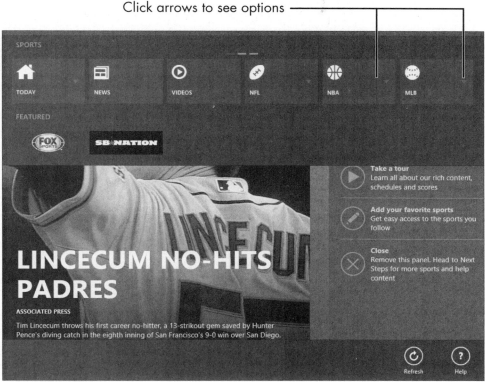

Figure 12-11

3. Click the screen again and then use the horizontal scroll bar to view categories of information such as the scoreboard, top stories, headlines, and more.

 To add a sport to your Favorites, scroll to the right to display the Get Started section, click the Add Your Favorite Sports tool, or scroll to the right to the Favorite Teams section and click the button with a + symbol, enter your team's name, and click Add.

Find Contacts with the People App

The People app is a combination address book and contact management app. It also provides you with access to your social networking accounts such as Facebook and Twitter.

You access the People app via the People tile on the Start screen, which sports a small icon of the head and shoulders of two "people" along with rotating pictures of your contacts from social networking sites, if you are logged in with an account that has social networking set up. When logged into an account, any contacts you have set up in that account, such as e-mail or Facebook, are imported into the People app automatically.

1. Click the People tile on the Start screen. In the top right corner, you see icons for any accounts you are connected to such as a Microsoft Live account or Facebook (see **Figure 12-12**).

Figure 12-12

2. Right-click and then click the New Contact button in the bottom right corner to add a contact.

3. Enter that person's details such as their name, company, e-mail address, phone numbers, and address, and then click the Save button to save that person's information (see **Figure 12-13**). Click the Back button to go back to the People Home page.

Enter the information...   ...click to Save

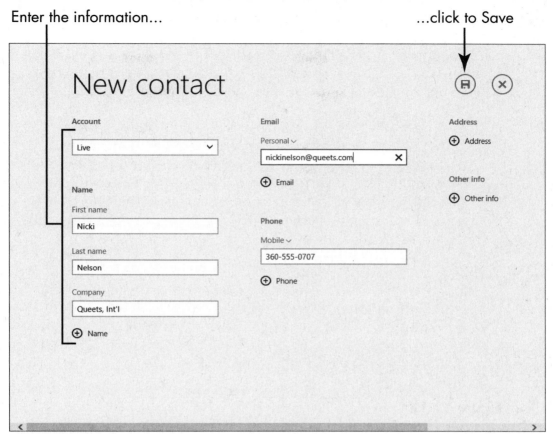

Figure 12-13

4. Click a contact in the list of contacts on the right to display contact details. From this screen, shown in **Figure 12-14**, you can send an instant message, call a phone, or send e-mail if you have stored that information for the contact.

 From the People home page, click the What's New area to read the latest postings by your friends on social networking sites.

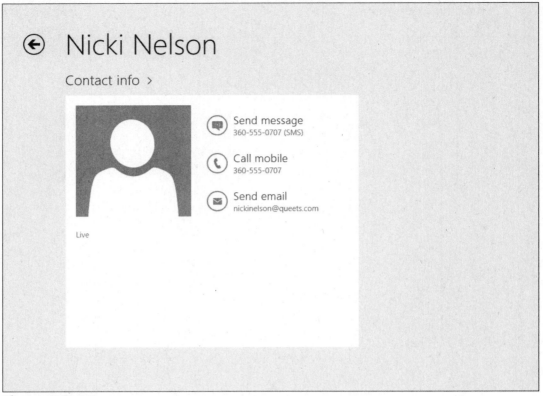

Figure 12-14

Stay on Schedule with the Calendar App

You can use the Calendar app to stay on schedule. Click the Calendar app tile on the Start screen (it contains, logically enough, a little calendar icon), and you can save information about various events and appointments. Those items generate an e-mail to remind you when the event is imminent.

1. Click the Calendar tile on the Start screen.

2. Right-click anywhere on the screen to display the toolbar shown in **Figure 12-15**. Click on a view: Day, Work Week, Week, or Month.

Figure 12-15

3. Right-click anywhere on the screen again and then click the New button to create a new event.

4. In the form that appears (see **Figure 12-16**), enter the details about the appointment and then click the Save button to save the item to your calendar.

Enter event details...   then click to save

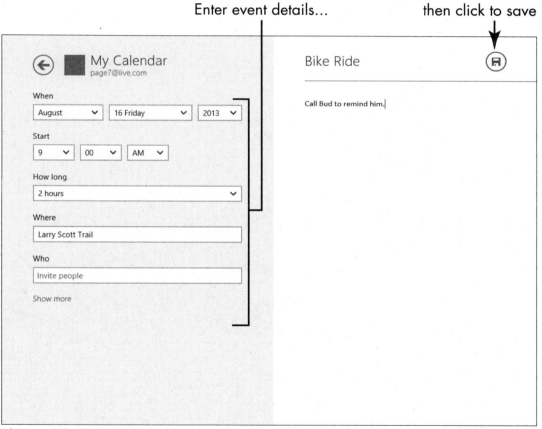

Figure 12-16

5. To edit an event saved to the Calendar app, simply click it. The entry form shown in Figure 12-16 opens for you to enter and save edits or delete the item.

 To quickly scroll forward or backward in time in the Calendar display, click the arrow buttons to the right and left at the top of the calendar display.

Hitting the Road with Your Laptop

Two preinstalled apps in Windows 8.1 take full advantage of your laptop's portability. When you want to take a business trip, visit family, or just hit the road for a vacation, you can use the Maps app to help you plan your route. You can also use the Travel app to find information about destinations from Paris to Niagara Falls, check on flights and buy tickets, and even find a hotel.

In this chapter, I give you ideas for using the Maps and Travel apps to plan your travel. Don't forget to bring your laptop along for the ride to get updates and more to help you enjoy the journey.

Use the Maps App

Most mapping applications make use of information about your location whenever you're connected to the Internet to provide directions, updates on traffic, and even listings of local restaurants, gas stations, and more.

The Maps app is preinstalled with Windows 8.1, so you will find a tile for it on the Windows Start screen.

Set Your Location

When you first click the Maps app tile on the Start screen, you will see a message (see **Figure 13-1**) asking you if Maps can use your location. If you click the Block button, Maps can only estimate your location, so directions and traffic information may be less exact. If you click the Allow button, Maps can use your location to provide more specific maps, but you are then allowing a remote service to pinpoint your location.

If children use your laptop, allowing a service to pinpoint your location could also allow people to find them. However, for most folks, allowing use of your location for a service such as Maps is pretty safe, so you can click Allow to continue. The map that appears will be specific to your location.

Figure 13-1

Show Traffic

1. After you open Maps, right-click and a toolbar appears along the bottom of your screen (see **Figure 13-2**). Click the My Location button to zoom in on your location.

Click to zoom in on your location

Figure 13-2

2. Right-click to display the toolbar and click the Show Traffic button. Traffic alerts such as those shown in **Figure 13-3** appear.

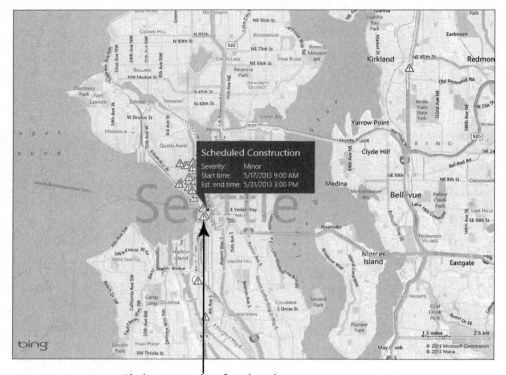

Click on an alert for details

Figure 13-3

3. Click an alert to display information about its severity, start time, and estimated end time (refer to **Figure 13-3**).

 You can right-click anywhere on the map and then click the Search tool to get a list of categories such as Eat & Drink, Hotels, and Banks. Click a category to display a list of nearby locations on the left side. You can then click a location and use buttons to access that business's website or place a call to them using Skype.

Get Directions

1. With the Maps app open, right-click and then then click the Directions button. A Directions panel appears (see **Figure 13-4**).

Enter a starting point

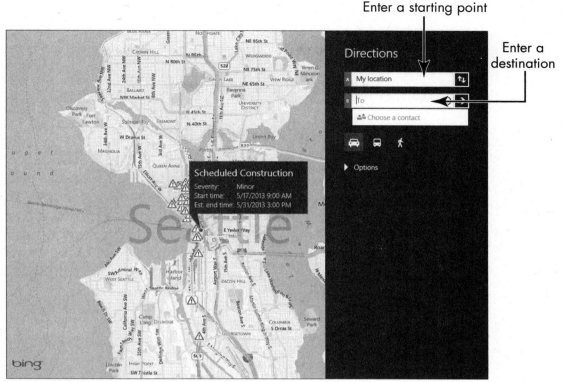

Enter a destination

Figure 13-4

2. Enter a start point in the field labeled A.

3. Enter a destination address in the field labeled B and click the arrow on the right side of that field.

4. If you are offered a few choices of start point or destination, click the correct one, and then click one of three icons: Drive (a car), Transit (a bus), or Walking (a person) to get directions for that mode of transportation (see **Figure 13-5**).

 When you open the Directions panel, click the Options button (refer to **Figure 13-4**) to choose to avoid highways or tolls.

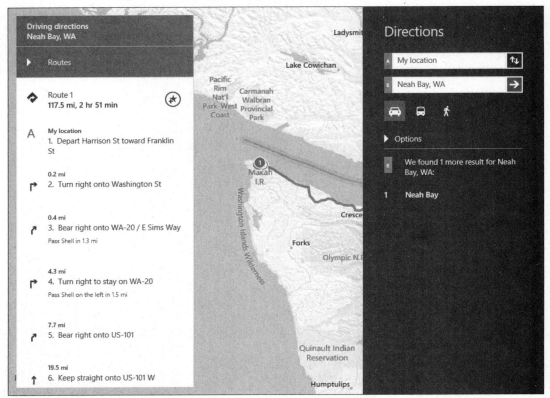

Figure 13-5

Use the Travel App

The Travel app uses the Bing Travel database to offer you information about travel destinations including current weather, maps, currency exchange, photos, restaurants and hotels, nearby attractions, and travel-booking services for flights and hotels.

The Travel app is preinstalled with Windows 8.1, and you access it from a tile on the Start screen. That tile sometimes shows text and sometimes a picture of a destination, but you can recognize it by the little suitcase icon when no picture is showing, or by the word *Travel* in the lower left corner of the tile (see **Figure 13-6**).

Figure 13-6

Find a Flight

1. Click the Travel tile on the Start screen.

2. Right-click the screen to display the tools shown in
Figure 13-7.

Figure 13-7

3. Click the Flights button. In the screen that appears (see **Figure 13-8**), enter information about departing and destination airports; if a suggested match appears below this field, click on it.

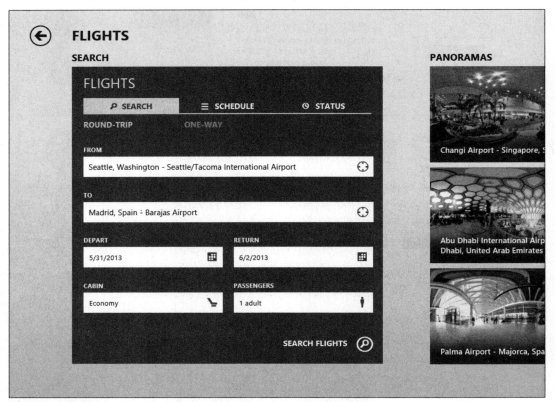

Figure 13-8

4. Continue by entering departure and return dates using the pop-up calendars that appear when you click in those fields; enter class such as Economy or First Class from the choices that appear when you click the Cabin field; and enter the number of people flying in the Passengers field.

5. Click the Search Flights button. In the list that appears, click a flight to see more details (see **Figure 13-9**).

PRICE PER PERSON, INCLUDING TAXES AND FEES. RATES BY **KAYAK**

← **SEATTLE, WASHINGTON (SEA) TO VANCOUVER, BRITISH COLUMBIA, CANA...**

PRICE : Show All ▾   AIRLINE : Show All ▾   DEPART : Show All ▾   RETURN : Show All ▾   STOPS : Show All ▾

Price ▲	Airline	Flight					Duration	Stops
$369	AIR CANADA	SEA	5:20 PM	✈	YVR	6:08 PM	48 min	–
		YVR	2:55 PM	✈	SEA	3:45 PM	50 min	–
$369	Alaska Airlines	SEA	8:10 PM	✈	YVR	9:00 PM	50 min	–
		YVR	8:30 PM	✈	SEA	9:20 PM	50 min	–
$369	Alaska Airlines	SEA	3:30 PM	✈	YVR	4:19 PM	49 min	–
		YVR	11:09 AM	✈	SEA	12:00 PM	51 min	–
$369	AIR CANADA	SEA	2:20 PM	✈	YVR	3:08 PM	48 min	–
		YVR	2:55 PM	✈	SEA	3:45 PM	50 min	–
$369	UNITED	SEA	4:10 PM	✈	YVR	4:58 PM	48 min	–
		YVR	8:05 AM	✈	SEA	8:58 AM	53 min	–
$369	Alaska Airlines	SEA	8:10 PM	✈	YVR	9:00 PM	50 min	–
		YVR	8:55 AM	✈	SEA	9:47 AM	52 min	–
$369	UNITED	SEA	7:10 PM	✈	YVR	7:58 PM	48 min	–
		YVR	4:05 PM	✈	SEA	4:55 PM	50 min	–
		SEA	4:10 PM	✈	YVR	4:58 PM	48 min	

Click a flight to see details

Figure 13-9

6. When you find the flight you want, click the Book button. In the window that appears, you can click the flight to go to a partner's website (such as American Airlines) to complete the transaction.

For help in planning your trip, click Best of Web in the tools shown in **Figure 13-7**. This displays brief descriptions and links to everything from Matador Network travel hub to GORP, which matches you with the right national park. There are even links to tutorials on packing efficiently and the U.S. Department of State travel information site.

Explore Destinations

1. Click the Travel tile on the Start screen and right-click to display the toolbar shown in **Figure 13-7**.

2. Click the Destinations button to display top travel destinations (see **Figure 13-10**) and click on one.

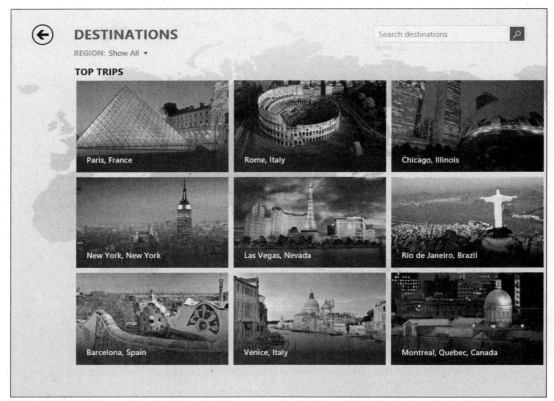

Figure 13-10

3. Use the horizontal scroll bar that appears when you move your mouse near the bottom of the screen to view a description, map, currency exchange, weather, Bing offers of the day, and information about attractions, hotels, restaurants, how to plan a trip, and nearby destinations. You can also use the Find Flights and Find Hotels tiles to buy tickets and book reservations (see **Figure 13-11**).

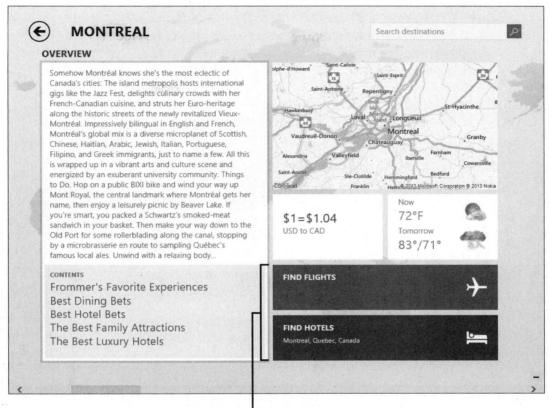

Find flights and hotels

Figure 13-11

 Check out the Panorama pictures, which you can view by scrolling to the right on the Travel home screen. Click one of these and the image appears. Click on the screen and drag to the left, right, up, or down to get a 360-degree view of your surroundings. Right-click to display tools that allow you to search for nearby hotels or flights to the destination.

Find a Hotel

1. Click the Travel tile on the Start screen, right-click, and then click the Hotels button.

2. In the screen that appears (see **Figure 13-12**), enter a city, and then choose a check-in and check-out date using the pop-up calendars that appear when you click in each of those fields.

Enter check-in and check-out dates

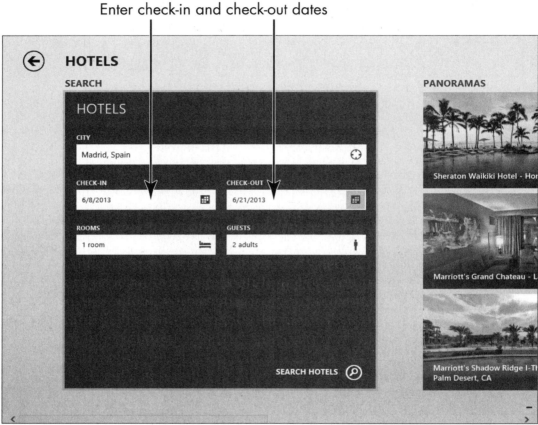

Figure 13-12

3. Enter the number of Rooms and Guests in those fields, and then click Search Hotels. In the results that appear, click the hotel that interests you to view more information (see **Figure 13-13**).

PRICE PER NIGHT, INCLUDING TAXES AND FEES. RATES BY **KAYAK**

VANCOUVER, BRITISH COLUMBIA, CANADA 8/3/201...

PRICE: Show All ▼   HOTEL CLASS: Show All ▼   AMENITIES: Show All ▼   Search by name or addres   **‹ ›**

Name		Price	Hotel Class	TripAdvisor® Rating	Amenities
Days Inn - Vancouver Metro 2075 Kingsway, Vancouver, B... 604-876-5531		$125	★ ★ ★ ★ ★	212 Reviews	
Howard Johnson Hotel Van... 1176 Granville St, Vancouver,... (604) 688-8701		$134	★ ★ ★ ★ ★	256 Reviews	
Loden Hotel 1177 Melville St, Vancouver,... 1-604-6695060		$337	★ ★ ★ ★ ★	885 Reviews	
Vancouver Marriott Pinnac... 1128 West Hastings Street, V... +1 604-684-1128		$304	★ ★ ★ ★ ★	614 Reviews	
Coast Plaza Hotel And Suites 1763 Comox Street, Vancouv... +1 520 760 5595		$275	★ ★ ★ ★ ★	396 Reviews	
Wedgewood Hotel And Spa 845 Hornby Street, Vancouve... +1 604 689 7777		$385	★ ★ ★ ★ ★	471 Reviews	

Figure 13-13

4. Scroll to the right to view information, photos, reviews, and more. Click the Book From button in the top right corner to get a list of travel services such as Kayak and Expedia through which you can book the room.

5. Click the offer you prefer, and you are taken to that service's site where you can book your room.

When you view a destination, you can click the Add to Favorites button. When you return to the Travel Home page, you'll see them listed under Favorites.

Getting Visual with Windows Media Player and the Video and Camera Apps

The world has discovered that it's fun and easy to share photos online, and that's why everybody is in on the digital image craze. Most people today have access to a digital camera (even if only on their cellphones) and have started manipulating and swapping photos like crazy, both online and off.

But today your phone, tablet, and computer not only let you upload and view pictures: You can use a built-in camera and the Windows 8.1 Camera app to take your own pictures or record videos and play them back. You can also buy videos (movies and TV shows, for example) and play them on your laptop.

In this chapter, you discover how to buy and play video, including movies and TV shows. I also give you some guidelines for uploading photos and videos from your digital camera, and explain how to view and share your visual treasures.

Work with Media Software

Your computer is a doorway into viewing and playing a media-rich world full of music, digital photos, and video. It also provides you with all kinds of possibilities for working with media.

Windows 8.1 has a useful media player built right into it: Windows Media Player. The Photos app provides another option for viewing photos. In addition, the Camera and Video apps, both newly arrived in Windows 8, help you create and view photos and video.

Here's what you can do with each of these programs:

➡ **Windows Media Player:** Is just what its name suggests: As you see in **Figure 14-1,** it's a program you can use to play music, watch movies, or view photos. It also offers handy tools to create *playlists* (customized lists of music you can build and play) and set up libraries of media to keep things organized. You can even burn media to a DVD so you can play it on your DVD player or another computer.

Figure 14-1

➡️ **Photos app:** Enables you to view digital photos; it opens automatically when you double-click a photo (as shown in **Figure 14-2**) in File Explorer and when you click the Photos tile on the Start screen. You can also share photos from within the Photos app by e-mail or by uploading to the SkyDrive file-sharing site.

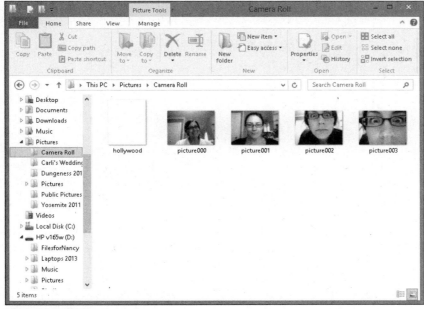

Figure 14-2

➡️ **Video app:** Takes you to the Windows Store (see **Figure 14-3**), where you can find TV shows and movies to buy and play on your computer or tablet.

➡️ **Camera app:** Allows anybody who has a computer with a built-in or external camera or webcam to take photos and record videos.

Figure 14-3

Buy Video Content at the Windows Store

1. The Windows Store offers a wonderful selection of content that you can buy or rent and play on your computer. Purchasing video involves making your selection and providing payment information to make your purchase. To shop for video, you use the Video app, which you access through a tile on the Start screen. Click the Video app tile to get started.

2. Click a featured title in the Windows Store or click the Movies or TV Store link above the featured listings and choose a category of movie to locate the one you want and then click on it.

3. Click the Buy button shown in **Figure 14-4**. (If you wanted to rent the movie, you'd click the Rent button at this point.) Depending on whether you're signed into your Microsoft account, you may be prompted to enter your password and asked whether you want to be asked for your password whenever you make a purchase; click Next.

4. In the screen that appears (see **Figure 14-5**), if you haven't provided payment information to Microsoft before, click Change Payment Options and add a credit card. Click Next. If you're renting, you may be asked to choose a viewing option, such as HD or SD, download or streaming, and click Next.

5. Click the Confirm button. In the screen that appears, click Done; your purchase downloads to your Video library.

Click to buy a movie

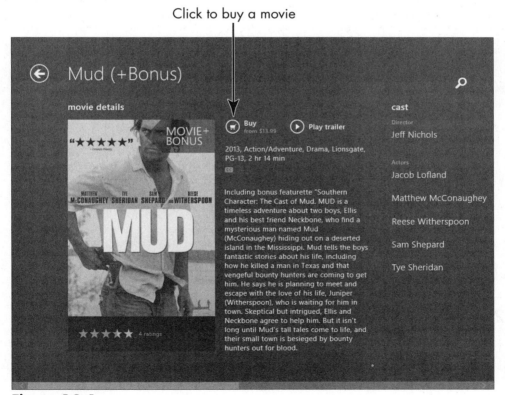

Figure 14-4

Add credit card info

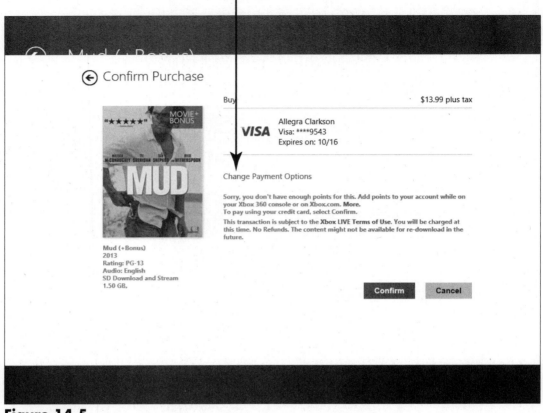

Figure 14-5

 To find videos you want, just start typing the name of the video on the Start screen. When the Search results appear, click the video to view more details or buy it.

Play Movies with Windows Media Player

1. From the Start screen, begin typing **Windows Media Player.** Click the app name in the results that appear. If this is your first time using the player, you may be prompted to select Recommended settings.

2. Click the Maximize button in the resulting Media Player window. (Maximize is in the upper-right corner of the window, next to the X-shaped Close button, represented by a square icon.)

3. Click Videos in the navigation pane to the left.

4. In the window listing video files, double-click the movie you want to play (as shown in **Figure 14-6**).

Double-click a video to play it

Figure 14-6

5. Use the tools at the bottom of the screen shown in **Figure 14-7** to do the following (if they disappear during playback, just move your mouse or tap your touch screen, if you have one, to display them again):

- **Adjust the volume** of any soundtrack by clicking and dragging the slider left (to make it softer) or right (to make it louder). Click the megaphone-shaped volume icon to mute the sound (and click it again to turn the sound back on).

- **Pause the playback** by clicking the round Play/Pause button in the center of the toolbar.

- **Stop the playback** by clicking the square-shaped Stop button to the left of the Pause/Play button.

- **Skip to the next or previous segment of the movie** by clicking the arrow buttons to the left or right of the Pause button.

Move to next or previous segment

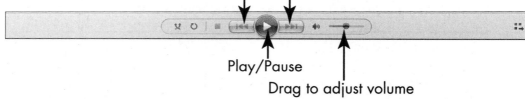

Play/Pause

Drag to adjust volume

Figure 14-7

6. Click the Close button to close Media Player.

 You can also use the Video app to play video content. Just click the Video tile on the Start screen, locate the video in the My Videos section, scroll to the left, and click to play it. The playback controls are almost identical to those discussed for Windows Media Player. This also works in playing movie trailers when you have a video selection's details displayed.

Upload Photos from Your Digital Camera

Uploading photos from a camera to your computer is a simple process, but it helps to understand what's involved. (This is similar to the process you can use to upload movies from a camcorder — in both cases, check your manual for details.) Here are some highlights:

➡ **Making the connection:** Uploading photos from a digital camera to a computer requires that you connect the camera to a USB port on your computer using a USB cable that typically comes with the camera. Power on the camera or change its setting to a playback mode as instructed by your user's manual.

➡ **Installing software:** Digital cameras also typically come with software that makes uploading photos to your computer easy. Install the software and then follow the easy-to-use instructions to upload photos. If you're missing such software, you can simply connect your camera to your computer and use File Explorer to locate the camera device on your computer and copy and paste photo files into a folder on your hard drive. (Chapter 11 tells you how to use File Explorer.)

➡ **Printing straight from the camera:** Digital cameras save photos onto a memory card, and many printers include a slot where you can insert the memory card from the camera and print directly from it without having to first upload pictures. Some cameras also connect directly to printers. However, if you want to keep a copy of the photo and clear up space in your camera's memory, you should upload the photos to your computer or an external storage medium such as a DVD or USB stick even if you can print without uploading.

Take Pictures and Videos with the Windows 8.1 Camera App

1. The Camera app was new with Windows 8. If your laptop has a camera (in the case of a computer, what you have may be a webcam), you can use the Camera app features to take both still photos and videos. Click the Camera app tile on the Start screen.

2. Aim your laptop towards your subject matter and click the Camera button (see **Figure 14-8**). The photo is captured.

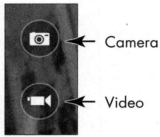

← Camera

← Video

Figure 14-8

3. Click the Video button to record a video.

4. Click the Video button again to stop recording.

> When you take a photo, you can right-click on the picture. Buttons then appear that you can use to open the picture in an app such as windows Photo Viewer or delete it. If you take multiple pictures, use the arrows that appear when you move your mouse to the sides of the screen to scroll through the photos.

> To adjust photo resolution or make settings for audio recordings when you're recording a video, right-click and then click the Exposure button to use a slider to adjust exposure brightness.

View a Digital Image in the Photos App

1. To peruse your photos and open them in the Photos app, click the Photos tile on the Start screen.

2. In the Photos app, double-click a photo library to display files within it. Double-click a photo to view it.

- You can then right-click the photo and use the tools shown in **Figure** 14-9 to do any of the following:

Figure 14-9

- The Delete button deletes the selected image.

- Click the Open With button to use another program, such as Paint, to edit the photo.

- Click the Set As button to set the image as your lock screen image, the image background for the Photos app tile, or as an app background.

- Click the Slide Show button to run a slide show (a topic covered later in this chapter).

- Use the Rotate button to rotate the image 90 degrees at a time.

- Use the Crop button to display handles you can drag to crop to a portion of the Image.

- Click the Edit button to make changes to the photo.

You can also press Win+I and then click the Options link to choose whether to shuffle photos on the Photos tile or not (see **Figure 14-10**).

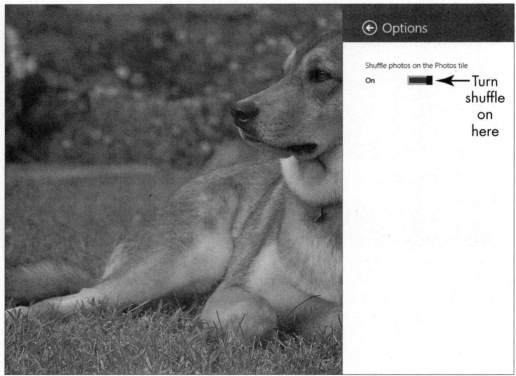

Figure 14-10

Share a Photo

1. Click the Photos app tile on the Start screen. Locate a photo you want to share and then press Win+C.

2. Click the Share charm (see **Figure 14-11**) for more sharing options in Photos. Click Mail.

Click for sharing options

Figure 14-11

3. In the e-mail form that appears (see **Figure 14-12**), enter an e-mail address or addresses, subject, and a message.

4. Click the Send button. An e-mail is sent from your default e-mail with your photo attached.

Figure 14-12

 If your photo is large, consider clicking the SkyDrive link, if available, rather than Mail to upload it to your SkyDrive account and share it with the recipient. See Chapter 18 for more about using the SkyDrive file-sharing service.

Run a Slide Show in Photos

1. You can use Photos to play a slide show, which continues until you stop it. Click the Photos tile on the Start screen and click a photo album or library to open it.

2. Right-click and click the Slide Show button shown in **Figure 14-13**.

Click to start a slide show

Figure 14-13

3. Click anywhere on the screen to stop the slide show.

Watch Movies Online

If you have an Internet connection, you can watch movies on your laptop using an online video sharing service such as YouTube or any of several free or paid movie sites such as Netflix and Hulu.

When you watch movies online, you're using a technology called *streaming*. The movie isn't downloaded to your laptop; rather, bits of the video are streamed to your computer over your Internet connection. When you play a trailer in the Video app, you are also streaming video.

The plus side of video streaming is that you can watch videos — many of which are free — without overloading your laptop's memory. The negative side is that, depending on your Internet connection, streaming can be less than smooth than playing a movie from a DVD. If you've tried watching a video online and gotten a message that the video is *buffering* (assembling content to show you), you know what I mean.

Try out YouTube (www.youtube.com) and Hulu (www.hulu.com) as a starting point. YouTube content is contributed by companies and people who want to share their shorter video clips, from the guy next door to movie studios and news stations. Hulu offers many movies and TV shows for free, or you can get a paid subscription to access more content. Either service will give you a taste of how well your connection will deliver video to your laptop. Just go to their websites, use the search feature to find a video, and then double-click a video to play it.

 Amazon.com recently added a lot of free instant video content to its Amazon Prime membership. If you pay the yearly fee for Amazon Prime ($79 as of this writing), it gives you unlimited second-day free shipping on anything you buy on the site and free video content. If you buy much at all each year from the online retailer, this works out to be a great deal.

Playing Music in Windows 8.1

Music is the universal language, and your laptop opens up many opportunities for appreciating it. Your laptop makes it possible for you to listen to your favorite music, download music from the Internet, play audio CDs and DVDs, and organize your music by creating playlists. You can also save (or *burn*, in computer lingo) music tracks to a CD/DVD or portable music device such as the hugely popular iPod.

With a sound card installed and speakers attached, you can set up your speakers and adjust volume, and then use Windows media programs to play music, manage your music library, burn tracks to a CD/DVD and use the Music app to buy music.

Set Up Speakers

1. Attach speakers to your laptop by plugging them into the appropriate connection (often labeled with a little megaphone or speaker symbol) on your CPU, laptop, or monitor.

2. From the Desktop, press Win+I, and then click Control
Panel in the top of the Settings panel.

3. Click Hardware and Sound; then click the Manage Audio
Devices link (under the Sound category).

4. In the resulting Sound dialog box (see **Figure 15-1**),
double-click the Speakers item and then click the
Properties button.

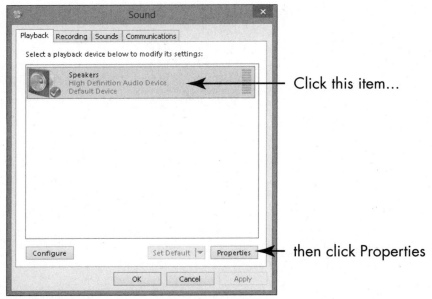

Figure 15-1

5. In the resulting Speakers Properties dialog box, click the
Levels tab, shown in **Figure 15-2**, and then use the
Speakers/Headphone slider to adjust the speaker volume.
Note: If you see a small red X on the speaker button, click
it to activate the speakers.

6. Click the Balance button. In the resulting Balance dialog
box, use the L(eft) and R(ight) sliders to adjust the balance of sounds between the two speakers.

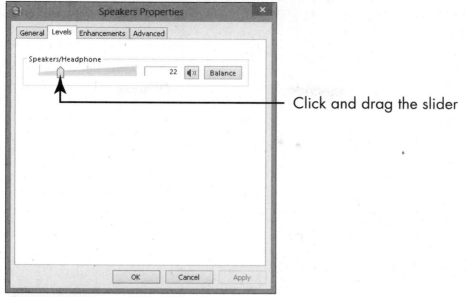

Click and drag the slider

Figure 15-2

7. Click OK three times to close all the open dialog boxes and save the new settings.

 If you use your laptop to make or receive phone calls, check out the Communications tab of the Sound dialog box. Here you can make a setting to have Windows automatically adjust sounds to minimize background noise.

Adjust System Volume

1. You can set the master system volume for your laptop to be louder or softer. From the Control Panel, click Hardware and Sound.

2. Click the Adjust System Volume link under Sound to display the Volume Mixer dialog box (shown in **Figure 15-3**).

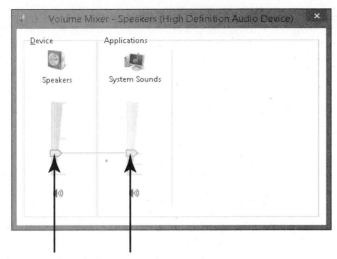

Move the sliders to adjust volume

Figure 15-3

3. Make any of the following settings:

- Move the Device slider to adjust the system's speaker volume up and down.

- For sounds played by Windows, such as a sound when you close an application (called *system sounds*), adjust the volume by moving the System Sounds slider.

- To mute either the main or application volume, click the speaker icon beneath either slider so that a red circle with a slash through indicating "no" appears.

4. Click the Close button twice.

 Here's a handy shortcut for quickly adjusting the volume of your default sound device. Click the Volume button (which looks like a little gray speaker) in the notification area on the right side of the taskbar. To adjust the volume, use the slider on the Volume pop-up that appears, or click the Mute Speakers button to turn off sounds temporarily.

 Today, many laptop keyboards include volume controls and a mute button to control sounds from your computer. Some even include buttons to play, pause, and stop audio playback. Having these buttons and other controls at your fingertips can be worth a little extra in the price of your keyboard.

 If you're using your laptop in a public place such as an Internet café and want to listen to music as you work, consider carrying a set of lightweight headphones with you and attach them to your laptop using the round headphone port. You can play your music or audio book as loud as you like and not disturb those around you.

Make Settings for Ripping Music

1. If your laptop has a CD/DVD drive and you place a CD/DVD in that drive, Windows Media Player will ask if you want to *rip* the music from the disc to your laptop. Doing so stores all the tracks on your laptop. To control how ripping works, begin clicking the All Apps button on the Start screen and locating and clicking Windows Media Player in the list of apps. Click the Organize button and choose Options.

2. Click the Rip Music tab to display it.

3. In the Options dialog box (see **Figure 15-4**), you can make the following settings:

Click to change where music is stored

Figure 15-4

- Click the **Change** button to change the location where ripped music is stored; the default location is your Music folder.

- Click the **File Name** button to choose the information to include in the filenames for music that is ripped to your laptop (see **Figure 15-5**).

- Choose the audio format to use by clicking the **Format** drop-down list on the Rip Music tab.

- Many audio files are copyright protected. If you have permission to copy and distribute the music, you may not want to choose the Copy Protect Music check box; however, if you're downloading music you paid for and therefore should not give away copies of, you should ethically choose to copy-protect music so that Windows prompts you or others using your laptop to download media rights or purchase another copy of the music when you copy it to another location.

Check to select which info
is included in filenames

Figure 15-5

- If you don't want to be prompted to rip music from CD/DVDs you insert in your drive, but instead want all music ripped automatically, select the **Rip CD Automatically** check box.

- If you want the CD/DVD to eject automatically after ripping is complete, select the **Eject CD after Ripping** check box.

4. When you finish making settings, click the OK button to save them and close the Options dialog box.

5. When you insert an audio CD/DVD in your internal or external drive if you haven't selected the Rip CD automatically option in the Options dialog box, Windows Media Player asks if you want to rip that music. Click Yes and the music is ripped into your Music library.

 Use the Audio Quality slider to adjust the quality of the ripped music. The smallest size file will save space on your laptop by compressing the file, but this causes a loss of audio quality. The Best Quality provides optimum sound, but these files can be rather large. The choice is yours based on your tastes and your computer's capacity!

 If you don't have a CD/DVD drive in your laptop, consider buying your music online and downloading it to your computer. With services such as Amazon. com's Cloud Player or Apple's iTunes, any music you buy can be stored online so you can play it from any computing device. See the task "Buy Music from the Windows Store" for more details about buying music online.

Find Music with Windows 8.1's Integrated Search

1. Windows 8.1's integrated search feature provides a great way to search for new music. From the Start screen, begin to type an artist name or song title.

2. In the search results, you can press Enter to see a variety of information about the search topic that may include images, articles, and music, or click a result such as "Lady Gaga songs" to narrow your search. Results appear as shown in **Figure 15-6**.

Figure 15-6

3. Scroll to the far right and click an album or song in the Windows Store results to view more details about tracks and artist, to play it using the Music app player, or to buy it (see **Figure 15-7**). Note that some results may take you to YouTube, an artist's web site, or sights such as MTV.

 The Music app lets you search the Windows Store for music selections you can buy.

Figure 15-7

Buy Music from the Windows Store

1. Purchasing music involves making your selection and providing payment information to make your purchase. Click the Music app tile on the Start screen. Click on a music selection to display details about it, and then click the Shopping Cart button. Depending on whether you're signed into your Microsoft account, you may be prompted to enter your password and asked whether you want to be asked for your password whenever you make a purchase. Click Next.

2. In the screen that appears (see **Figure 15-8**), if you haven't provided payment information to Microsoft before, click Change Payment Options and add a credit card.

3. Click the Confirm button. In the screen that appears, click Done. Your purchase downloads.

Figure 15-8

Create a Playlist

1. A *playlist* is a saved set of music tracks you can create yourself — like a personal music album. From the Start screen, begin to type **Windows Media Player** and then click the Windows Media Player app when it appears in the results.

2. Click a Library in the Navigation pane on the left and then click the Create Playlist button. A new playlist appears in the Navigation pane. Type a name for the playlist, and then click anywhere outside the playlist to save the name.

3. Click a category (for example, Music) to display libraries, and then click a library in the left pane; the library contents appear (see **Figure 15-9**). Click an item and then drag it to the new playlist in the Navigation pane. Repeat this step to locate additional titles to add to the playlist.

Click a library

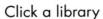

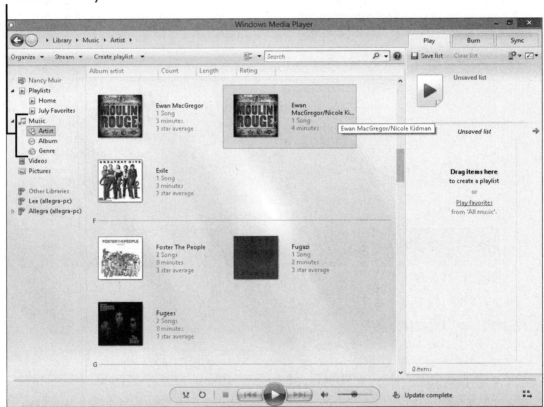

Figure 15-9

4. To play a playlist, click it in the Library pane and then click the Play button at the bottom of the screen.

5. You can organize playlists by clicking the Organize button (see **Figure 15-10**) and then choosing Sort By. In the submenu that appears, sort by features such as title, artist, or release date.

Click here

and then here

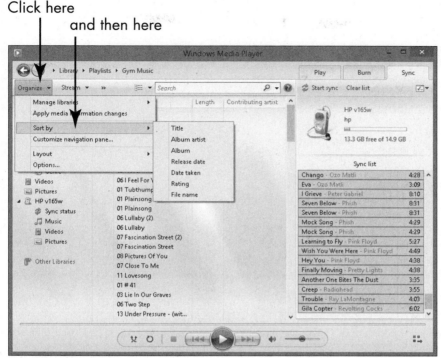

Figure 15-10

 You can also right-click a playlist in the Library pane and choose Play to play it or choose Delete to delete the list, although the original tracks that were added to the list still exist.

Burn Music to a CD/DVD

1. Saving music files to a storage medium such as a CD or DVD is referred to as *burning*. You might burn music to a disc so you can take it to a party or another computer location. If your laptop has a CD/DVD drive, insert a blank CD or DVD suitable for storing audio files in your drive.

2. Open Windows Media Player, click the Burn tab, and then click one or more songs, albums, or playlists in the middle of the screen and drag them to the Burn pane on the right (see **Figure 15-11**).

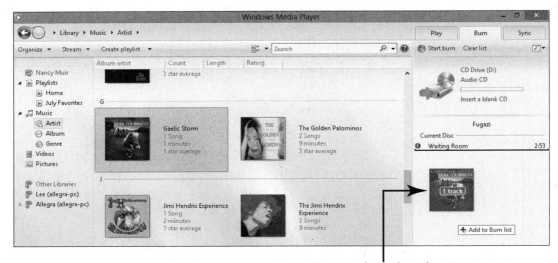

Songs placed in the Burn pane

Figure 15-11

3. Click Start Burn in the right side of the screen. Windows Media Player begins to burn the items to the disc. The Status column for the first song title reads `Writing to Disc` and changes to `Complete` when the track is copied.

4. When the burn is complete, your disc is ejected (although you can change this option by clicking the Burn Options button (a small button on the top right of the Burn tab) and choosing Eject Disc After Burning to deselect it).

 If you swap music online through various music-sharing services and then copy them to CD/DVD and pass them around to your friends, always do a virus check on the files before handing them off. Also, be sure you have the legal right to download and swap that music with others.

Note that optical discs come in different types, including CD-R (readable), CD-RW(read/writable), DVD+, DVD–, and DVD+/–. You must be sure your optical drive is compatible with the disc type you're using or you can't burn the disc successfully. Check your laptop user manual or the manufacturer's site to see what disc format it takes and check the disc packaging for the format before you buy!

Sync with a Music Device

1. If you have a portable music player, you can sync it to your laptop to transfer music files to it. Connect a device to your laptop and open Windows Media Player.

2. Click the Sync tab; a Device Setup dialog box appears (see **Figure 15-12**).

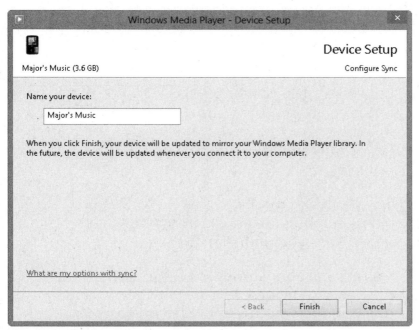

Figure 15-12

3. Name the device and click Finish. The device is now synced with Windows Media Player and will be automatically updated whenever you connect it to your laptop.

 To add items to be synced to a device, with the Sync tab displayed, simply drag items to the right pane. If your device is connected, or the next time you connect it, the items are copied onto the device automatically.

 If you want to be sure that the sync is progressing, click the Sync Options button (it's on the far right of the top of the Sync tab and looks like a little box with a check mark in it) and choose View Sync Status.

Play Music with Windows Media Player

1. Open Windows Media Player clicking the All Apps button on the Start screen, and then scrolling to the right and then clicking Windows Media Player in the list of apps that appears.

2. Click the Library button and then double-click Music or Playlists to display a library like the one shown in **Figure 15-13**. Double-click an album or playlist to open it; the song titles are displayed in the right pane.

3. Use the buttons on the bottom of the Player window (as shown in **Figure 15-14**) to do the following:

- Click a track, and then click the **Play** button to play it. When a song is playing, this button changes to the **Pause** button.

- Click the **Stop** button to stop playback.

- Click the **Next** or **Previous** button to move to the next or previous track in an album or playlist.

- Use the **Mute** and **Volume** controls to pump the sound up or down without having to modify the Windows volume settings.

Click a library

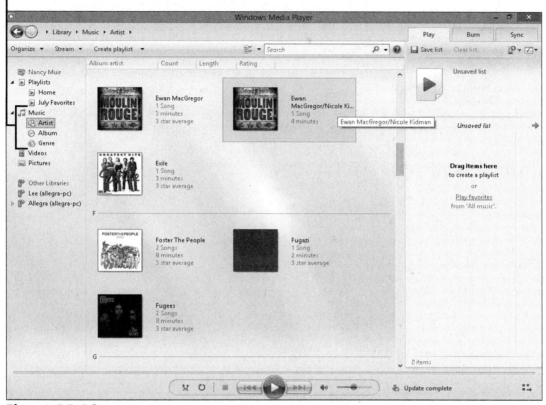

Figure 15-13

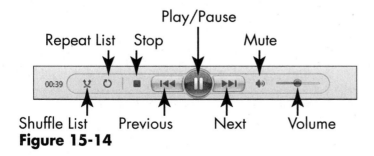

Figure 15-14

Tired of the order in which your tracks play? You can use the List Options button (the button looks like a box with a down arrow near the top on the far right on the Play pane) and choose Shuffle List to have Windows Media Player move around the tracks on your album randomly. Click this button again (it sports wavy arrows) to turn the shuffle feature off.

 To jump to another track, rather than using the Next and Previous buttons, you can double-click a track in the track list in the Media Player window. This can be much quicker if you want to jump several tracks ahead or behind of the currently playing track.

Part IV

Exploring the Internet

Understanding Internet Basics

Many people buy a laptop mainly to tap into the wonderful opportunities the Internet offers. You can use the Internet to check stock quotes, play interactive games with others, and file your taxes, for example. For seniors especially, the Internet can provide wonderful ways to keep in touch with family and friends located around the country or on the other side of the world via e-mail, video phone calls, or instant messaging. You can share photos of your grandchildren or connect with others who share your hobbies or interests.

But before you begin all those wonderful activities, it helps to understand some basics about the Internet and how it works.

This chapter helps you to understand what the Internet and World Wide Web are, as well as providing some basics about connecting to the Internet and navigating it.

Understand What the Internet Is

The Internet, links, the web . . . people and the media bounce around many online-related terms these days, and folks sometimes use them incorrectly. Your first step in getting familiar with the Internet is to understand what some of these terms mean.

Here's a list of common Internet-related terms:

➠ The *Internet* is a large network of computers that contains information and technology tools that can be accessed by anybody with an Internet connection. (See the next task for information about Internet connections.)

➠ Residing on that network of computers is a huge set of documents, which form the *World Wide Web*, usually referred to as just the *web*.

➠ The web includes *websites*, which are made up of collections of *web pages*, just as a book is made up of chapters that contain individual pages. Websites can be informational and/or host communication tools such as *chats* or *discussion boards* that allow people to "talk" via text messages. They may also provide entrance to an online retail business where you can shop, or allow you to share files with others or use software applications without having to install them on your computer.

➠ You can buy, bid for, or sell a wide variety of items in an entire online marketplace referred to as the world of *e-commerce*.

➠ To get around online, you use a software program called a *browser*. There are many browsers available, and they're free. Internet Explorer is Microsoft's browser; others include Mozilla Firefox, Google

Chrome, and Opera. Browsers offer tools to help you navigate from website to website and from one web page to another.

➡ When you open a website, you might see colored text or graphics that represent *hyperlinks*, also referred to as *links*. You can click links using your mouse to move from place to place within a web page, on a website, or between web documents. **Figure 16-1** shows some hyperlinks indicated by highlighted text (such as Start Searching Apps) or graphics (such as the Music and Games buttons).

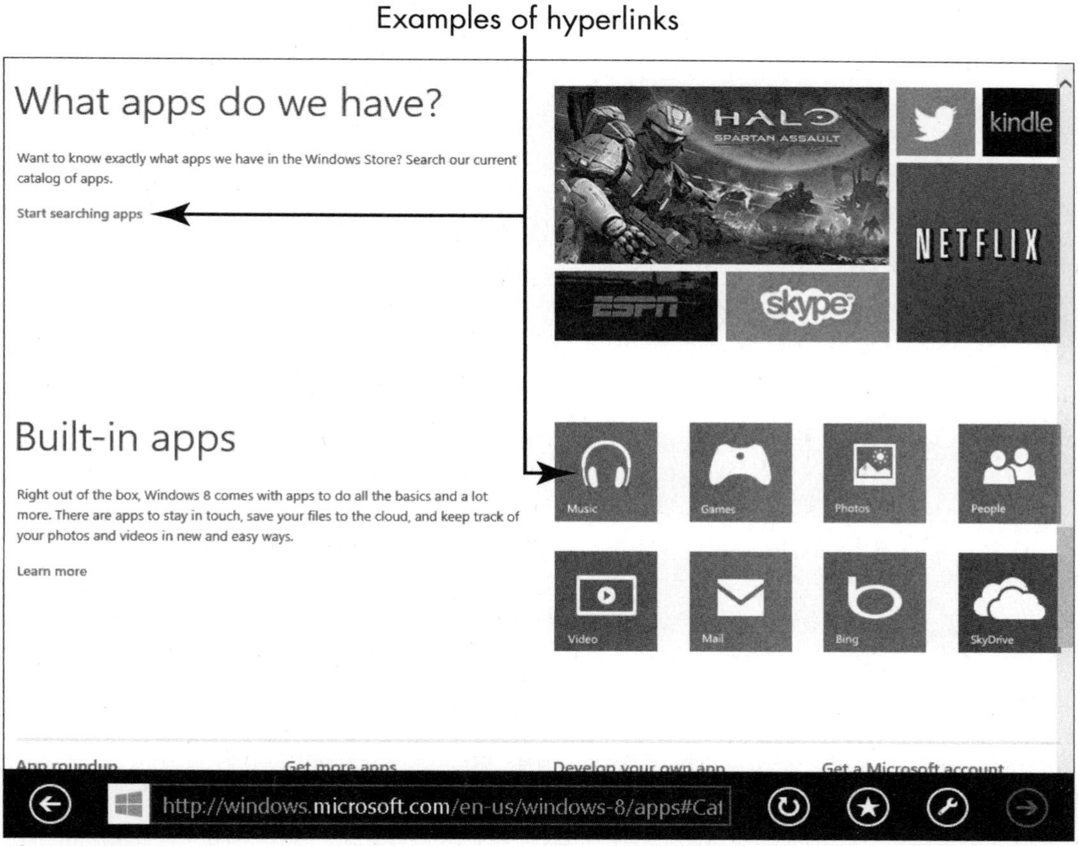

Examples of hyperlinks

What apps do we have?

Want to know exactly what apps we have in the Windows Store? Search our current catalog of apps.

Start searching apps

Built-in apps

Right out of the box, Windows 8 comes with apps to do all the basics and a lot more. There are apps to stay in touch, save your files to the cloud, and keep track of your photos and videos in new and easy ways.

Learn more

App roundup   Get more apps   Develop your own app   Get a Microsoft account

http://windows.microsoft.com/en-us/windows-8/apps#Cat

Figure 16-1

A link can be a graphic (such as a company logo) or text. A text link is identifiable by colored text, and it's usually underlined. After you click a link, it usually changes color to show that you've followed the link.

Explore Different Types of Internet Connections

Before you can connect to the Internet for the first time, you have to have certain hardware in place and choose your *Internet service provider* (also referred to as an *ISP* or simply a *provider*). An ISP is a company that owns dedicated computers (called *servers*) that you use to access the Internet. ISPs charge a monthly fee for this service.

In the past, you could sign up with an ISP such as Microsoft's MSN to get dial-up access (that is, access via your regular phone line) to the Internet. Today, many people pay to access the Internet through their telephone or cable-television provider, whose connections are much faster than a dial-up connection.

You can choose the type of connection you want to use to go online. Depending on the type of connection you want, you'll go to a different company for the service. For example, a DSL connection might come through your phone company, whereas a cable connection is available through your cable-TV company.

Wireless connections provide a convenient and sometimes free way to go online when you travel with your laptop. You can use them for free at Wi-Fi hotspots such as an Internet cafe, or you can subscribe to a wireless network so that you can pick up Wi-Fi signals as you roam.

Some laptops and tablet devices can pick up a connection from a 3G or 4G-enabled cellphone if they are out of range of a network, although this usually involves paying an additional fee to your cellphone company for a personal hotspot.

Not every type of connection is necessarily available in every area, so check with phone, cable, and small Internet providers in your town to find out your options and costs. (Some offer discounts to AARP members, for example.)

Here are the most common types of connections:

➡ **Dial-up connections:** With a dial-up connection, you plug your laptop into a phone line at home or at a hotel room or friend's house to connect to the Internet, entering a phone number that's provided by your ISP. This is the slowest connection method, but it's relatively inexpensive. Your dial-up Internet provider will give you *local access numbers*, which you use to go online. Using these local access numbers, you won't incur long distance charges for your connection. However, with this type of connection, you can't use a phone line for phone calls while you're connected to the Internet, so it's no longer a very popular way to connect.

➡ **Digital Subscriber Line:** DSL also uses a phone line, but your phone is available to you to make calls even when you're connected to the Internet. DSL is a form of broadband communication, which may use phone lines and fiber-optic cables for transmission. You have to subscribe to a broadband service (check with your phone company) and pay a monthly fee for access.

➡ **Cable:** You can go through your local cable company to get your Internet service via the cable that brings your TV programming rather than your phone line. This is another type of broadband service, and it's also faster than a dial-up connection. Check with your cable company for monthly fees.

➡ **Satellite:** Especially in rural areas, satellite Internet providers may be your only option. This requires that you install a satellite dish. BlueDish and Comcast are two providers of satellite connections to check into.

➠ **Wireless hotspots:** If you take a wireless-enabled laptop computer with you on a trip, you can piggy-back on a connection somebody else has made. You will find wireless hotspots in many public places, such as airports, cafes, and hotels. If you're in range of such a hotspot, your laptop usually finds the connection automatically, making Internet service available to you for free or for a fee. You may need to ask the folks at the hotspot for a password to log in.

Internet connections have different speeds that depend partially on your laptop's capabilities and partially on the connection you get from your provider. Before you choose a provider, it's important to understand how faster connection speeds can benefit you:

➠ Faster speeds allow you to send data faster (for example, to upload a photo to a photo sharing site). In addition, web pages and images display faster.

➠ Dial-up connection speeds run at the low end, about 56 kilobits per second, or Kbps. Most broadband connections today are around 500 to 600 Kbps. If you have a slower connection, a file might take minutes to upload (for example, a file you're attaching to an e-mail). This same operation might take only seconds at a higher speed.

Depending on your type of connection, you'll need different hardware:

➠ A broadband connection uses an Ethernet cable and a modem, which your provider should make available, as well as a connection to your phone or cable line.

➠ Some laptops come with a built-in modem for dial-up connections (though these are being left out more and more as people move to wireless connections) or are enabled for wireless service. If you choose a broadband connection, your phone or cable company provides you with an external modem and wireless router (usually for a price). Remember, however, that you can't use this connection when you travel with your laptop.

➡ If you have a laptop that doesn't have a built-in wireless modem, you can add this hardware by buying a wireless CardBus adapter PC card at any office supply or computer store. This card enables a laptop to pick up wireless signals.

◎ Many providers offer free or low-cost setup when you open a new account. If you're not technical by nature, consider taking advantage of this when you sign up.

◎ If you fly with your laptop, you may not be able to connect to the Internet during the flight. Also, it's important to remember that during takeoff and landing, you'll be asked to turn off electronics so that they don't interfere with air traffic communications. Be alert to the announcement if you intend to use your laptop on the plane. Some tablet computers and smartphones come with an Airport setting that disables any disruptive communications while in flight.

Set Up an Internet Connection

1. The first step in going online is to set up a connection in Windows so that you can access the Internet. From the Desktop, press Win+I to display the Settings, and then click Control Panel.

2. Click Network and Internet and in the resulting window, click Network and Sharing Center.

3. In the resulting Network and Sharing Center window (see **Figure 16-2**), click the Set Up a New Connection or Network link.

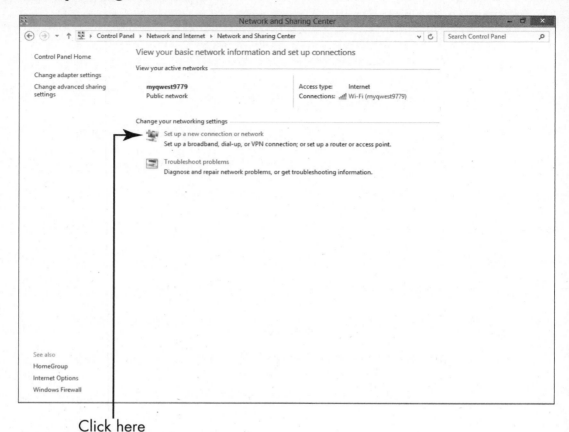

Click here

Figure 16-2

4. In the Choose a Connection Option window, click Next to accept the default option of creating a new Internet connection. If you are already connected to the Internet, a window appears; click Set Up A New Connection Anyway.

5. In the resulting dialog box, click your connection. (These steps follow the selection of Broadband. Other options could include Dial Up.)

6. In the resulting dialog box, as shown in **Figure 16-3,** enter your username, password, and connection name (if you want to assign one) and then click Connect. Windows detects the connection automatically, and the Network and Sharing Center appears with your connection listed.

Figure 16-3

 In many cases, if you have a disc from your ISP, you don't need to follow the preceding steps. Just pop that DVD into your DVD-ROM drive, and in no time, a window appears that gives you the steps to follow to get set up.

Compare Popular Browsers

A *browser* is a program that you use to navigate around the Internet. Popular browsers include Internet Explorer from Microsoft, Firefox from Mozilla, Opera from Opera Software, Chrome from Google, and Safari from Apple.

Most browsers have similar features and all are free. Internet Explorer is preinstalled on Windows-based laptops, but you can download any browser by going to its associated website (see Chapter 17 for more about browsing to websites). You can install and use multiple browsers if you like. Here are some features to consider when choosing a browser:

➠ **Safety features:** Browsing the web can be dangerous; certain sites will attempt to download dangerous programs such as viruses to your computer. Even if you have an antivirus program installed on your computer, choose a browser with robust security and privacy features. An advisor feature that ranks sites based on their safety record when they appear in search results is a good feature to have.

➠ **Favorites and Bookmarking:** The ability to save links to sites you like to visit often is very useful. Just about every browser has Favorites and Bookmarking features, and some also provide a feature such as IE's Frequent page, which appears whenever you open a new tab. It provides icons for accessing your most-often visited sites.

➠ **Tabs:** Browsers that use *tabs* allow you to open more than one site at a time so you can jump back and forth among them or open an additional site easily. Most of the current browsers use the tab approach, but an older version of a browser may not. Don't worry, you can always update a browser by going to the browser creator's site and downloading the latest version.

Navigate the Web

1. You need to learn how to get around the web using a browser such as the popular Internet Explorer (IE) from Microsoft. If you have Windows 8 or 8.1, you can actually access two different versions of IE depending on whether you open it from the Start Screen or Desktop. You open IE from the Desktop by clicking the Internet Explorer tile. Open IE Desktop by clicking the Internet Explorer icon in the Windows Taskbar.

2. In the Desktop IE, enter a web address in the Address bar, as shown in **Figure 16-4,** and then press Enter.

Enter a web address here

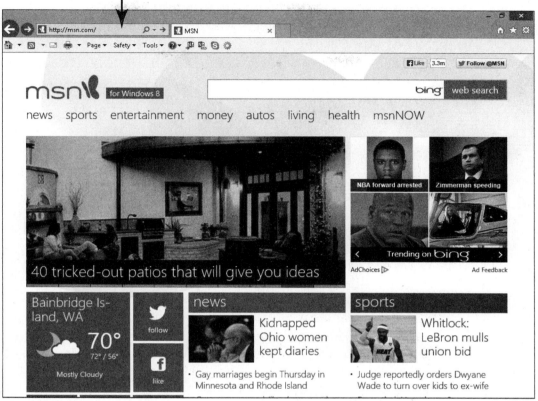

Figure 16-4

3. On the resulting web site, click a link (short for *hyperlink;* a *link* takes you to another online page or document), display another page on the site using navigation tools on the page (such as an About Us or Contact Us link common on most retail sites), or enter another address in the address bar to proceed to another page.

> A text link is identifiable by colored text, usually blue. After you click a link, it usually changes to another color (such as purple) to show that it's been followed.

4. Click the Back button to move back to the first page that you visited. Click the Forward button to go forward to the second page that you visited.

5. Click the down-pointing arrow at the far right of the
Address bar to display a list of sites that you visited
recently, as shown in **Figure 16-5**. Click a site in this list
to go there.

Click a site to visit   Click to see recently visited sites

Figure 16-5

 The Refresh and Stop buttons that appear on the right
end of the Address bar are useful for navigating sites.
Clicking the Refresh button (it's a circle with an arrow
at the end) redisplays the current page. This is especially useful if a page updates information frequently,
such as on a stock market site. You can also use the
Refresh button if a page doesn't load correctly; it
might load correctly when refreshed. Clicking the Stop
button (an X shape that appears when a site is load-
ing) stops a page you've begun to access from appear-
ing. If you made a mistake entering the address, or if

the page is taking longer than you'd like to load, click the Stop button to halt the process.

Use Tabs in Browsers

1. Tabs allow you to have several web pages open at once and easily switch among them. With Desktop Internet Explorer open, click New Tab (the smallest, blank tab on the far right side of the tabs).

2. When the new tab appears, your most frequently visited sites are displayed (see **Figure 16-6**). You can click on a frequent site, or enter a URL in the Address bar and press Enter. The web site opens in that tab. You can then click other tabs to switch among open sites.

A new tab

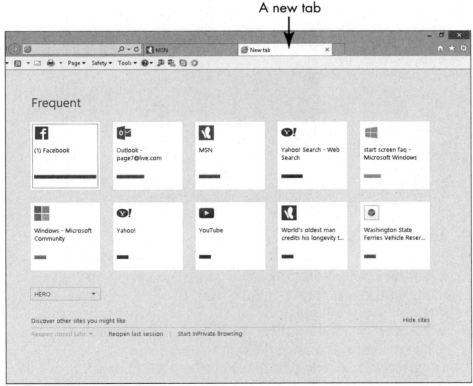

Figure 16-6

3. You can return to a page by clicking that page's tab, thumbnail, or name in the drop-down list (see **Figure 16-7**) that you display by clicking the arrow in the Address bar.

Click x to close a tab

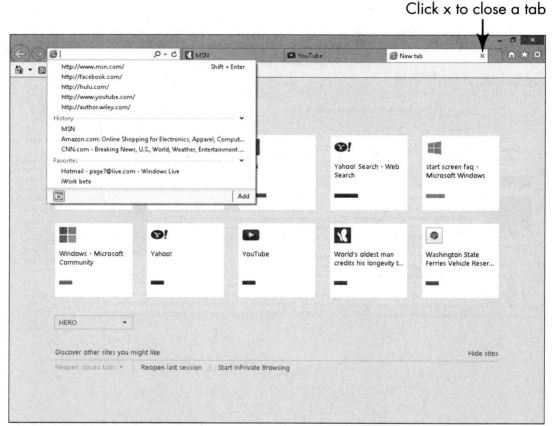

Figure 16-7

4. Close an active tab by clicking the Close button on the right side of the tab.

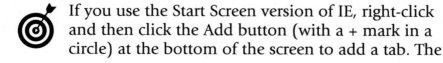 If you use the Start Screen version of IE, right-click and then click the Add button (with a + mark in a circle) at the bottom of the screen to add a tab. The

black area at the bottom of the screen shows any currently open tabs and you can enter a new URL to add a tab.

 You can also press Ctrl+T to open a new tab in either version of Internet Explorer. Also, if you want to keep one tab open and close all others, right-click the tab you want to keep open and choose Close Other Tabs.

Set Up a Home Page

1. Your home page(s) appears automatically every time you log on to the Internet, so choose one or a few sites that you go to often for this setting. Open Desktop Internet Explorer and click the Tools icon in the upper right corner. Then choose Internet Options from the resulting menu.

2. In the resulting Internet Options dialog box, on the General tab, enter a website address to use as your home page, as shown in **Figure 16-8,** and then click OK. Note that you can enter several home pages that will appear on different tabs every time you open IE, as shown in **Figure 16-8.**

Alternatively, click one of the following preset option buttons shown in **Figure 16-8:**

- **Use Current:** Sets whatever page is currently displayed in the browser window as your home page.

- **Use Default:** This setting sends you to the MSN web page.

- **Use New Tab:** If you're a minimalist, this setting is for you. No web page displays; you just see the Frequent blank tab.

Enter home page addresses here

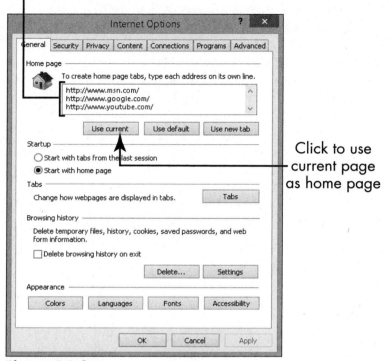

Figure 16-8

3. Click the Home button (see **Figure 16-9**) on the IE tool-bar (it looks like a little house) to go to your home page.

Click to go to your home page

Figure 16-9

 If you want to have more than one home page, you can create multiple home-page tabs that appear onscreen when you click the Home button. Click the arrow on the Home button and choose Add or Change Home Page. In the Add or Change Home Page dialog box that appears, click the Add This Web

Page to Your Home Page Tabs radio button, and then click Yes. Display other sites and repeat this procedure to add all the home-page tabs you want.

 To remove one home page when you have set up multiple home pages, click the Home Page button, choose Remove, and then choose a particular home page or choose Remove All from the submenu that appears.

Browsing the Web with Internet Explorer

A *browser* is a program that you can use to move from one web page to another, but you can also use it to perform searches for information and images. Most browsers, such as Internet Explorer (IE) and Mozilla Firefox, are available for free. Macintosh computers come with a browser called Safari preinstalled with the operating system.

Chapter 16 introduces browser basics, such as how to go directly to a site when you know the web address, how to use the Back and Forward buttons to move among sites you've visited, and how to set up the home page that opens automatically when you launch your browser.

In this chapter, you discover the ins and outs of using the Desktop version of Internet Explorer (Desktop IE) and the Start screen version.

Using IE, you can

➠ **Navigate all around the web.** Use the IE navigation features to go back to places you've been (via the Favorites and History features), work with tabs to move among several open websites, and use a search engine to find new places to visit.

➡ **Customize your web-browsing experience.** You can modify what tools are available to you on Internet Explorer toolbars to make your work online easier.

➡ **Subscribe to RSS feeds.** You can request that a site alert you when it adds new content, so that you can stay up to date on news or opinions from various sources.

➡ **Print content from web pages.** When you find what you want online, such as an image or article, just use IE's Print feature to generate a hard copy.

Understand Differences between the Two Versions of IE

With Windows 8, Microsoft also introduced two new versions of Internet Explorer 11: the first you access through the Start screen and the other you access through the Desktop. Here's how they differ:

➡ **Start screen IE:** This version was designed along the lines of Windows 8/8.1: a less-cluttered screen (see **Figure 17-1**); no drop-down menus and dialog boxes for making settings, just a few simple buttons and an address field along the bottom of the screen; tabs you can display showing thumbnails of recently visited sites; and Internet Options you can manage from the Settings charm. You may have to right-click the screen to display the address field and tabs.

➡ **Desktop IE:** More familiar to users of previous versions of IE, Desktop IE 11 offers an address field across the top of the screen, toolbars with drop-down menus such as File and Favorites, as well as tools for going to your home page and changing safety and other settings (see **Figure 17-2**).

This chapter focuses on Desktop IE.

Figure 17-1

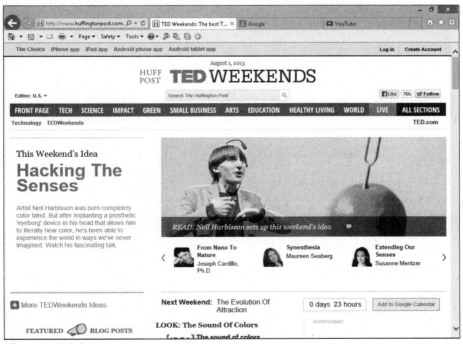

Figure 17-2

Search the Web Using Desktop IE

1. You can use words and phrases to search for information on the web using a search engine no matter which browser you use. In this example, you'll use Desktop IE and Google, a popular search engine. From the Desktop, click the Internet Explorer icon in the taskbar and type www.google.com in the address bar and press Enter.

2. Type a search term in the search box and then click the Google Search button.

3. In the search results that appear (see **Figure 17-3**), you can click a link to go to that web page. If you don't see the link that you need, click and drag the scroll bar to view more results.

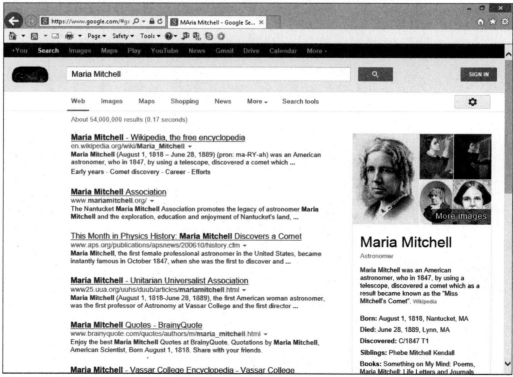

Figure 17-3

4. Click the cog-shaped Options button near the top-right corner of the Google search screen (refer to **Figure 17-3**), and then click Advanced Search to change Search parameters.

5. In the resulting Advanced Search page, shown in **Figure 17-4**, modify the following parameters:

- **Find Web Pages With:** These options let you narrow the way words or phrases are searched; for example, you can find matches for only the exact wording you enter or enter words that you want to exclude from your results. For example, you could search *flu* and specify you don't want results that involve *swine flu*.

- **Then Narrow Your Results By:** Here you can select language and region. You can also limit results based on when information on the site was last updated, if you're looking for the most current information on the subject you're searching. You can specify a site address and where on the page to search. You can also adjust safety settings for your search by using the SafeSearch drop-down list, or adjust the reading level, file type, and *usage rights settings* (in other words, any copyrights that prohibit you from reusing content).

When you're done with the settings, click the Advanced Search button to run the search again with the new criteria.

 Knowing how search engines work can save you time. For example, if you search by entering *golden retriever*, you typically get sites that contain both words or either word. If you put a plus sign between these two keywords (*golden+retriever*), you get only sites that contain both words.

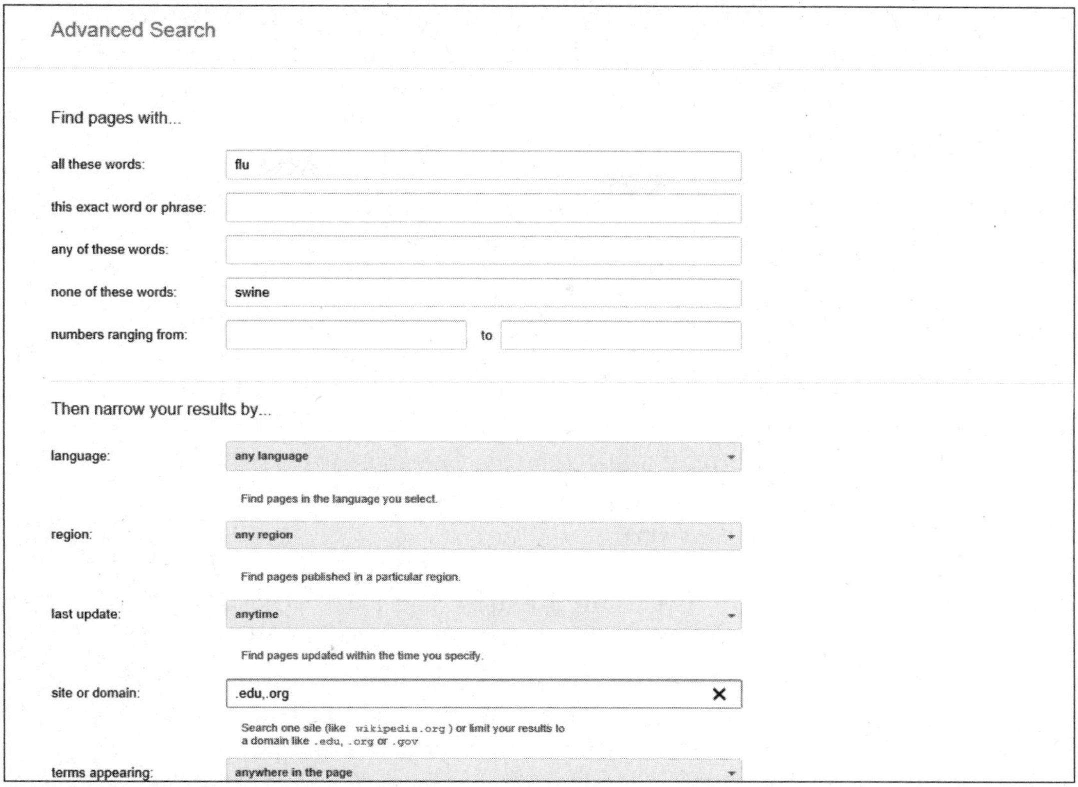

Advanced Search

Find pages with...

all these words:	flu
this exact word or phrase:	
any of these words:	
none of these words:	swine
numbers ranging from:	to

Then narrow your results by...

language: | any language ▼

Find pages in the language you select.

region: | any region ▼

Find pages published in a particular region.

last update: | anytime ▼

Find pages updated within the time you specify.

site or domain: | .edu,.org | ✕

Search one site (like wikipedia.org) or limit your results to a domain like .edu, .org or .gov

terms appearing: | anywhere in the page ▼

Figure 17-4

Find Content on a Web Page

1. With Desktop Internet Explorer open, enter a URL in the address field, and press Enter. Click the Edit menu on the IE toolbar (if this doesn't appear on your screen, right-click in the toolbar area and click Menu bar to display it) and choose Find on this Page.

2. In the resulting Find toolbar that appears on the top of the page, as shown in **Figure 17-5**, enter the word that you want to search for. As you type, all instances of the word on the page are highlighted.

3. Click the Next button to the right of the Find field and you move from one highlighted instance of the word to

the next (see **Figure 17-6**). If you want to move to a previous instance, click the Previous button.

Enter a search term here

Figure 17-5

4. When you're done searching on a page, click the Close button at the left end of the Find on this Page toolbar.

 Many websites have a Search This Site feature that allows you to search not only the displayed web page but all web pages on a website, or to search by department or category of item in an online store. Look for a Search text box and make sure that it searches the site — and not the entire Internet.

Previous and Next

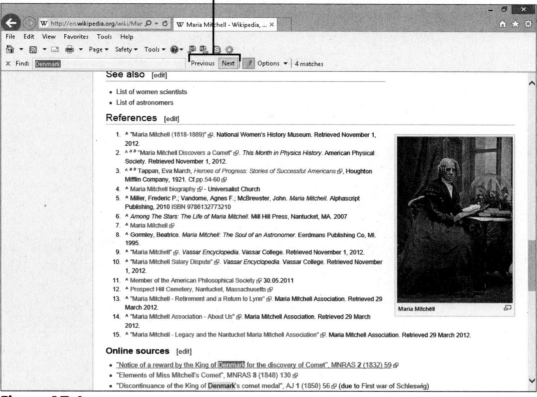

Figure 17-6

Add a Website to Favorites

1. If there's a site you intend to revisit, you may want to save it to IE's Favorites folder so you can easily go there again. To use this feature, open IE from the Desktop, enter the URL of a website that you want to add to your Favorites list, and then press Enter.

2. Click the Favorites button (a star near the top-right corner of the browser screen) to display the Favorites pane.

3. In the resulting Add a Favorite dialog box, shown in **Figure 17-7**, modify the name of the Favorite listing to

something easily recognizable. If you wish, choose another folder or create a folder to store the Favorite in.

Figure 17-7

4. Click the Add button to add the site.

When you want to return to the site, click the Favorites button and then click the name of the site from the list that's displayed (see **Figure 17-8**).

Figure 17-8

Regularly cleaning out your Favorites list is a good idea — after all, do you really need the sites that you used to plan last year's vacation? With the Favorites Center displayed, right-click any item and then choose Delete or Rename to modify the Favorites listing.

 You can keep the Favorites Center as a side pane in Internet Explorer by displaying it and then clicking the Pin the Favorites Center button (it has a left-facing green arrow on it and is located in the top-left corner of the pane).

Organize Favorites

1. You can organize favorites into folders to make them easier to find. With Internet Explorer open from the Desktop, click the Favorites button to open the Favorites pane. Click the arrow on the right of the Add to Favorites button and then choose Organize Favorites.

2. In the resulting Organize Favorites dialog box (see **Figure 17-9**), click New Folder to create a new folder to store items in and give it a name, or click an item in the Favorites list and then click Move, Rename, or Delete to organize or clean up your favorites list.

3. When you finish organizing your Favorites, click Close.

 If you create new folders in these steps, you need to manually transfer files into those folders. To do this, just display the Favorites Center and click and drag a file listed there into a folder.

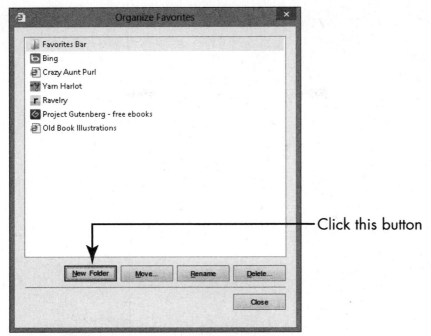

Figure 17-9

View Your Browsing History

1. If you went to a site recently and want to return there again but can't remember the name, you might check your browsing history to find it. In the Desktop Internet Explorer application, click the Favorites button and then click the History tab to display the History pane (see **Figure 17-10**).

History
tab

Figure 17-10

2. Click the down-arrow on the View By button (see
Figure 17-11) and select a sort method:

- **View By Date:** Sort favorites by date visited.

- **View By Site:** Sort alphabetically by site name.

- **View By Most Visited:** Sort with the sites visited
  most at the top of and those visited least at the
  bottom of the list.

- **View By Order Visited Today:** Sort by the order in
  which you visited sites today.

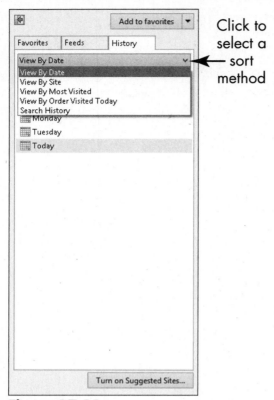

Click to select a sort method

Figure 17-11

3. In the History pane, you can click to drill down to sites or pages on a particular site visited on a particular day and then click an item to go to it. The History pane closes.

> You can also choose the arrow on the right of the Address bar to display sites you've visited.

> Choose Search History on the menu on the History tab to display a search box you can use to search for sites you've visited.

Customize the Internet Explorer Toolbar

1. You can customize the toolbars that offer common commands in IE 11 so that the commands you use most often are included. Open IE from the Desktop and be sure the Command bar is displayed (if it's not, right-click in the toolbar area and click to select Command bar in the list that appears).

2. Click the Tools button on the right side of the Command bar, choose Toolbars, and then choose Customize. The Customize Toolbar dialog box (shown in **Figure 17-12**) appears.

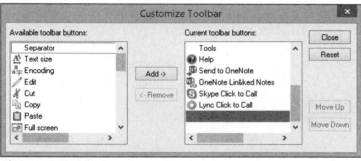

Figure 17-12

3. Click a tool on the left and then click the Add button to add it to the toolbar.

4. To remove a tool from the toolbar, click a tool on the right and then click the Remove button.

5. When you're finished, click Close to save your new toolbar settings. The new tools appear (see **Figure 17-13**); click the double-arrow button on the right of the toolbar to display any tools that IE can't fit onscreen.

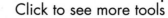

Click to see more tools

Figure 17-13

 You can use the Move Up and Move Down buttons in the Customize Toolbar dialog box to rearrange the order in which tools appear on the toolbar. To reset the toolbar to defaults, click the Reset button in that same dialog box.

 If you want to add some space between tools on the toolbar so they're easier to see, click the Separator item in the Available Toolbar Buttons list and add it before or after a tool button.

Print a Web Page

1. If a web page includes a link or button to print or display a print version of a page, click that and follow the instructions.

2. If the page doesn't include a link for printing, click the Print button on the Desktop IE toolbar or press Ctrl+P on your keyboard.

3. In the resulting Print dialog box, decide how much of the document you want to print (All, Selected content, or a range of pages) in the Page Range area, as shown in **Figure 17-14**.

 Note that choosing Current Page or entering page numbers in the Pages text box of the Print dialog box doesn't mean much when printing a web page — the whole document might print because web pages aren't divided into pages as word-processing program documents are.

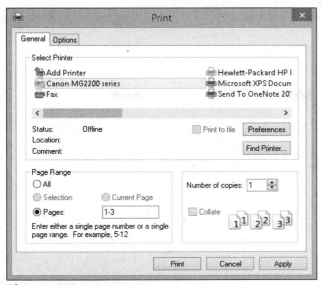

Figure 17-14

4. Click the up arrow in the Number of Copies text box to print multiple copies. If you want to collate multiple copies, select the Collate check box.

5. After you adjust all settings as needed, click Print.

Enter a Web Site Address Using Start Screen IE

1. The version of Internet Explorer you access from the Start screen looks and behaves a bit differently from Desktop IE. To open Start screen IE, click the Internet Explorer tile on the Start screen.

2. Right-click to display the tabs and address bar at the bottom of the screen (see Figure 17-15).

3. Enter a website URL in the Address bar and press Enter. The page is displayed.

To go the displayed site in Desktop IE, click the Page Tools button (shaped like a wrench) to the far right of the Address bar and choose View On the Desktop.

Figure 17-15

Navigate among Pages

1. With Start screen IE open, right-click and enter a URL in the Address bar.

2. Click the left-facing arrow to the left of the Address field to go back to the previous page (see **Figure 17-16**).

3. Move your mouse over the right side of the web page and an arrow appears in the middle of the page on that side (see **Figure 17-16**).

4. Click the right-facing arrow in the middle of the page to move to the next page. You can use the previous and next arrows in the Address bar and on the sides of the displayed page interchangeably to move to previously viewed pages.

Figure 17-16

Display Tabs

1. With Start screen IE open, right-click to display the tabs shown in **Figure 17-17**.

Figure 17-17

2. Click the New Tab button on the far right (it's shaped like a big plus sign).

3. In the field that opens, enter the URL of the site you want to open on a new tab and press Enter, or click a site from the Pinned, Frequent, or Favorite items displayed above the field. The site is opened in a new tab. To move among tabs, right-click and then click on the tab you want to view.

 InPrivate browsing is a feature that prevents IE from saving data about your browsing habits. To turn on

the InPrivate browsing feature, right-click and then click the Tab Tools button on the right, which sports three dots. Select New InPrivate Tab from the menu that appears. To turn off In Private browsing, display the tabs and click the close button on the InPrivate tab to close it and the feature.

Use Start Screen IE Settings

1. When you are working in an app such as Internet Explorer, the Settings you access from the Windows 8.1 Charm bar are specific to that app. With the Start screen IE open, press Win+C to open the Charm bar.

2. Click Settings and then click Options in the list of settings that appears.

3. In the panel that appears (see **Figure 17-18**), make selections for the following settings:

- **Appearance:** Use the On/Off slider to always show the address bar and tabs, and the Zoom feature to enlarge or reduce the size of pages in your browser.

- **Home Pages:** Click the Customize button here to choose your IE home pages.

- **History:** Click the Select button here to control what browsing data you want to retain or delete from your laptop.

- **Passwords:** Turn on this feature to be able to go to the next page on a website; information will be sent to Microsoft if you turn this feature on so that they can "improve" your browsing experience.

- **Phone Numbers**: Turn this setting on to be able to call phone numbers you find on a web site.

- **Fonts and Encoding:** With this on, IE adjusts for text on a web page that doesn't seem to be in your preferred language.

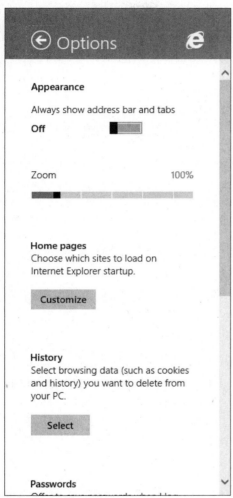

Figure 17-18

Working in the Cloud

You may have heard the term *cloud* bandied about. The term comes from the world of computer networks, where certain functionality isn't installed on computers but resides on the network itself, in the so-called cloud, where it can be accessed by individual computers.

Today, definition of the term has broadened to include functionality that resides on the Internet. If you can get work done without using an installed piece of software — or if you store and share photos online or work with an e-mail service such as Gmail or Outlook — you're working in the cloud. The cloud is especially useful to you if you travel with your laptop as you can store content online and access it wherever you are (if you have an Internet connection) without having to carry it on a USB stick, DVD, or store it on your hard drive.

Chapter 18

Get ready to . . .

In this chapter, you discover the types of applications you might use in the cloud, saving you the cost and effort of buying and installing software. In addition, I explore two Windows 8.1 features that help you access your own data in the cloud: Sync and SkyDrive. Sync allows you to share the settings you've made in Windows 8.1 on one computer with other Windows 8.1 computers. SkyDrive is a file-sharing service that has been around a while, but with Windows 8.1, sharing files from your laptop with others or with yourself on another computer is more seamless than ever.

Use Applications Online

Certain apps, such as Maps and People, are built into Windows 8.1. You may purchase or download and install other apps, such as Fresh Paint or Angry Birds, or applications such as Microsoft Word or Excel. Although these apps and applications may connect to the Internet to get information — such as the latest traffic info or software help files — the software itself is installed on your laptop.

Today, you have the option of using software in the cloud, meaning that you never install the software on your laptop but simply make use of it online. Here are some examples you can explore:

➡ **Google Docs via Google Drive:** This service offers the ability to view, copy, comment, and print your uploaded files (available at `www.docs.google.com`; see **Figure 18-1**). This feature is compatible with popular office software such as Microsoft Word and PowerPoint as well as graphics file formats such as PNG or JPEG.

➡ **E-mail clients:** When you log into Gmail or into Outlook.com to work with your Microsoft e-mail accounts such as Hotmail, you're using the software in the cloud. In addition, some e-mail clients which access various email accounts, such as Outlook, connect with file-sharing sites so that, rather than

attaching files to e-mail messages, you are given the option of uploading and sharing them on the file sharing site. Windows Live Hotmail using SkyDrive is one example of this scenario.

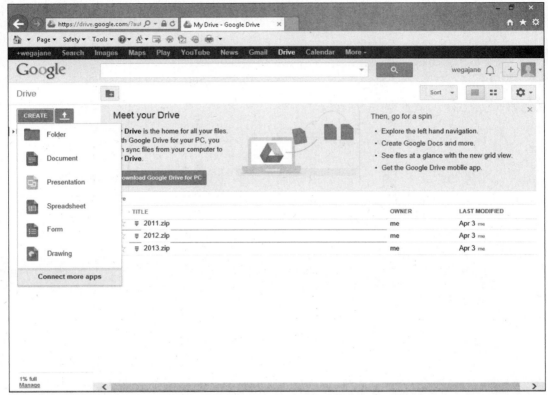

Figure 18-1

⇒ **Photo-sharing sites:** Sites such as Flickr (`www.flickr.com`), shown in **Figure 18-2,** allow you to upload and download photos to them without ever installing an app on your computer. A variation on this is a site such as Viewbook (`www.viewbook.com`), where you can create an online portfolio of art samples or business presentations, for example, to share with others.

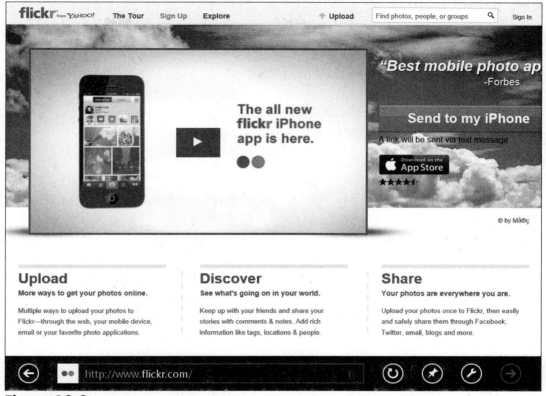

Figure 18-2

➠ **Financial applications:** You might use a site such as Portfolio Monkey (www.portfoliomonkey.com) to maintain an online portfolio of investments and generate charts to help you keep track of trends. You can also use online versions of popular money-management programs, such as Intuit's free online service Mint (www.mint.com), through which you can access your data from any computer or mobile device.

Add Files to SkyDrive

1. You can easily add files to SkyDrive at any time to back them up or share them with others. Click the SkyDrive tile on the Start screen.

2. Click a folder, such as Documents (see **Figure 18-3**), and then in the list of sub-folders and files that appears, click a folder or file and it opens.

Figure 18-3

3. Right-click the screen, then click the Add Items button in the toolbar.

4. Locate the folder where the file you want to upload is placed (see **Figure 18-4**). (If you don't see the file you need, scroll down in the list of folders on the left, click the Go Up button, or click the down-arrow to the right of the SkyDrive header; more folders are displayed.)

5. Click a file.

6. Click Open.

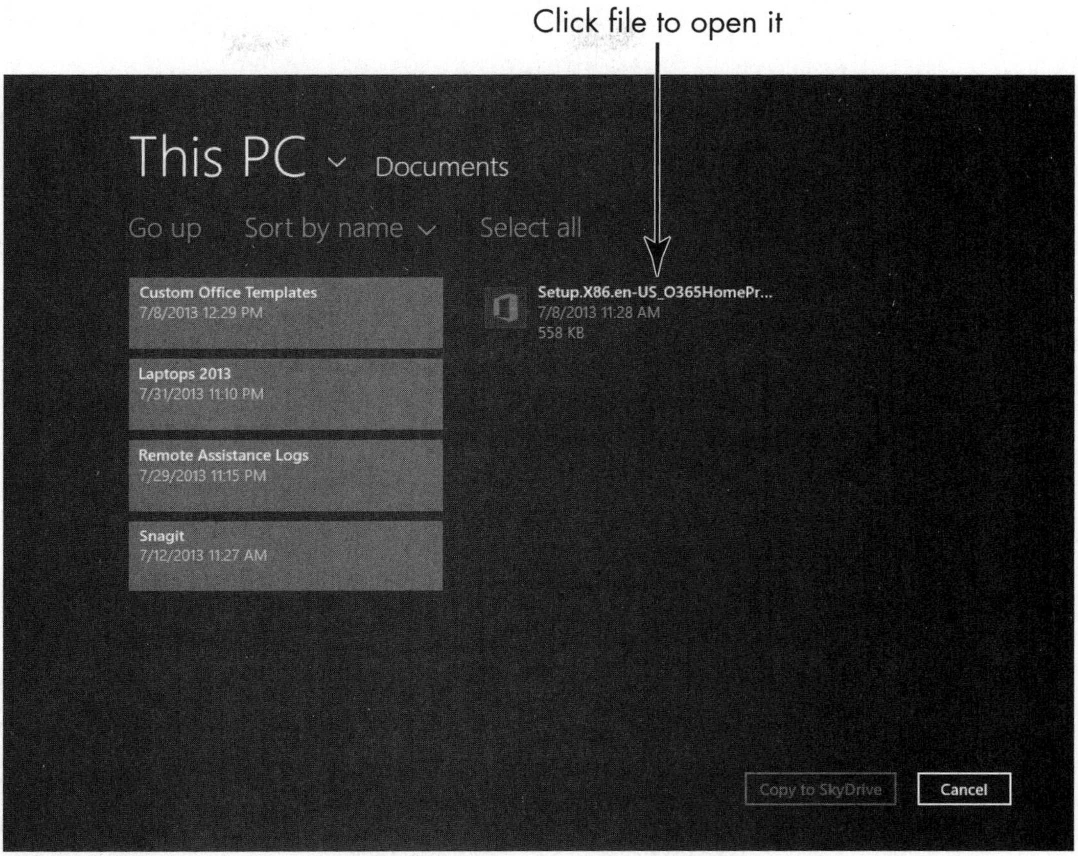

Click file to open it

This PC ⌄ Documents

Go up   Sort by name ⌄   Select all

Custom Office Templates
7/8/2013 12:29 PM

Laptops 2013
7/31/2013 11:10 PM

Remote Assistance Logs
7/29/2013 11:15 PM

Snagit
7/12/2013 11:27 AM

Setup.X86.en-US_O365HomePr...
7/8/2013 11:28 AM
558 KB

Copy to SkyDrive   Cancel

Figure 18-4

You may want to delete a file from SkyDrive, as the free storage is limited to 7 gigabytes (GB). First, find the file in SkyDrive that you want to delete, and right-click it. Click Delete. In the pop-up menu that appears, click Delete.

Share Files Using SkyDrive

1. SkyDrive allows you to upload and share files with others. With Windows 8.1, you can share larger files such as videos and photos via SkyDrive as you're working with the Mail app. Sharing files online can be easier than sending them as attachments because e-mail programs typically limit how much data you can send at one time.

You can share items from within apps such as Camera (assuming you have a camera built into your laptop, which most computers today have). Click the Camera tile on the Start screen.

2. Click the camera button to take a picture.

3. Return to Start screen, click the SkyDrive tile, and click to display a photo.

4. Press Win+C, and then click Share. You can choose a sharing options on the right such as posting to Facebook or sending via Mail (options may vary depending on other settings in Windows; see **Figure** 18-5).

Figure 18-5

5. Click Send E-mail.

6. Enter the e-mail address for the person you're sharing with.

7. Enter a message if you like, use the check boxes below the message to set whether the recipient can edit the content and whether those accessing content have to sign in, and then click Share.

8. Now when your recipient opens his e-mail account, he can click the link to view the item on SkyDrive.

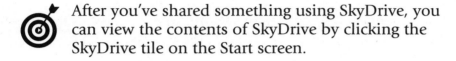 After you've shared something using SkyDrive, you can view the contents of SkyDrive by clicking the SkyDrive tile on the Start screen.

Create a New SkyDrive Folder

1. You can keep your shared files in order by placing them in folders on SkyDrive. After you've placed content in folders, you can then share those folders with others. This ability to share individual folders gives you a measure of security, as you don't have to share access to your entire body of SkyDrive content with anybody. Click the Internet Explorer tile on the Start screen.

2. Right-click to display the Address field (see **Figure 18-6**). Type https://skydrive.live.com and press Enter.

Figure 18-6

3. Click the Create button and then click Folder and enter a name for the new folder.

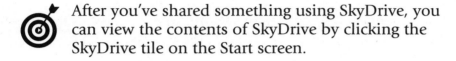 When you click the SkyDrive tile on the Start screen, you see folders of content stored online. When you go to the SkyDrive site by entering www.skydrive.com into any browser's address field, you have more

options for displaying your content by criteria such as name, date modified, and with whom your folders are shared.

Share a SkyDrive Folder with Others

1. SkyDrive's purpose is to allow you to share files with others, but you can only share folders from SkyDrive if you go to the site online (rather than using the SkyDrive tile on your Start screen). Sharing can involve allowing others to view content, or granting permission to edit it. Open SkyDrive in a browser (www.skydrive.com) and then click Files to display the Files list (see **Figure 18-7**).

Click files

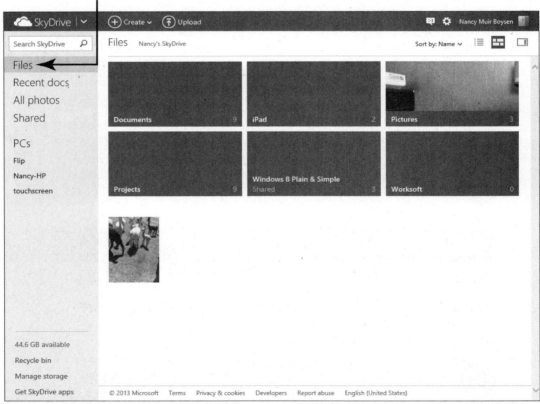

Figure 18-7

2. Right-click a folder.

3. Choose Sharing. A warning may appear about sharing and your privacy; click Share this Folder to proceed. Enter an e-mail address (see **Figure 18-8**).

Enter an email address

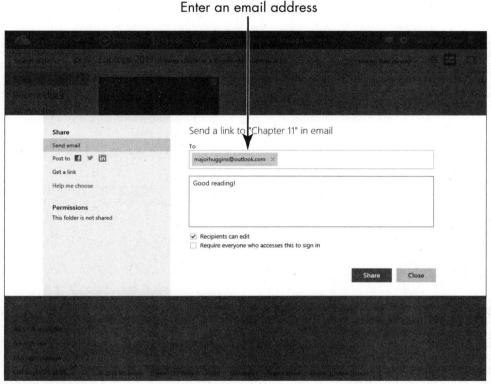

Figure 18-8

4. You can enter a note, although this is optional.

5. If you don't want to allow the person you're sharing with to edit files, deselect the Recipients Can Edit check box.

6. Click Send.

 When you share a word-processing file with another person on SkyDrive and grant permission to edit it, she can edit it in a Word Web App (a cloud version of Microsoft Word) or open the document in Microsoft Word on her computer.

Turn On the Sync Feature

1. You can use the Sync feature to share your PC settings among Windows 8.1 devices so you don't have to redo the settings on each device. To sync, you have to turn on the sync feature. With the Sync feature turned on, sign into your Windows Live account on another device, and all your settings will be synced from the cloud. To begin, press Win+I.

2. Click Change PC Settings, and then click SkyDrive⇨Sync Settings.

3. Click the Sync Settings on This PC On/Off button (see **Figure 18-9**).

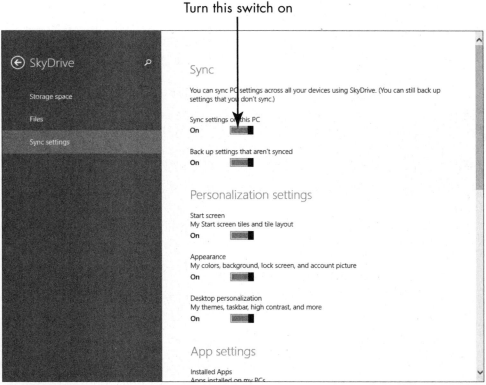

Turn this switch on

Figure 18-9

Syncing works only with Windows 8 or 8.1 settings and settings for apps that you buy from the Windows Store.

Choose Which Settings You Want to Sync

1. When you turn on syncing, you can choose what you want to share. For example, you can share language preferences, passwords, or Ease of Access settings — it's up to you. To set up what you want to sync, begin by pressing Win+I.

2. Click Change PC Settings.

3. Click SkyDrive⇨Sync Settings.

4. Click the On/Off buttons for the various settings you want to share such as Personalization or App settings (refer to **Figure 18-9**). With Sync turned on, selected settings are synced automatically among Windows 8.1 devices.

If you're charged for data or Internet connection time — for example on a Windows 8.1 tablet with 3G — go to Sync Settings in the PC Settings and click the On/Off button under Sync and Back Up Settings over Metered Internet Connections. You might want to keep the next item, Sync and Back Up Settings over Metered Connections Even When I'm Roaming, off, as syncing settings while roaming can cost you a lot.

Staying Safe While Online

*I*f you're using your laptop to go online, you're probably enjoying all the Internet has to offer. But going online also brings with it some risks. If you understand those risks, you can learn to avoid most of them and stay relatively safe online.

In this chapter, you discover some of the risks and safety nets that you can take advantage of to avoid risk, starting with these points:

➡ **Understand what risks exist.** Some risks are human, in the form of online predators wanting to steal your money or abuse you emotionally; other risks come from technology, such as computer viruses. For the former, you can use the same common sense you use when interacting offline to stay much safer. For the latter, there are tools and browser settings to protect you.

➡ **Be aware of what information you share.** Abuses such as identity theft occur most often when you or somebody you know shares information about you that's nobody's business. Find out how to spot who is exposing information (including you) and what information to keep private, and you'll become much safer online.

Chapter 19

Get ready to . . .

➡ **Avoid scams and undesirable content.** You can use the Internet Explorer Family Safety settings to limit the online locations that you can visit so that you don't encounter sites you consider undesirable. You can also find out how to spot various e-mail scams and fraud so that you don't become a victim.

➡ **Create safe passwords.** Passwords don't have to be hard to remember — just hard to guess. I provide some guidance in this chapter about creating passwords that are hard to crack.

Understand Technology Risks on the Internet

When you buy a car, it has certain safety features built in. Sometimes after you drive it off the lot, you might find that the manufacturer slipped up and either recalls your car or requests that you go to the dealer's service department for replacement of a faulty part.

Your laptop is similar to your car in terms of the need for safety. It comes with an operating system (such as Microsoft Windows) built in, and that operating system has security features. Sometimes new flaws or threats to that operating system emerge after it's installed. You need to download and install regular updates to keep your computer secure.

As you use your laptop, you're exposing it to dangerous conditions and situations that you have to guard against. Threats to your laptop security can come from a file you copy from a disc you insert into your laptop, but most of the time, the danger is that you'll download a harmful program from the Internet. These downloads can happen when you click a link, open an attachment in an e-mail, or download a piece of software without realizing that *malware* (malicious software) is attached to it.

You need to be aware of these three main types of malware:

➡ A *virus* is a little program that some nasty person thought up to spread around the Internet and infect computers. A virus can do a variety of things, but typically, it attacks your data, deleting files, scrambling

data, or making changes to your system settings that cause your laptop to grind to a halt.

➡ *Spyware* consists of programs that help somebody track what you do with your laptop. Some spyware simply helps companies you do business with track your activities so that they can figure out how to sell things to you; other spyware is used for more insidious purposes, such as stealing your passwords.

➡ *Adware* is the computer equivalent of telemarketing phone calls at dinner time. After adware is downloaded onto your laptop, you'll see annoying pop-up windows trying to sell things or tempt you to illicit sites all day long. Beyond the annoyance, adware can quickly clog up your laptop. Your laptop's performance slows down, and it's hard to get anything done at all.

To protect your information and your laptop from these various types of malware, you can do several things:

➡ **You can buy and install an antivirus, anti-spyware, or anti-adware program.** It's critical that you install an antivirus program, such as those from McAfee, Symantec, AVG Free (see **Figure 19-1**), or Trend Micro, or the freely downloadable AVG Free. People are coming up with new viruses every day, so it's also important that you update the software regularly with the latest virus definitions. Many antivirus programs are purchased by yearly subscription, which gives you access to regularly updated virus definitions that the company constantly makes available throughout the year with the click of a button. Also, be sure to run a scan of your laptop on a regular basis. For convenience, you can use settings in the software to set up automatic updates and scans. Consult your program's Help tool for instructions on how to use these features.

Figure 19-1

→ **Install a program that combines tools for detecting adware and spyware.** Windows 7, 8, and 8.1 have a built-in program, Windows Defender, which includes an anti-spyware feature. (I cover Windows Defender tools later in this chapter.) If you don't have Windows 7, 8, or 8.1, you can purchase programs such as Spyware Doctor from PC Tools (www.pctools.com) or download free tools such as Spybot (http://spybot-download.net) or Spyware Terminator (www.spywareterminator.com).

→ **Use Windows 8.1 tools to keep Windows up-to-date with security features and fixes to security problems.** You can also turn on a *firewall*, which is a feature that stops other people or programs from accessing your laptop over an Internet connection

without your permission. I cover firewalls in Chapter 23.

➠ **Use privacy and security features of your browser,** such as the SmartScreen Filter, Tracking Protection, and InPrivate Browsing features in Internet Explorer 9, 10, and 11.

 Laptop users who travel with their laptops face another type of security concern. Because you carry your laptop with you, it is exposed to potential theft or loss. See Chapter 23 for more about protecting laptops while travelling.

Download Files Safely

1. Open a website that contains downloadable files (such as www.adobe.com, which offers its popular Adobe Flash add-on and Adobe Reader program for free). Typically, websites offer a Download button or link that initiates a file download.

2. Click the appropriate link to proceed. Windows might display a dialog box asking your permission to proceed with the download; click Yes.

3. In the toolbar that appears along the bottom of the screen, as shown in **Figure 19-2,** choose either option:

  • **Click Run to download the file to a temporary folder.** You can run a software installation pro- gram, for example. However, beware: If you run a program you download from the Internet, you could be introducing dangerous viruses to your system. You might want to set up an antivirus pro- gram to scan files before downloading them.

  • **Click Save to save the file to your hard drive.** In the Save As dialog box, select the folder on your

laptop or removable storage media (a USB flash drive, for example) where you want to save the file. If you're downloading software, you need to locate the downloaded file and click it to run the installation.

Figure 19-2

 If you're worried that a particular file might be unsafe to download — for example, if it's from an unknown source or it's an executable (a file that executes a procedure and whose name ends with `.exe`) file type, which could contain a virus — click Cancel in the File Download dialog box.

 If a particular file will take a long time to download (some can take 20 minutes or more), you may have to babysit it. If your laptop goes into standby mode, it could pause the download. If your laptop automatically downloads Windows updates, it may cause your laptop to restart automatically as well, cancelling or halting your download. Check in periodically to keep things moving along.

 Make sure you choose a folder that's easy for you to remember and return to later when you need the file. If you're downloading software, you need to locate the downloaded file (in whichever folder you saved it) and double-click it to install it.

Turn on InPrivate Browsing and Filtering

1. InPrivate Browsing is a feature that stops Internet Explorer version 9, 10, or 11 from saving information about your browsing session, such as cookies that form a record of your activities on some sites and your browsing history. InPrivate Filtering allows you to block or allow

activity from sites that are automatically collecting information about your browsing habits. InPrivate Browsing
is turned off by default. To activate InPrivate for your
browsing session, first open IE from the Start Screen.

2. Right-click a blank spot on the desktop and then click the
Tab Tools button (with three dots on it) in the tab area
shown in **Figure 19-3**.

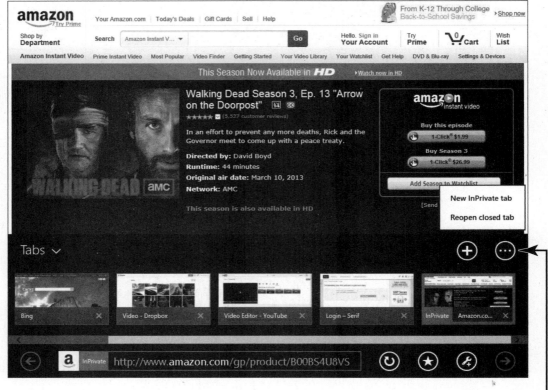

Click the Tab Tools button

Figure 19-3

3. Choose New InPrivate Tab. A message appears, telling
you that InPrivate Browsing is on.

4. To surf the web privately, click in the Address bar and do
one of the following: Type a web address, click a
Frequent tile, or click a Pinned tile.

5. To turn InPrivate Browsing off, right-click to display tabs, and then click the Close button on the InPrivate tab to close it, as shown in **Figure 19-4**.

Figure 19-4

 If you don't want to use InPrivate Browsing but would like to clear your browsing history manually from time to time, with IE open, press Win+I and click Options. In the History section, click Select and then click to choose what you want to delete. Finally, click the Delete button to delete selected items.

Use SmartScreen Filtering

When you activate SmartScreen Filter, you allow Microsoft to check its database for any information on the websites you visit. Microsoft alerts you if any of those websites are known to generate phishing scams or download malware to visitors' computers. SmartScreen Filter is on by default; if it has been turned off, to turn SmartScreen Filter on, open IE from the Desktop (click the Desktop tile from the Start screen if you are not in Desktop and then click the Internet Explorer button in the taskbar) and then follow these steps:

1. Click the Safety menu, and then choose SmartScreen Filter⇨Turn On SmartScreen filter. In the confirmation dialog box that appears (shown in **Figure 19-5**), click OK.

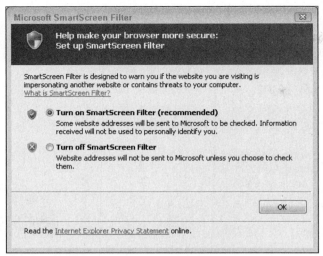

Figure 19-5

2. To use SmartScreen Filter, go to a website you want to check. Click the Safety menu, hover your mouse over the SmartScreen Filter command and choose Check This Website. Click OK to authorize the check.

3. The SmartScreen Filter window appears, indicating whether it found any threats. Click the OK button to close the message.

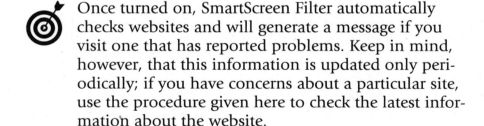 Once turned on, SmartScreen Filter automatically checks websites and will generate a message if you visit one that has reported problems. Keep in mind, however, that this information is updated only periodically; if you have concerns about a particular site, use the procedure given here to check the latest information about the website.

Change Privacy Settings

1. You can modify how Internet Explorer 11 deals with privacy settings to keep information about your browsing habits or identity safer. From the Desktop, press Win+I and click the Control Panel app in the panel that appears.

2. Click Network and Internet, and then click Internet Options.

3. In the Internet Properties dialog box, click the Privacy tab, as shown in **Figure 19-6.**

Privacy tab

Figure 19-6

4. Drag the slider up or down to make different levels of security settings.

5. Read the choices and select a setting that suits you.

6. Click the Sites button to specify sites to always or never allow the use of cookies. In the resulting Per Site Privacy Actions dialog box (as shown in **Figure 19-7**), enter a site in the Address of Website field and click either Block or Allow.

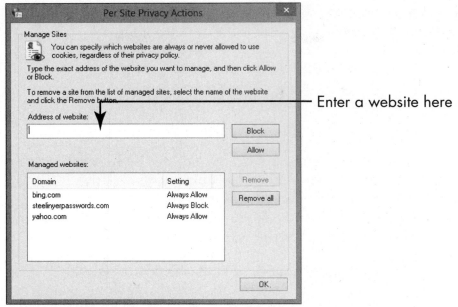

Enter a website here

Figure 19-7

7. Click OK and then click OK in the remaining dialog box
to save your new settings.

The default setting, Medium, is probably a good bet for
most people. To restore the default setting, click the
Default button on the Internet Options dialog box's
Privacy tab or drag the slider to Medium.

 You can also use pop-up blocker settings on the
Privacy tab to specify which pop-up windows to
allow or block. Just click the Settings button, enter a
website name, and then click Add to allow pop-ups
from that site.

Understand Information Exposure

Many people think that if they aren't active online, their information
isn't exposed. But you aren't the only one sharing your information.
Consider how those in your life might expose your information:

➠ **Employers:** Many employers share information about employees. Consider carefully how much information you're comfortable with sharing through, for instance, an employee bio posted on your company website. How much information should be visible to other employees on your intranet? When you attend a conference, is the attendee list shown in online conference documents? And even if you're retired, there may still be information about you on your former employer's website. Review the site to determine if it reveals more than you'd like it to — and ask your employer to take down or alter the information if needed.

➠ **Government agencies:** Some agencies post personal information, such as documents concerning your home purchase and property tax (see **Figure 19-8**), on publicly available websites. Government agencies may also post birth, marriage, and death certificates, and these documents may contain your Social Security Number, loan number, copies of your signature, and so on. You should check government records carefully to see if private information is posted — if it is, demand that it be removed.

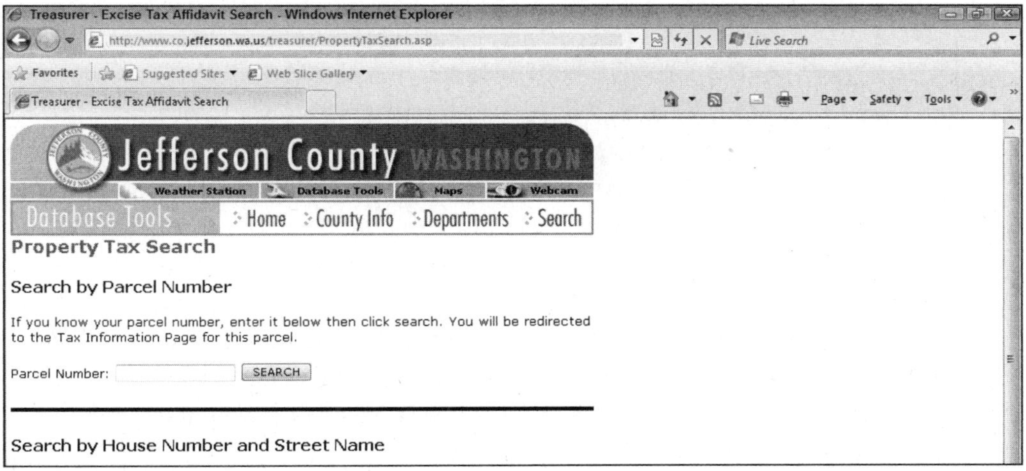

Figure 19-8

➠ **Family members and friends:** They may write about you in their blogs or social networking sites or mention you on revealing special-interest sites, such as those focused on genealogy.

➠ **Clubs and organizations:** Organizations with whom you volunteer, the church you attend, and professional associations you belong to may reveal facts such as your address, age, income bracket, and how much money you've donated.

➠ **Newspapers:** If you've been featured in a newspaper article, you may be surprised to find the story, along with a picture of you or information about your work, activities, or family, by doing a simple online search. If you're interviewed, ask for the chance to review the information that the newspaper will include, and be sure that you're comfortable with exposing that information.

➠ **Online directories:** Services such as www.white pages.com, shown in **Figure 19-9,** or www.any who.com list your landline phone number and address, unless you specifically request that these be removed. You may be charged a small fee associated with removing your information — a so-called privacy tax — but you may find the cost worthwhile. Online directories often include the names of members of your family, your e-mail address, the value of your home, your neighbors' names and the values of their homes, an online mapping tool to provide a view of your home, driving directions to your home, and your age. The record may also include previous addresses, schools you've attended, and links for people to run background checks on you. A smart con person can use all that information to convince you that he's a friend of a friend or even a relative in distress who needs money.

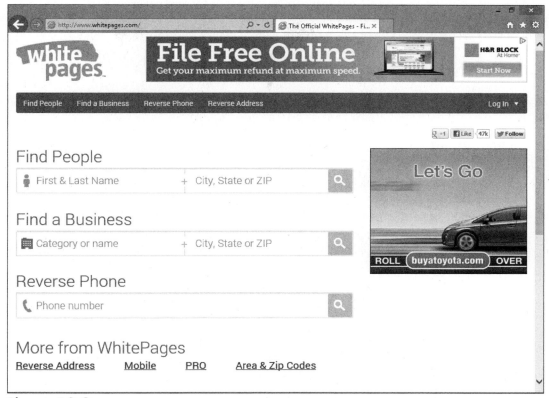

Figure 19-9

 Because services get new information from many sources, you'll need to check back periodically to see if your information has again been put online — if it has, contact the company or go through their removal process again.

 Try entering your home phone number in any browser's address line; chances are that you'll get an online directory listing with your address and phone number (although this doesn't work for cellphone numbers).

Keep Your Information Private

Sharing personal information with friends and family enriches your relationships and helps you build new ones. The key is to avoid sharing information with the wrong people and shady companies —

because exposing your personal information online is one of your biggest risks, just as it is in the real world.

Criminals come in all flavors, but the more savvy ones collect information online in a very systematic way. Each bit of information is like another piece of a puzzle that, over time, collects to form a very clear picture of your life. And be aware that after criminals collect and organize the information, they never throw it away because they may be able to use it many times over.

Fortunately, information exposure is a risk you have a great deal of control over. Before sharing information such as your date of birth, make sure that you're comfortable with how the recipient will use it. Consider the following points regarding the types of information you might be asked for:

➠ **Address and phone number:** Abuse of this information results in you receiving increased telemarketing calls and junk mail. Although less common, this information may also increase a scammer's ability to steal your identity and make your home a more interesting target for break-ins.

➠ **Names of husband/wife, father, and mother (including mother's maiden name), siblings, children, and grandchildren:** This information is very interesting to criminals, who can use it to gain your confidence and then scam you, or use it to guess your passwords or secret question answers, which often include family members' names. This information may also expose additional family members to ID theft, fraud, and personal harm.

➠ **Information about your car:** Limit access to license plate numbers; VINs (vehicle identification numbers); registration information; make, model, and title number of your car; your insurance carrier's name, coverage limits, loan information, and driver's license number. The key criminal abuse of this

information includes car theft (or theft of parts of the car) and insurance fraud. The type of car you drive may also indicate your financial status, and that adds one more piece of information to the pool of data criminals collect about you.

➡ **Information about work history:** In the hands of criminals, your work history can be very useful for "authenticating" the fraudsters and convincing people and organizations to provide them with more about your financial records or identity.

➡ **Information about your credit status:** This information can be abused in so many ways that any time you're asked to provide this online, your answer should be no. Don't fall for the temptation to check your credit scores for free through sites that aren't guaranteed as being reputable. Another frequent abuse of credit information is found in free mortgage calculators that ask you to put in all kinds of personal information in order for them to determine what credit you qualify for.

Many people set automatic responders in their e-mail letting people know when they'll be away from their offices. This is really helpful for colleagues, but exercise caution and limit who you provide the information to. Leaving a message that says, "Gone 11/2-11/12. I'm taking the family to Hawaii for ten days," may make you a prime target for burglary. And you'll probably never make the connection between the information you exposed and the offline crime.

You may need to show your work history, and so may post your résumé on Internet job or business networking sites. Be selective about where you post this information, create a separate e-mail account to list on the résumé, and tell what kinds of work you've done rather than give specifics about which

companies and what dates. Interested, legitimate
employers can then contact you privately, and you
won't have given away your life history to the world.
After you've landed the job, **take down** your résumé.
Think of it as risk management — when you need a
job, the risk of information exposure is less vital than
the need to get the job, but make that info private
again when it's served its purpose.

Spot Phishing Scams and Other E-mail Fraud

As in the offline world, the Internet has a criminal element. These cyber-
criminals use Internet tools to commit the same crimes they've always
committed, from robbing you to misusing your good name and financial information. Know how to spot the types of scams that occur
online, and you'll go a long way toward steering clear of Internet crime.

Before you click a link that comes in a forwarded e-mail message or
forward a message to others, ask yourself:

➥ **Is the information legitimate?** Sites such as www.
truthorfiction.com, www.snopes.com (see
Figure 19-10), or http://urbanlegends.about.
com can help you discover if an e-mail is a scam.

➥ **Does a message ask you to click links in the e-mail
(see Figure 19-11) or instant message?** If you're
unsure whether a message is genuinely from a company or bank that you use, call them, using the number from a past statement or the phone book.
Remember: Don't call a phone number in the e-mail;
it could be fake. To visit a company's or bank's website, type the address in yourself if you know it or
use your own bookmark rather than clicking a link.
If the website is new to you, search for the company
using a search engine and use that link to visit its
site. Don't click the link in an e-mail, or you may
land on a site that looks right — but is, in reality,
just a good fake.

Figure 19-10

Figure 19-11

➠ **Does the e-mail have a photo or video to download?** If so, exercise caution. If you know the person who sent the photo or video, it's probably fine to download, but if the photo or video has been forwarded several times and you don't know the person who sent it originally, be careful. It may deliver a virus or other type of malware to your laptop.

In addition to asking yourself these questions, also remember the following:

➠ **If you decide to forward (or send) e-mail to a group, always put their e-mail addresses on the Bcc: (or Blind Carbon Copy) line.** This keeps everyone's e-mail safe from fraud and scams.

➠ **Think *before* you click.** Doing so will help save you and others from scams, fraud, hoaxes, and malware.

Keeping In Touch via Mail

An e-mail program is a tool you can use to send messages to others. These messages are delivered to the recipient's e-mail **inbox**, usually within seconds. You can attach files to e-mail messages and even put images within the message body. You can get an e-mail account through your Internet provider or through sites such as Yahoo! and Microsoft Live Hotmail. These accounts are typically free.

When you have one or more e-mail accounts, you can set them up in the Mail app in Windows 8.1, and then use that app to send and receive e-mail for all your Windows Live Hotmail, Outlook, AOL, Yahoo!, and Gmail accounts in one place. Mail uses the information you store in the People app for addressing your e-mails, and it can sync contacts from your individual e-mail accounts to People if you choose.

Chapter 20

Get ready to . . .

If you prefer, you can instead use your provider's e-mail interface in your Internet browser. Some of these programs provide more tools for working with e-mail, such as more sophisticated tools to format message text or add a signature (for example, your company name and phone number) to every message you send. Check out `www.gmail.com` to sign in and see the Google interface you'll be using if you get a Google account, for example.

To make your e-mailing life easier, this chapter takes a look at these tasks:

⟶ **Choose an e-mail provider.** Find out how to locate e-mail providers and what types of features they offer.

⟶ **Set up your e-mail accounts in the Mail app.** Make settings to access your Windows Live Hotmail or other e-mail account from within the Mail app so you can check all your messages in one place. This is useful if you use both work and home e-mail accounts, for example.

⟶ **Receive, send, and forward messages.** Deal with the ins and outs of receiving and sending e-mail.

⟶ **Make settings for each account.** Set up how often content is downloaded, and whether to sync your e-mail, contacts, and calendar information from each account.

Set Up an Internet-Based E-mail Account

Your Internet service provider (ISP) — whether that's your cable or phone company, or a small local provider — probably offers you a free e-mail account along with your service. You can also get free

accounts from many online sources, such as Yahoo!, AOL, Gmail, and Windows Live Mail. Note that the Mail app in Windows 8.1 is currently set up to work with Windows Live Hotmail, Outlook, AOL, Yahoo!, and Gmail accounts — as well as Microsoft Exchange accounts, which are typically business accounts such as your company might provide.

Here are some tips for getting your own e-mail account:

➠ **Using e-mail accounts provided by an ISP:** Check with your ISP to see whether an e-mail account comes with your connection service. If it does, your ISP should provide instructions on how to choose an *e-mail alias* (that's the name on your account, such as SusieXYZ@aol.com) and password, and instructions on how to sign into the account.

➠ **Searching for an e-mail provider:** If your ISP doesn't offer e-mail, or you prefer to use another service because of the features it offers, use your browser's search engine to find out what's available. Don't use the search term *free e-mail* because results for any search with the word *free* included are much more likely to return sites that will download bad programs such as viruses and spyware onto your laptop. Besides, just about all e-mail accounts today are free. Alternatively, you can go directly to services such as Yahoo!, AOL, or Gmail by entering their addresses in your browser's address field (for example, www. gmail.com).

➠ **Finding out about features:** E-mail accounts come with certain features that you should be aware of. For example, each account includes a certain amount of storage for your saved messages. (Look for one that provides 10 gigabytes or more.) The account should also include an easy-to-use address book feature to

save your contacts' information. Some services provide better formatting tools for text, as well as calendar and to-do list features.

Whatever service you use, make sure it has good junk-mail filtering to protect you from unwanted e-mails. You should be able to modify junk-mail filter settings so that the service places messages from certain senders or with certain content in a junk-mail folder, where you can review the messages with caution or delete them.

➡ **Signing up for an e-mail account:** When you find an e-mail account you want to use, sign up (usually there will be a Sign Up or Get An Account button or link to click) by providing your name and other contact information and selecting a username and password. The username is your e-mail address, in the form of `UserName@`**`service`**`.com`, where the *service* is, for example, Yahoo!, Windows Live Hotmail, or AOL. Some usernames might be taken, so have a few options in mind.

➡ **Making sure your username is a safe one:** If possible don't use your full name, your location, age, or other personal information. Such personal identifiers might help scam artists or predators find out more about you than you want them to know.

Set Up Accounts in Mail

1. You can set up the Windows 8.1 Mail app to manage Hotmail and other accounts so you can receive all your e-mail messages in one place. Click the Mail tile on the Start screen.

2. Press Win+I and click the Accounts link shown in
   Figure 20-1.

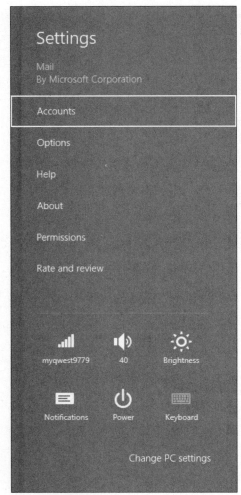

Figure 20-1

3. Click the Add an Account link shown in **Figure 20-2.**

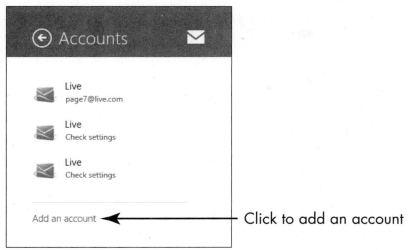

Figure 20-2

4. Click a provider option as shown in **Figure** 20-3.

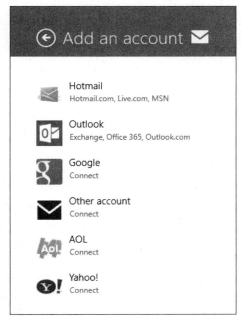

Figure 20-3

5. In the resulting window (see **Figure 20-4**), enter the account address and your password and click Connect.

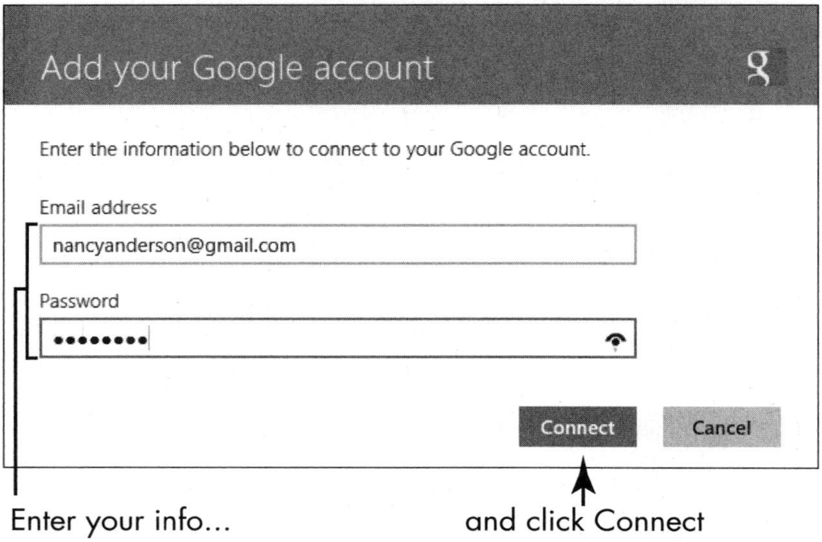

Add your Google account

Enter the information below to connect to your Google account.

Email address

nancyanderson@gmail.com

Password

••••••••

Connect   Cancel

Enter your info...   and click Connect

Figure 20-4

6. Mail takes a moment to set up the account. Click the account in the list of accounts on the left side of the Mail screen to open its inbox and view messages.

Get to Know Mail

Mail (see **Figure 20-5**) may look a bit different from other e-mail programs that use menus and tools to take actions such as deleting an e-mail, creating a new e-mail, and so on. Mail has a sparser, cleaner interface in line with the whole Windows 8.1 approach. You have a list of e-mail accounts and a list of folders for the selected account on the left. Some typical folders are your Inbox, where most incoming mail appears; your Outbox, where items you send that haven't completed sending sit; your Drafts folder, where drafts of e-mails are saved ready to be sent; and your Sent folder, where copies of sent e-mails are stored. You can set up any other folders in your original e-mail program such as Hotmail or Gmail, because you can't set these up in Mail.

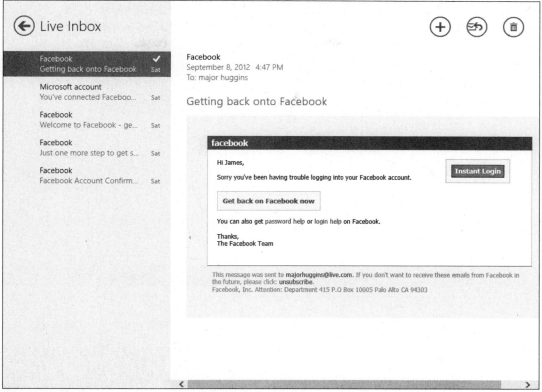

Figure 20-5

The section on the left displays inbox content, and the right portion of the screen shows the contents of a selected message in the Inbox or other folder whose contents are in the middle column of the screen (see **Figure 20-6**).

 To move a message from your inbox, right-click it and then click the Move button on the toolbar that appears. Click a folder, and the message is moved there.

 When you access Windows Live Mail and many of the other online e-mail services, you're using a program that's hosted online, rather than software on your laptop. That makes it easy to access your mail from any computer because your messages and

folders are kept online. If you use an e-mail client such as Outlook to access your e-mail accounts, the client software and your downloaded messages are stored on your laptop. Outlook.com is an online version of Outlook and can be accessed from anywhere.

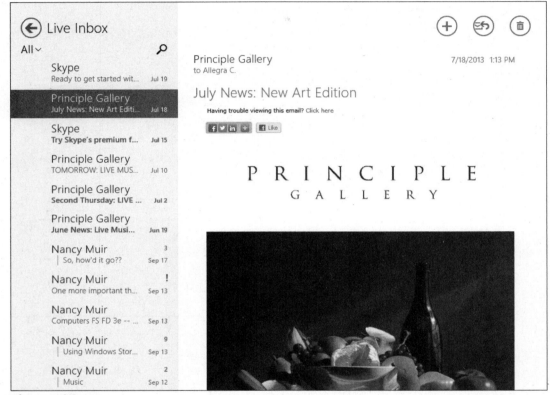

Figure 20-6

Open Mail and Receive Messages

1. Click the Mail tile on the Start screen.

2. Click the account you want to read mail from, and the contents of the inbox are displayed, as shown in **Figure 20-7**.

Click a message here

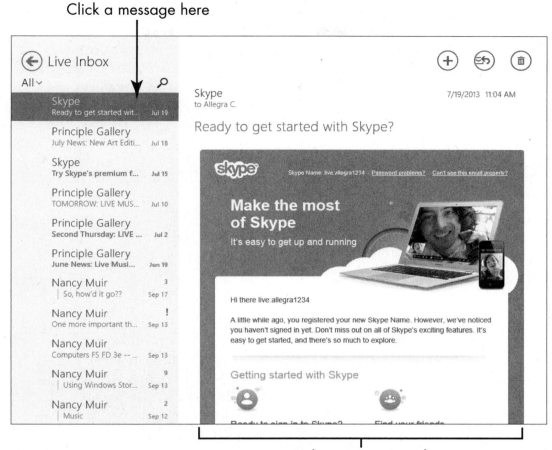

... and see its contents here

Figure 20-7

3. Click a message, and its contents appear on the right side of the screen. Use the scroll bar on the right to move through the message contents.

4. If the message has an attachment, you'll see a paper clip symbol (refer to **Figure 20-8**) next to it in the inbox. Click to display the message and then click the attachment thumbnail. Choose one of the following from the menu that appears:

- **Open:** The file opens in the app that Windows 8.1 associates it with.

- **Open With:** Use this option when you want to choose which program in which the attachment opens.

- **Save:** Windows 8.1 opens the associated library (such as Pictures for an image), where you can enter a name and click Save to save the file in that library.

This message has an attachment

Figure 20-8

 If your mail doesn't come through, it's probably because your e-mail provider's servers are experiencing technical problems. Just wait a little while. If you still can't get mail, make sure your connection to the Internet is active. Mail may show your Inbox, but if you've lost your connection, it can't receive new messages.

 Note that if an e-mail has a little exclamation point next to it in your Inbox, somebody has flagged it as urgent. It's usually best to check out those e-mails first.

Create and Send E-mail

1. Creating e-mail is as simple as filling out a few fields in a form. Open Mail and click the account from which you want to send the e-mail.

2. Click the New button (it's in the upper-right corner with a + symbol). See **Figure 20-9.**

Click to create a new message

Figure 20-9

3. Type the e-mail address of the recipient(s) in the To field. If you want to send a courtesy copy of the message to other people enter addresses in the Cc field, or to send a blind copy, click the Show More link and enter an address(es) in the Bcc field. You can also choose a priority for the message by clicking the Priority field and making your selection.

4. Click in the Add a Subject field (in **Figure 20-10** this is the field at the top on the right) and type a concise yet descriptive subject.

5. Click in the message pane beneath the subject and type your message (see **Figure 20-10**).

Don't press Enter at the end of a line when typing a message. Mail and most e-mail programs have an automatic text-wrap feature that does this for you. Do be concise. If you have lots to say, consider sending a letter by snail mail or overnight delivery. Most people tire of reading text onscreen after a short while.

Keep e-mail etiquette in mind as you type. For example, don't type in ALL CAPITAL LETTERS. This is called shouting, which is considered rude. Do be polite even if you're really, really angry. Your message could be forwarded to just about anybody, just about anywhere, and you don't want to get a reputation as a hothead.

Type your subject here   Type your message here

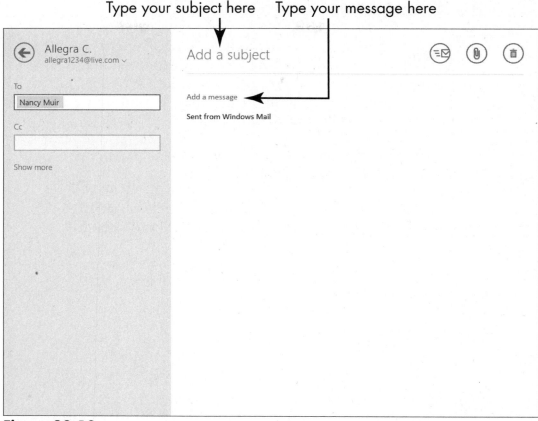

Figure 20-10

6. When you finish typing your message, click the Send button. The message is on its way!

Remember that when you're creating an e-mail, you can address it using a stored address in the People app. Click the To, CC, or BCC link in the address area and the People app appears. You can then select a contact(s) from there and click the Add button. Mail also allows you to just begin to type a stored contact in an address field (To, Bcc, or Cc), and it provides a list of likely options as you type. Just click the correct name when it appears in the list to enter it.

Send an Attachment

1. It's very convenient to be able to attach a document or image file to an e-mail that the recipient can open and view on his end. To do this, open Mail and click your e-mail account. Click New to create a new e-mail message, address it, and enter a subject.

2. Click the Attachments icon (it's shaped like a paperclip) at the top of the page (see **Figure 20-11**).

3. The This PC library appears. Locate the file or files that you want using the Go Up link if necessary and click to select it (or them).

Click to attach files

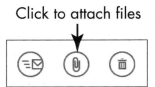

Figure 20-11

4. Click the Attach button. A thumbnail of the attached file appears in the message body (see **Figure 20-12**) indicating that it's uploaded. If you have other attachments you want to make from other folders on your laptop, you can click the Attachments link again and repeat the previous steps as many times as you like to add more attachments.

5. Click the Send button to send the message and attachment.

 If you change your mind about sending a message while you're creating it, just click the Close button (it's in the top-right corner with an X in it) and choose Save Draft or Delete.

A thumbnail of attachment

Figure 20-12

Read a Message

1. When you receive an e-mail, your next step is usually to read it. Click an e-mail message in your Inbox. Unread messages are in bold and messages you've read are unbolded.

2. Click in the message body and use the scroll bar in the message window to scroll down through the message and read it (see **Figure 20-13**).

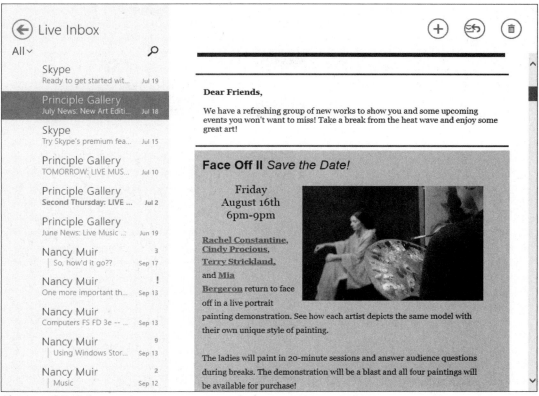

Figure 20-13

3. If you want to delete the message, simply click the Trash button in the top-right corner. If you want to save it, right-click and click the Move icon to move it into a folder, or just leave it in your inbox.

> If you'd like to save an attachment to a storage disc or your hard drive, right-click the thumbnail of it in the message, click Save, and then choose the location to save the file to.

> When you're travelling around with a laptop and reading e-mails, remember that people can look over your shoulder. If you're reading or writing sensitive information, consider displaying it when you get to the privacy of your home.

Reply to a Message

1. If you receive an e-mail and want to send a message back, use the Reply feature. Open the message you want to reply to, click the Respond button, and then select one of the following reply options, as shown in **Figure 20-14:**

- **Reply:** Send the reply to only the author.

- **Reply All:** Send a reply to the author as well as to everyone who received the original message.

Figure 20-14

2. In the resulting e-mail form (see **Figure 20-15**), enter any additional recipient(s) in the To and/or Cc text boxes; to send a blind copy, you can click Show More to display the Bcc field. Type your message in the message window.

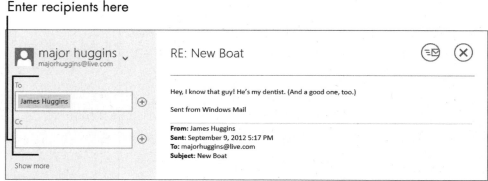

Figure 20-15

3. Click the Send button to send the reply.

Forward E-mail

1. To share an e-mail you receive with others, use the Forward feature. Open the e-mail message that you want to forward in Mail.

2. Click the Respond button, and then click Forward.

3. In the message that appears with FW: added to the beginning of the subject line, enter a new recipient(s) in the To and/or Cc and Bcc fields, and then enter any message that you want to include in the message window, as shown in the example in **Figure 20-16**.

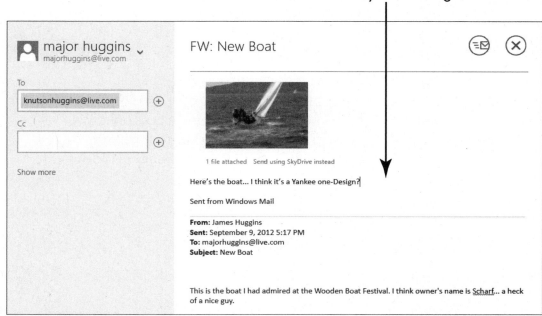

Figure 20-16

4. Click Send to forward the message.

Change Account Settings in Mail

1. Each account that you set up in Mail has its own settings. Click the Mail tile on the Start screen.

2. From within Mail, press Win+I, and then click Accounts in the Settings panel (see **Figure 20-17**).

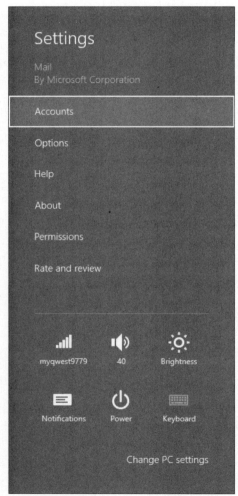

Figure 20-17

3. Click the account for which you want to change settings. In the panel displayed in **Figure 20-18,** you can make the following changes:

- **Download New E-mail.** You can click this field and, from the drop-down list that appears, choose to download content when a message arrives or every 15, 30, or 60 minutes. If you prefer, you can choose to download items manually by clicking the Manual option here.

- **Download E-mail From.** This is a handy setting if you're away from Mail for a while and have been checking messages in your browser. If so, you may not want to download a month's worth of messages you've already read, so choose another setting from this drop-down list, such as The Last 3 Days.

- **Content to Sync.** Syncing involves having certain actions and content delivery or deletions coordinated among different accounts. You can choose to download various items, depending on your e-mail provider, such as e-mail, contacts, or calendar appointments using this command.

- **Automatically Download External Images.** Turn this setting off if you're concerned about the content of images and prefer that you manually download them rather than having them automatically downloaded.

- **Use an E-mail Signature.** To automatically add a signature such as your name and phone number to every e-mail you send, click this field so it reads Yes and then use the text box below the setting to enter the signature you want to use.

- **Show E-mail Notifications for This Account.** If you want Windows 8.1 to notify you when e-mail

arrives, turn this on. To activate this, you must also check Mail in the list of apps from which you can get notifications in the Search & Apps⇨ Notifications area of PC Settings (see **Figure 20-19**).

- **Remove Account.** If you decide you don't want Mail to access an account anymore, click the Remove Account button. For the account you use to log in to Windows 8.1, you'll have to do this procedure though the PC Settings window (press Win+I and then click Change PC Settings).

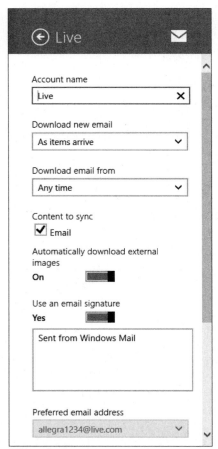

Figure 20-18

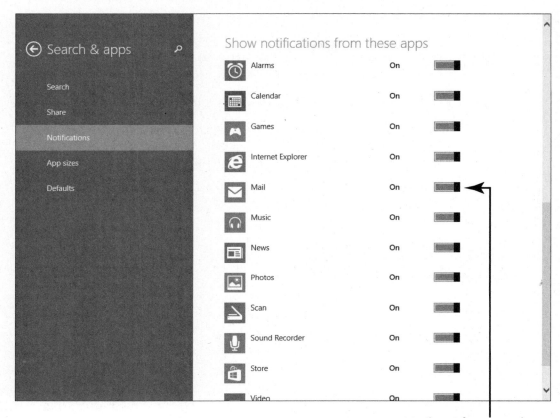

Turn on Mail notifications here

Figure 20-19

Connecting with People Online

The Internet is a great place to find people with similar interests and share information.

You'll find discussion boards, blogs, and chat features on a wide variety of sites, with people sharing information from news to recipes. There are some great senior chat rooms for making friends, and many sites allow you to create new chat rooms on topics that interest you at any time.

Another great way to use the Internet to communicate is by making calls using services such as Skype, and even using your laptop's web camera (called a *webcam*) to make video calls where you and the other person can see each other as you talk.

You can use handy event planning sites to schedule your next meeting, send greeting cards in electronic form, and more.

In this chapter, I look at some ways you can share information with others online, and I tell you how to do so safely.

Chapter 21

Get ready to . . .

Use Discussion Boards and Blogs

A *discussion board*, also sometimes referred to as a *forum*, is a place where you can post written messages, pictures, and videos on a topic. Others can reply to you, and you can reply to their postings. In a variation on discussion boards, you'll find *blogs* (short for web logs) everywhere you turn, and you can also post your comments about blog entries.

Discussion boards and blogs are *asynchronous*, which means that you post a message (just as you might on a bulletin board at the grocery store) and wait for a response. Somebody might read it that hour — or ten days or several weeks after you make the posting. In other words, the response isn't instantaneous, and the message isn't usually directed to a specific individual.

You can find a discussion board or blog about darn near every topic under the sun, and the information on them can be tremendously helpful when you're looking for answers. They're also a great way to share your expertise — whether you chime in on how to remove an ink stain, provide history trivia about button styles on military uniforms, or announce the latest breakthroughs in your given field. Postings are likely to stay on the site for years for people to reference, so be aware that what you read there may be up to date or not that current.

1. To try out a discussion board, enter this URL in your browser address field: `http://answers.microsoft.com/en-us/`. (Note that some discussion boards require that you become a member with a username and that you sign in before you can post comments. If you want to post a reply in Step 4, you will first have to join the site.)

2. Click a topic area, such as Internet Explorer (see **Figure 21-1**), to see discussion subtopics. Continue to click on subtopics until you get to a discussion of interest and then read the original posting and any responses.

3. When you click a posting that has replies, you'll see that the replies are organized in chronological order (see **Figure 21-2**). You can review the various participants' comments as they add their ideas to the conversation.

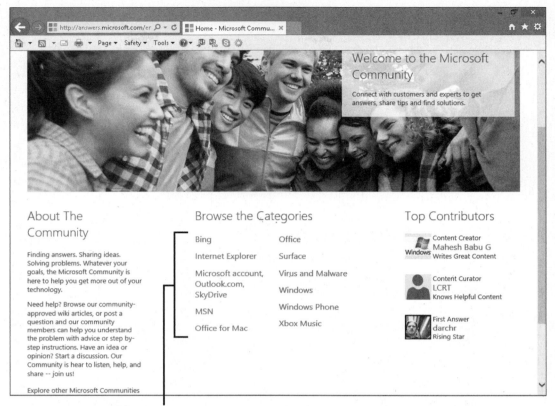

Choose a topic

Figure 21-1

4. To reply to a posting yourself, first click the posting (refer to **Figure 21-2**), and then click the Reply link, enter your comments, and click Submit.

With any site where users share information, you can stay safer if you know how to sidestep some abuses, including *data mining* (gathering your personal information for commercial or criminal intent), *social engineering* ploys that try to gain your trust and access to your money, ID theft scams, and so forth. Throughout this chapter, I provide safety tips, but remember that if you're careful to protect your privacy, you can enjoy socializing online with little worry.

Click to reply to a message

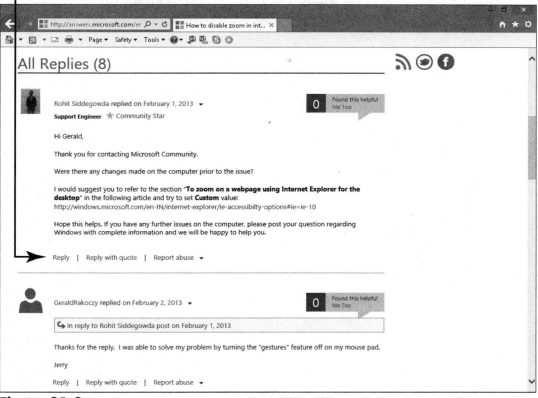

Figure 21-2

Participate in Chat

A *chat room* is an online space where groups of people can talk back and forth via text, audio, web camera, or a combination of media. (See **Figure 21-3,** which shows a web site that links to hundreds of chat rooms.) In chat, you're having a conversation with one or more people in real time (without delay, as you experience with a discussion board), and your entire conversation appears in the chat window. Here are some characteristics of chat that you should know about:

➡ When the chat is over, unless you save a copy, the conversation is typically gone.

➟ Several people can interact at once, although this can take getting used to as you try to follow what others are saying and jump in with your own comments.

➟ When you find a chat you want to participate in, sign up to get a screen name, and then you simply enter the chat room, enter your comment, and submit it. Your comment shows up in the stream of comments, and others may — or may not — reply to it.

Figure 21-3

 When you're talking to someone in a chat room with multiple people, if the site offers the option, you could invite him to enter a *private chat room*, which keeps the rest of the folks who wandered into the

chat room out of your conversation. Also, others can invite you into private chat rooms. Be careful who you interact with in this way, and be sure you understand the motivations for making your conversation private. This may be entirely reasonable, or it may be that you're dealing with someone with suspect motivations.

 Warning: Before you get started, check out the website's Terms of Use, privacy, and monitoring and abuse reporting procedures to understand the safety protections in place before joining a conversation. Some sites are well monitored for signs of abusive content or interactions; others have no monitoring at all. If you don't like the terms, find a different site.

Use Webcams

Webcams are small video cameras you can use to transmit your picture to somebody in an online conversation or meeting. They are relatively inexpensive, and most laptops now come with webcams embedded in their lids. (See **Figure 21-4**.) You can use a webcam with apps like Skype to make calls over the Internet, or other apps to have face-to-face live meetings.

Each computer manufacturer includes a software program to use with your built-in webcam or you can find another online, such as CyberLink YouCam (`www.cyberlink.com/products/youcam`). Some software even allows you to record, edit, and post video to video sharing sites such as YouTube (`www.youtube.com`).

When you use instant messaging software or join an online meeting, your webcam is likely to begin displaying video automatically. Use the tools in that program to control your webcam.

A webcam can be a great way to communicate with friends and family, but it can quickly become risky when you use it for conversations with strangers.

A webcam

Figure 21-4

➡ Giving your image away, especially one that may show your emotional reactions to a stranger's statements in real-time, simply reveals too much information that can put you at risk.

➡ If you use a webcam to meet with someone you don't know online, they may expose you to behavior you'd rather not see.

➡ Note that webcams can also be high-jacked and turned on remotely. This allows predators to view and listen to individuals without their knowledge. When you aren't using your webcam, consider turning it off — or disconnecting it, if it isn't a built-in model.

 Warning: Teens in particular struggle to use good judgment when using webcams. If you have grandchildren or other children in your care, realize that normal inhibitions seem to fall away when they aren't physically present with the person they're

speaking to — and many expose themselves, figuratively and literally. In addition to having a conversation about appropriate webcam use with children and teens, it may be wise to limit access to webcams.

Use Skype to Make Calls Online

Skype is a popular site for making phone calls using your Internet connection and a technology called VoiP (Voice over Internet Protocol). There are several benefits to using Skype to make phone calls, including

➡ Calls to other users of Skype are absolutely free, even it the other person is located around the world from you. If you call landlines or mobile phones, you still get low rates for your calls using credits that you purchase.

➡ You can use the video feature of Skype along with a webcam to make video calls to others. This is an awesome way to keep in touch with the grandkids or other friends in distant places.

➡ You can store contact information for others and call them with a click.

➡ If you're not at your computer when a call comes in, you can set up a voicemail feature to take messages.

Skype comes preinstalled by manufacturers on some computers. If there is no Skype tile on your Start screen, from the Start Screen, type Skype, and then click on the Store category. In the results, click on Skype, and then on the next page, click Install.

To get set up to use Skype, follow these steps:

1. Click the All Apps button on the Start screen and then click the Skype app on the list of apps.

2. On the following screen, Allow or Block Skype from using your webcam and microphone; allowing it enables you to make video calls.

3. On the next screen, click Allow or Don't Allow to let Skype run in the background so you can get notifications on the lock screen and open it quickly.

4. On the screen shown in **Figure 21-5,** click the New to Skype button to sign in (this sign-in will be based on the Microsoft account with which you signed into Windows 8.1). On the following screen, click to select whether Skype can contact you by e-mail or SMS or not, and then click the I Agree – Join Skype button to accept the terms.

Figure 21-5

5. The Skype main screen appears (see **Figure 21-6**). When you have saved people as contacts, their names appear along the right side. Click a contact, and then click the phone button that appears on the screen to call that person.

6. If you don't have any saved contacts or want to call a different person, click the Call Phones button at the top of the screen shown in **Figure 21-6**.

7. In the following screen shown in **Figure 21-7,** click the numerical pad to enter a number to call. Note that if you need to buy Skype Credit to make a call, you can do that from this screen by clicking the Buy Skype Credit or Get a Subscription links, depending on what type of plan you prefer.

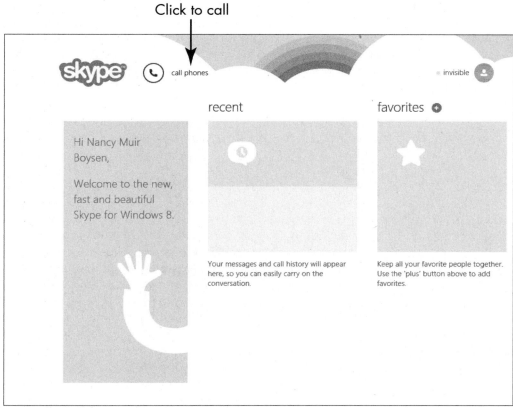

Figure 21-6

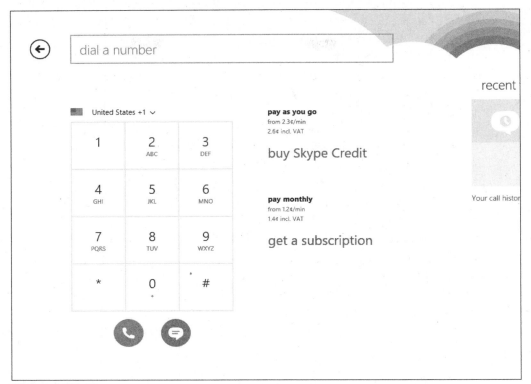

Figure 21-7

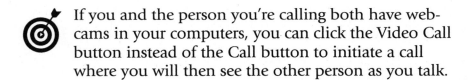 If you and the person you're calling both have web-cams in your computers, you can click the Video Call button instead of the Call button to initiate a call where you will then see the other person as you talk.

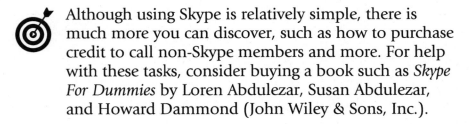 Although using Skype is relatively simple, there is much more you can discover, such as how to purchase credit to call non-Skype members and more. For help with these tasks, consider buying a book such as *Skype For Dummies* by Loren Abdulezar, Susan Abdulezar, and Howard Dammond (John Wiley & Sons, Inc.).

Schedule Events

You know what an annoyance it can be to schedule a meeting or party? You e-mail or call a few people to see if they're available. One person can make it, but another can't. You leave phone messages for

two other people who you don't hear back from. Then you reschedule the event only to find that two people you never heard back from are out of town that day.

Today you can use online event planning sites such as Evite (`www.evite.com`) or Doodle (`www.doodle.com`), shown in **Figure 21-8,** to plan events by sending out electronic invitations that offer recipients a range of dates and times. The invitees let you know when they can come, and the service helps you to easily identify the best time and date for your event.

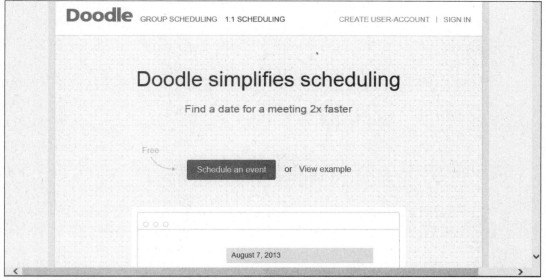

Figure 21-8

Most of these services are free, and you can use handy views such as calendars and tables to help you organize your various events.

Send E-greeting Cards

Who among us hasn't had the experience of suddenly realizing a dear friend or relative's birthday is tomorrow and we forgot to get and mail a card? The Internet to the rescue: You can now use online greeting card services to send fun e-cards that include animation and music. The convenient part is that your greeting can get to recipients at the very last minute.

Visit sites such as www.hallmark.com (shown in **Figure 21-9**) and www.123greetings.com to check out what they have to offer. Some of these sites are free; some offer a few free cards but charge you a yearly fee to access their full range of cards.

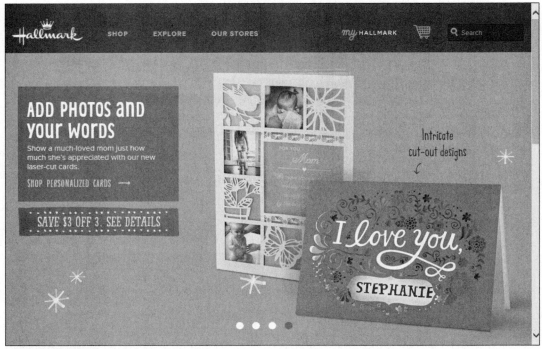

Figure 21-9

 When you use some sites that are entirely free, you run a greater risk of downloading viruses or having advertising placed on your cards. The yearly subscriptions to legitimate sites are very low, allowing you to send out as many greetings as you like for the entire year, so you might consider spending the money to use one.

Most online greeting card sites offer easy instructions on how to use them, but you typically follow these steps in a similar order:

1. Search the site to find a card.

2. Personalize the card with a greeting and select certain formatting for text.

3. Preview the card.

4. Enter the recipient's e-mail address.

5. Send the card on its way. The recipient gets an e-mail notification with a link to click to view the card.

Share Content with Others

Windows 8.1 apps allow you to share various types of content with others via e-mail or several social networking services.

For example, if you display your Collection from the Music app — or you're searching the web and find an interesting site — press Win+C to display the Charms bar, click the Share charm, and then click either Mail or People (see **Figure 21-10**).

Click either Mail or People to share

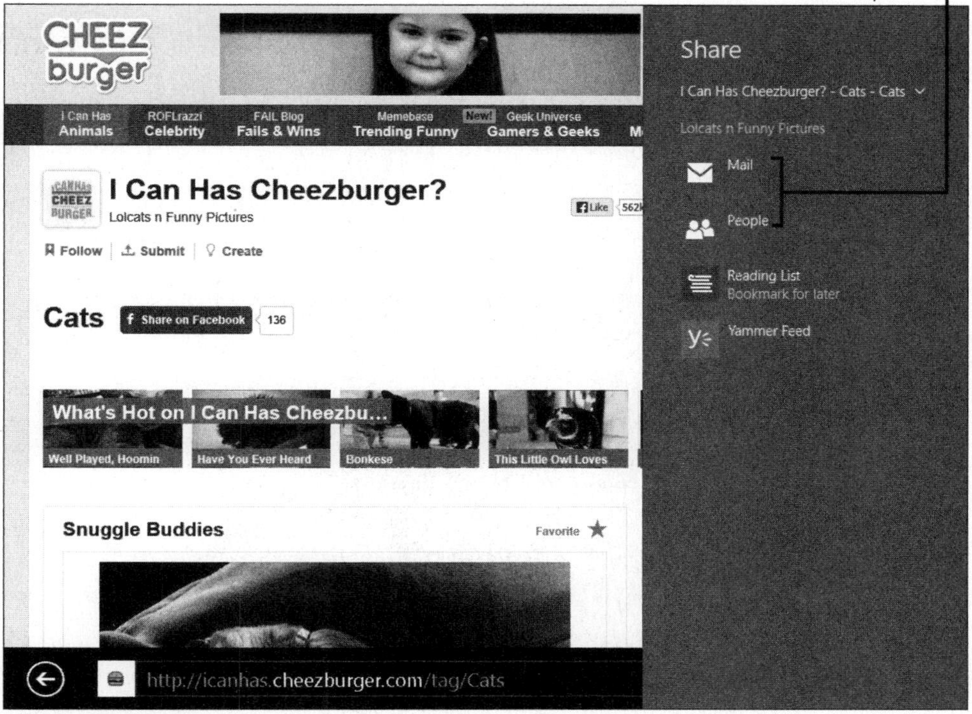

Figure 21-10

Clicking Mail allows you to forward the item (a music file or a web link, for example) via e-mail. Clicking People lets you view Facebook or Twitter contacts and post the info or link to them on one of those services.

Recommend a Site to Others

A phenomenon called *social bookmarking* allows you to share your likes and dislikes for online sites and content with others. Web sites that sport icons from services such as Digg, StumbleUpon, Delicious, and Diigo provide a way for you to report your opinion about articles, videos, and more.

Figure 21-11 shows one site with several social bookmarking icons on display. Services such as Facebook and Twitter also allow you to rate content by posting a comment on their sites.

Social media icons

Figure 21-11

When you click any of these icons, you're taken to a web page where you can sign in to an account or open a new account with a service. You can then type your comment in to whatever form that service provides, such as the one from StumbleUpon shown in **Figure 21-12**. With social sites such as Facebook and Twitter, you can share a comment and link with your Facebook friends or those following you on Twitter.

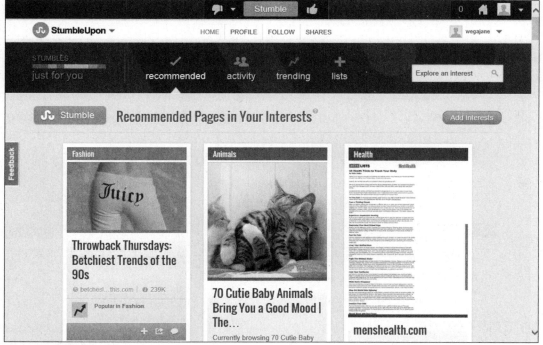

Figure 21-12

Getting Involved in the Social Net

1n this chapter, I look at the world of the social net. Social networking sites such as Facebook are a great way for you to connect with others and share your thoughts, your images, and your activities.

If you're new to social networking, this chapter gives you an overview of what it's all about, shows you the different types of services available, and even takes you through the signup process on one popular social networking site. In addition, I provide some advice on online dating services and image-sharing sites (which are discussed in more detail in Chapter 18).

Overview of Collaborative and Social Networking Sites

Although you may think kids are the most active group using social networking, statistics prove that isn't the case. In fact, people 35–54 years old make up a large segment of social networkers.

There are several types of sites where people collaborate or communicate socially. As you explore this new social world, the following definitions may be useful:

➡ **Wiki:** A website that allows anyone visiting to contribute (add, edit, or remove) content. Wikipedia, for example, is a virtual encyclopedia built by users providing information in their areas of expertise. Because of the ease of collaboration, wikis are often used when developing group projects or sharing information collaboratively. Wikipedia (`http://en.wikipedia.org`) is shown in **Figure 22-1**.

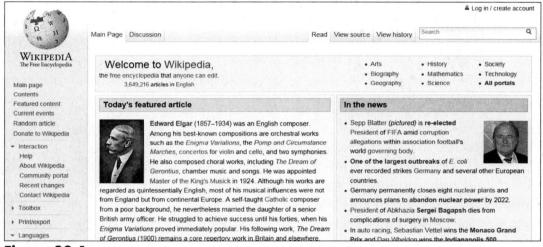

Figure 22-1

➡ **Blog:** An online journal (*blog* is short for *web log*) that may be entirely private, open to select friends or family, or available to the general public. You can usually adjust your blog settings to restrict visitors from commenting on your blog entries, if you'd like.

➡ **Social networking site:** This type of website (see **Figure 22-2**) allows people to build and maintain an online web page and create networks of people that they're somehow connected to — their friends, work associates, and/or other members with similar interests. Most social networking sites also host blogs and have social networking functions that allow people to view information about others (in the form of member profiles), post photos, and contact each other.

Figure 22-2

➡ **Social journaling sites:** Sites such as Twitter (http://twitter.com) allow people to go online with short notes (fewer than 140 characters) that are typically about what they're doing or thinking at the moment. Many companies and celebrities are now *tweeting,* as the act of posting comments on Twitter is referred to. You can follow individuals on Twitter so you're always informed if somebody you're a fan of makes a post.

Compare Popular Services

Many social networking sites are general in nature and attract a wide variety of users, such as Facebook, Bebo, or Myspace. Facebook, which

was begun by some students at Harvard as a college student–only site, has become today's most popular social site, and many seniors use its features to blog, exchange virtual "gifts," and post photos. Other social networking sites revolve around particular interests or age groups. For example, LinkedIn (www.linkedin.com) is aimed at those who want to network with a focus on their careers, and SeniorPeopleMeet (www.seniorpeoplemeet.com) is a social site for seniors.

There are also sites that provide social networking features that are focused around issues such as grief and healthcare, and sites that host politics- or consumer-oriented discussions.

 Visit TopTenReviews for a detailed comparison of social websites at http://social-networking-websites-review.toptenreviews.com/. You can find out handy information such as which sites have mostly under 18 users, which have stronger privacy settings, and which allow you to share videos, music, and other types of contents with others.

Sign Up for a Social Networking Service

Here's where you can walk through the signup process for Facebook, one of the most popular social networking sites, to see the kinds of information they ask for. Follow these instructions to get your Facebook account:

1. Type this URL into your browser address line: www.facebook.com.

2. In the signup form that appears (see **Figure 22-3**), enter your name, e-mail address, a password, your birthdate, gender, and then click Sign Up.

Note that the site requires your birthdate so that Facebook can provide certain safeguards for accounts of younger children, but you can choose to hide this information from others later if you don't want it displayed.

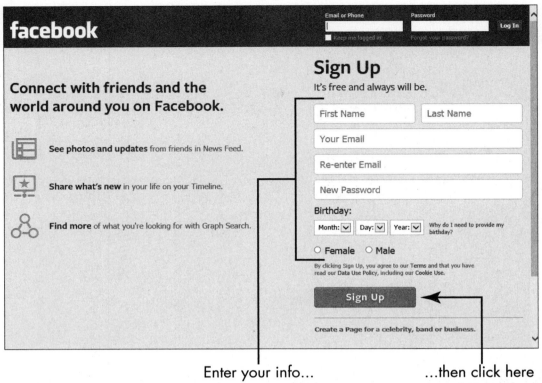

Enter your info...   ...then click here

Figure 22-3

3. On the screen that appears (see **Figure 22-4**), you can click Find Friends to have Facebook search for contacts in your e-mail account address book and invite them to be your friends, or click Skip This Step to continue creating your account. In this case, click Skip This Step.

4. In the next screen, enter profile information that you can choose to have visible to others or not. Details you can enter here include your schools, employers, current city of residence, and hometown.

5. Click Save and Continue.

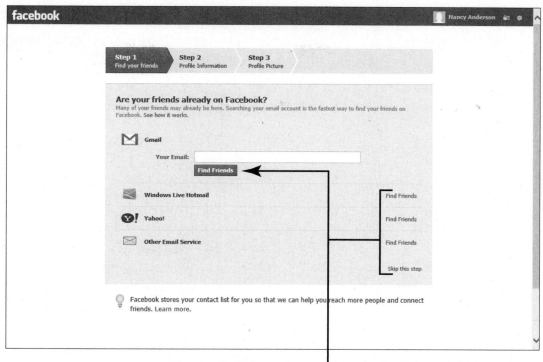

Click to find friends in your email address book

Figure 22-4

6. On the next screen (see **Figure 22-5**), click Upload a Photo or Take a Photo if you'd like a picture associated with your account. If you have a photo on your computer you'd like to use, click Upload a Photo and, in the form that appears, click the Browse button to display File Explorer. Locate the picture and then click Open.

7. Click the Save & Continue button. Your account is now set up. On the following screen, you can locate friends, check privacy settings, or find individuals you know who might have a Facebook account.

 Click the cog-shaped Options icon at the top right of your page at any time and then choose Privacy Settings to manage settings for who can access information you post on your page.

Click to access Privacy Settings ———

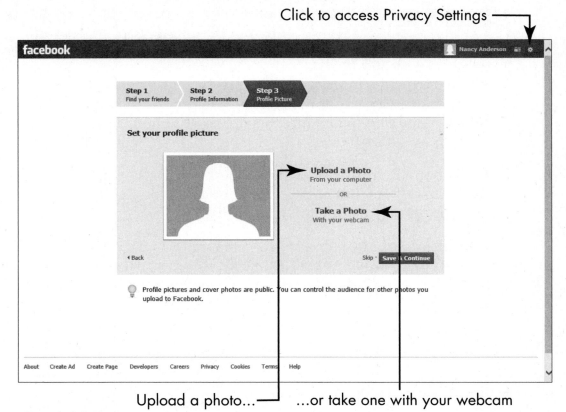

Upload a photo...——— ...or take one with your webcam

Figure 22-5

Create a Profile

When signing up for a service, understand what is *required* information and what is optional. You should clearly understand why a web service needs any of your personally identifiable information and how they may use that information — before providing it. Consider carefully the questions that sites ask users to answer in creating or modifying a profile.

 Warning: Accepting a social networking service's default settings may expose more information than you intend.

Follow these steps to create a profile in Facebook (there are similar steps for adding to your profile in other popular social networking sites):

1. After creating an account (see the previous task), log in to Facebook by going to www.facebook.com. Enter your screen name or e-mail address and password and click the Log In button.

2. Click the Edit Profile link below your name in the upper left corner. If you've entered Profile information before, this button may be called Update Info.

3. Click the Edit button in a section such as Living or Contact info (see **Figure 22-6**), make changes to that section of your profile, and then click Done Editing.

Click on Edit button to edit that section

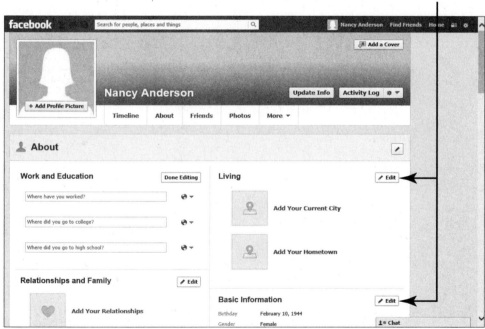

Figure 22-6

4. Continue to enter information, being sure to click the Done Editing button to save any changes in each section as you go.

5. Click Save to save all changes.

Invite Friends

1. Having logged in to your Facebook account, with your home page displayed, click Friends.

2. Click find Friends, and in the page that appears, shown in **Figure 22-7**, click the Add Friend button next to a suggested Facebook member's name, or enter a name and any information you have for somebody else you know such as high school or hometown, and then click the Add Friend button for that person in the results that appear.

Click to add friend

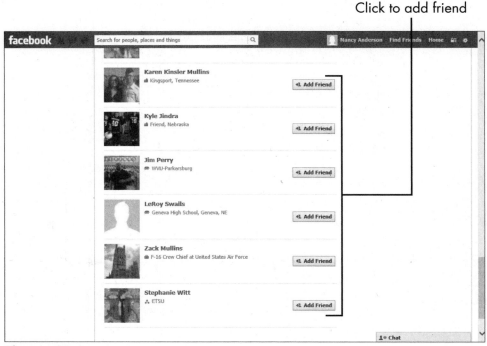

Figure 22-7

To view people who have sent you friend requests, click the Friend Requests icon at the top (it looks like two silhouettes) and on the list that appears, click the Add Friend button to add that person as a friend.

3. The Add Friend button changes to read Friend Request Sent (see **Figure 22-8**).

Your friend receives an invitation in her e-mail inbox; by clicking a link in the invitation, she becomes your friend on Facebook.

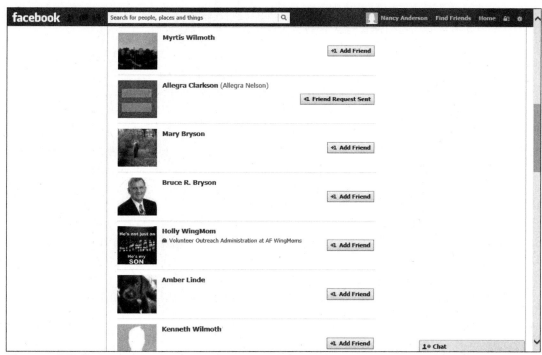

Figure 22-8

 Display a list of friends by clicking your name on your home page and clicking the Friends tab.

See How Online Dating Works

Many seniors are making connections with others via online dating services. In fact, finding a possible partner online can be a good way to gradually get to know somebody (and make sure he or she is right for you) before you meet in person. If you've been wondering if this route could be for you, here's how you can jump into the world of online dating:

➠ Choose a reputable dating site. (See the next task.)

➠ Sign up and provide information about your likes, dislikes, preferences, and so on. This often takes the form of a self-guided interview process.

➠ Create and modify your profile to both avoid exposing too much personal information and ensure that you're sending the right message about yourself to prospective dates.

➠ Use search features on the site (see **Figure 22-9**) to find people who interest you and send them messages or invitations to view your profile.

➠ You'll get messages from other members of the site, to which you can respond (or not). Use the site's chat and e-mail features to interact with potential dates. You may also be able to read comments about the person from others who've dated him or her, if the site offers that feature.

➠ When you're comfortable with the person and feel there might be a spark, decide whether you want to meet the person offline.

Figure 22-9

 Formal dating sites aren't the only places that people meet online, but they typically have the best privacy safeguards in place. Many dating sites screen participants and provide strong reporting measures that are missing on other types of sites, so be particularly careful if you're trying to find love on general interest sites. If you want to interact with people you meet on other sites, you should provide your own safeguards. Create a separate e-mail account (so you can remain anonymous and abandon the e-mail address if needed). Take your time getting to know someone first before connecting in person.

Select a Dating Service

Select your online dating service carefully:

➡ Look for an established, popular site with plenty of members and a philosophy that matches your own.

➡ Review the site's policy regarding your privacy and its procedures for screening members. Make sure you're comfortable with these.

➡ Use a service that provides an e-mail system that you can use for contacting other members only (sometimes called *private messaging*). By using the site's e-mail rather than your own e-mail address, you can maintain your privacy.

➡ Some sites, such as `http://saferdates.com`, shown in **Figure 22-10,** offer stronger levels of authenticating members. Safer Dates, for example, uses fingerprint identification and screening to make you more confident that you know who you're interacting with.

Figure 22-10

➡ Visit a site such as www.onlinedatingsites.net for comparisons of sites. Whether you choose a senior-specific dating site such as www.datingfor seniors.com/ or a general-population site such as www.match.com, reading reviews about the sites ahead of time will help you make the best choice.

 Most people have good experiences with online dating, but if you try a site and experience an unpleasant incident involving another member, report it and make sure the service follows through to enforce its policies. If it doesn't, find another service.

Explore Twitter

Twitter (http://twitter.com) is a *microblogging* service, which means you can share your thoughts with others in text, but with a limit of 140 characters. When you join Twitter, you can create a profile and gain followers who can read your postings (see **Figure 22-11**). You can also follow others. It's an interesting way to get quick updates on what your friends or family members are doing, or to follow a public figure or celebrity's activities and thoughts.

You can also set up Twitter on your mobile phone and get notifications when people you're following post new messages, called *tweets*. You can include location information with your tweets, share photos and videos, and include links so your followers can go to another site to read more detailed information than the limited characters allowed in a tiny tweet. If you follow news or informational sites, you can also stay up-to-date with hot news items using Twitter on your phone.

Figure 22-11

Get Involved in Video and Photo Sharing

The ability to share photos and videos online is a wonderful way to connect to others. You can use services such as YouTube (www.you tube.com), Flickr (www.flickr.com), or PhotoBucket (http://photobucket.com), or you can simply share your images on your social networking page.

 See Chapter 18 to read the steps you can follow to share photo and video files using Microsoft's SkyDrive sharing service.

Do be cautious about what images you share if your page isn't totally private. It's easy to copy images from the web and distribute them widely, so if you wouldn't want anybody in your life to see a particular image, don't post it.

Part V

Taking Care of Your Laptop

Laptop Security and Safety

Your laptop contains software and files that can be damaged in several different ways.

One major source of damage is from malicious attacks that are delivered via the Internet. Some people create programs called *viruses* that are specifically designed to get onto your laptop's hard drive and destroy or scramble data.

Companies might download *adware* to your laptop, which causes pop-up ads to appear, slowing down your laptop's performance.

Spyware is another form of malicious software that you might inadvertently download by clicking a link or opening a file attachment; *spyware* sits on your laptop and tracks your activities, whether for use by a legitimate company in selling you products or by a criminal element seeking to steal your identity.

Microsoft provides security features within Windows 8 that help to keep your laptop and information safe, whether you're at home or travelling.

In this chapter, I introduce you to the major concepts of laptop security, including how to

➡ Understand laptop security and why you need it.

➡ Run periodic updates to Windows that install security solutions and patches to the software (*patches* fix security problems).

➡ Enable a *firewall*, which is a security feature that keeps your laptop safe from outsiders and helps you avoid several kinds of attacks on your data.

➡ Change the Windows password to protect your laptop from others accessing it.

➡ Protect yourself against spyware.

➡ Use devices such as a laptop lock or fingerprint reader to keep bad guys away from your laptop.

➡ Protect your laptop from physical damage.

➡ Find your laptop or protect the data on it from thieves if it's lost or stolen.

Understand Laptop Security

Every day you carry around a wallet full of cash and credit cards, and you take certain measures to protect its contents. Your computer also contains valuable items in the form of data, and it's just as important that you protect it from thieves and damage.

Your laptop comes with an operating system (such as Microsoft Windows) built in, and that operating system has security features that protect your data. Sometimes that operating system has flaws or new threats appear, and you need to get updates to it to keep your laptop secure. (I tell you more about that in the next two tasks.)

In addition, as you use your laptop, you're exposing it to dangerous conditions and situations that you have to guard against.

Some files contain programs that threaten your laptop security. Such files may get transferred to your laptop when you copy them from a disc you insert into your laptop, but most of the time, the danger is from a program that is downloaded from the Internet. These downloads can happen without your knowledge when you click a link or open an attachment in an e-mail; or you may download a legitimate piece of software without realizing that another program is attached to it. Downloads can also happen when you click on a link or image in that cute kitty picture e-mail that got forwarded to you and several dozen others.

There are three main types of dangerous programs (collectively called *malware*) you should be aware of:

➠ A *virus* is a little program that some nasty person thought up to spread around the Internet and infect computers. A virus can do a variety of things, but typically it attacks your data, deleting files, scrambling data, or making changes to your system settings that cause your laptop to grind to a halt.

➠ *Spyware* consists of programs whose main purpose in life is to track activities on your laptop. Some spyware simply helps companies you do business with to track what you do online so they can figure out how to sell you things; other spyware is used for more insidious purposes, such as stealing your passwords.

➠ *Adware* is the computer equivalent of telemarketing phone calls at dinner time. After adware is downloaded onto your laptop, you'll get annoying pop-up windows trying to sell you things all day long. Beyond the annoyance, adware can quickly proliferate, slowing down your laptop's performance until it's hard to get anything done at all.

To protect your information and your laptop from these various types of malware, you can do several things:

➡ **Buy and install an antivirus, antispyware, or anti-adware program.** Programs such as McAfee Antivirus, Norton Antivirus from Symantec (see **Figure 23-1**), or the freely downloadable AVG Free from Grisoft can help prevent the downloading of malicious files. These types of programs can also detect files that have somehow gotten through and delete them for you. Remember that after you install such a program, you have to download regular updates to it to handle new threats, and you need to run scans on your system to catch items that might have snuck through. Many antivirus programs are purchased by yearly subscription, which gives you access to updated virus definitions that the company constantly gathers throughout the year.

Figure 23-1

➠ **Some other programs, such as Spyware Doctor from PC Tools, combine tools for detecting adware and spyware.** Windows 8 has a built-in program, Windows Defender, that includes an antispyware feature.

➠ **Use Windows tools to keep Windows up to date with security features and fixes to security problems.**

➠ **Turn on a firewall, which is a feature that stops other people or programs from accessing your laptop without your permission.**

The last two features of Windows are covered in this chapter.

Understand Windows Update Options

When a new operating system such as Windows 8 is released, it has been thoroughly tested; however, when the product is in general use, the manufacturer finds a few problems or security gaps that it couldn't anticipate. For that reason, companies such as Microsoft release updates to their software, both to fix those problems and deal with new threats to laptops that appeared after the software release.

Windows Update is a tool you can use to make sure your laptop has the most up-to-date security measures in place. You can set Windows Update from the Control Panel by choosing System and Security⇨ Windows Update⇨Change Settings. In the resulting dialog box (see **Figure 23-2**), click the Important Updates drop-down list and you find these settings:

➠ **Install Updates Automatically:** With this setting, Windows Update starts at a time of day you specify, but your laptop must be on for it to work. If you've turned off your laptop, the automatic update will start when you next turn on your laptop, and it might shut down your laptop in the middle of your work to reboot (turn off and then on) and complete the installation.

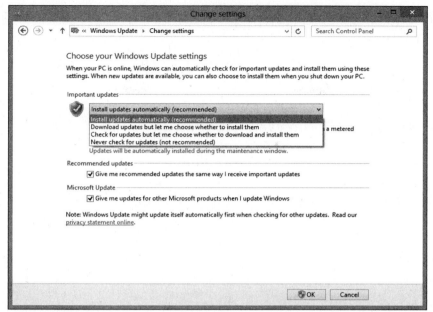

Figure 23-2

➠ **Download Updates But Let Me Choose Whether to Install Them:** You can set up Windows Update to download updates and have Windows notify you (through a little pop-up message on your taskbar) when they're available. You get to decide when the updates are installed and when your laptop reboots to complete the installation. This is my preferred setting because I have control and won't be caught unaware by a sudden laptop reboot.

➠ **Check for Updates But Let Me Choose Whether to Download and Install Them:** With this setting, you neither download nor install updates until you say so, but Windows notifies you that new updates are available.

➠ **Never Check for Updates:** You can stop Windows from checking for updates and check for them yourself, manually. (See the following task for instructions.) This puts your laptop at a bit more risk because you may neglect to download important

updates, but it's useful for you to know how to perform a manual update if you discover a new update
such as a new printer driver or language pack is
available that you need.

Run Windows Update

1. Press Win+I and click Change PC Settings.

2. In the PC Settings window, click Update & Recovery.

3. In the resulting window, as shown in **Figure 23-3**, click
the Check Now link to see all updates.

Click to see updates

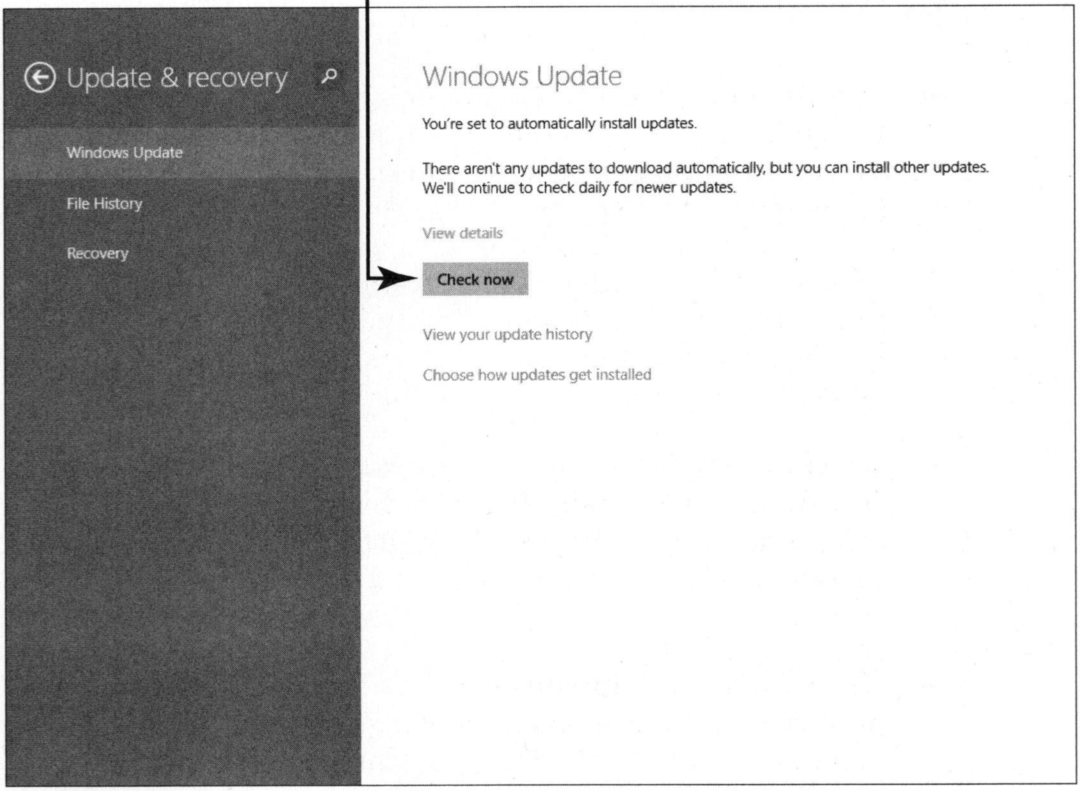

Figure 23-3

4. In the following window, which shows the available updates (see **Figure** 23-4), click to select available critical or optional updates that you want to install. Then click the Install button.

Figure 23-4

5. A window appears, showing the progress of your installation. When the installation is complete, you might get a message telling you that it's a good idea to restart your computer to complete the installation. Click Restart Now.

You can make settings for Windows Update by clicking the Choose How Updates Get Installed link in the window shown in Figure 23-3. If you leave the setting for Windows Update to Never Check for Updates, it's very important that you perform a manual update on a regular basis.

Running Windows Update on a regular basis — either automatically or manually — ensures that you get the latest security updates to the operating system. It's a good idea to stay current with those updates to avoid the latest threats.

Set Up Trusted and Restricted Websites

1. You can set up Internet Explorer to recognize websites you trust — and those to which you don't want Internet Explorer to take you or anybody else who uses your laptop. Click the Internet Explorer icon in the Desktop taskbar to start your browser.

2. Choose Tools⇨Internet Options.

3. In the Internet Options dialog box (see **Figure 23-5**), click the Security tab.

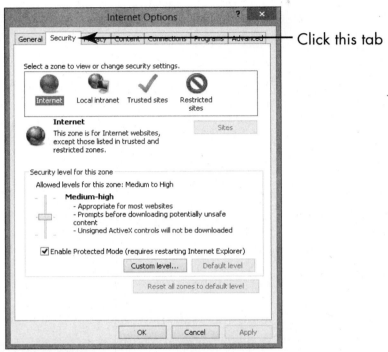

Click this tab

Figure 23-5

4. Click the Trusted Sites icon and then click the Sites button.

5. In the resulting Trusted Sites dialog box, enter a URL (website address) in the Add This Web Site to the Zone text box for a website you want to allow your laptop to access.

If you wish to allow any locations for particular companies, such as Microsoft, you can use a *wildcard* (a character that tells the computer to trust all sites that include that word in the URL). **Figure 23-6** shows the asterisk (*) wildcard in use in the Websites field.

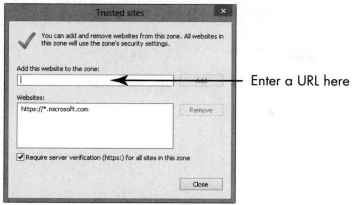

Enter a URL here

Figure 23-6

6. Click Add to add the site to the list of websites.

7. Repeat Steps 3–6 to add more sites.

8. When you're done, click Close and then click OK to close the Internet Options dialog box.

9. To designate sites that you don't want your laptop to access, repeat Steps 1–8, clicking the Restricted Sites icon rather than Trusted Sites in Step 4 to designate sites that you don't want your laptop to access.

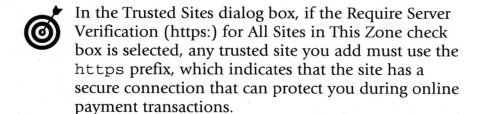 In the Trusted Sites dialog box, if the Require Server Verification (https:) for All Sites in This Zone check box is selected, any trusted site you add must use the https prefix, which indicates that the site has a secure connection that can protect you during online payment transactions.

You can establish a Privacy setting on the Privacy tab of the Internet Options dialog box to control which sites are allowed to download *cookies* to your laptop. *Cookies* are tiny files that a site uses to track your online activity and recognize you when you return to the site. Some sites need to use cookies to allow you to use your account — and that's fine — but other sites may use cookies to track (and even sell information

about) your online activities that could put you at risk. *Trusted sites* are ones that you allow to download cookies to your laptop even though the privacy setting you have made might not allow other sites to do so. *Restricted sites,* on the other hand, can never download cookies to your laptop, no matter what your privacy setting is.

Enable the Windows Firewall

1. A firewall keeps outsiders from accessing your laptop via an Internet connection. Right-click the Start button on the Desktop and then click on Control Panel in the menu that appears.

2. Click System and Security➪Windows Firewall.

3. In the Windows Firewall window that appears (see **Figure** 23-7), check that the Windows Firewall is marked as On. If it isn't, click the Turn Windows Firewall On or Off link in the left pane of the window.

Make sure this is set to On

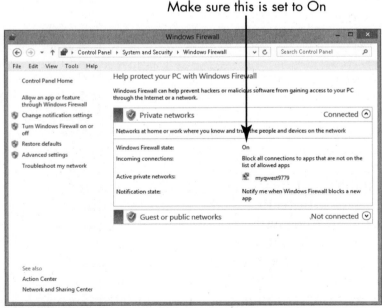

Figure 23-7

4. In the resulting Customize Settings window (see **Figure 23-8**), select the Turn on Windows Firewall radio button for Private Networks (such as your home network) and/or Public Networks (such as in a coffee shop) and then click OK.

 It's always a good idea to have the firewall turned on when you go online using a public "hot spot" connection, such as at an Internet café. If you have a home network, you may already have a firewall active in the router (a piece of equipment used to set up the network), so the Windows firewall setting could be optional in that situation.

Turn either/both of these options on

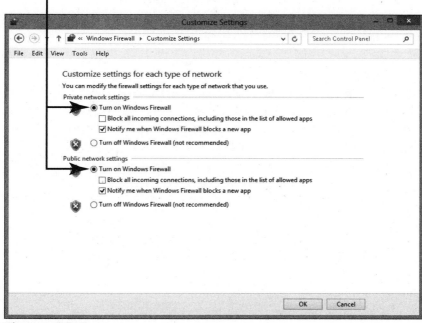

Figure 23-8

5. Click the Close button to close Windows Security Center and the Control Panel.

> A *firewall* is a program that protects your laptop from the outside world. This is generally a good thing. If you have set up a Virtual Private Network (VPN), often used by corporations, that you connect your laptop to, be aware that using a firewall with a VPN results in your being unable to share files and use some other VPN features.

> Antivirus and security software programs may offer their own firewall protection and may display a message asking whether you want to switch. Check their features against Windows and then decide, but usually most firewall features are comparable. The important thing is to have one activated.

Change Your Laptop Password

1. If you log into Windows using an online account, your password is the password associated with your Windows Live account. If you set up a local account not associated with an online account, you create a password when you set up the account. To change a password, press Win+I, click Change PC Settings, and then click Accounts.

2. In the Accounts panel, shown in **Figure 23-9**, click the Sign-In Options, and then click the Change button under Password. You may be asked to enter your current password to proceed.

Click here   ...and then here

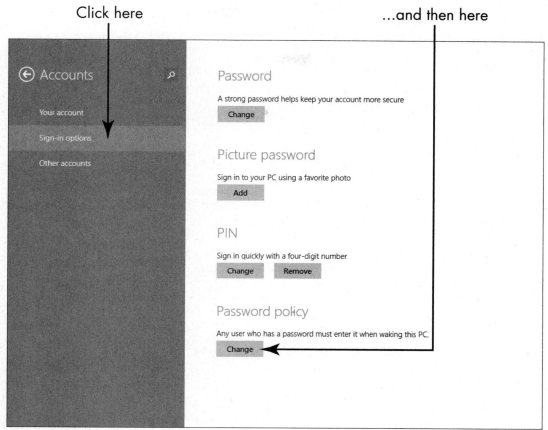

Figure 23-9

3. In the Change Your Microsoft Account Password screen, shown in **Figure 23-10**, enter your current password, and then enter the new password and confirm it.

4. Click Next.

5. Click Finish.

 You can use a similar procedure by clicking Change PIN Sign-in Settings in the PC User Settings to assign a four character PIN for logging into your account, rather than a password. PIN's are typically shorter than passwords (four characters), so they save you time if you log on and off Windows throughout the day.

Enter your old password here

Enter your new password in both of these fields

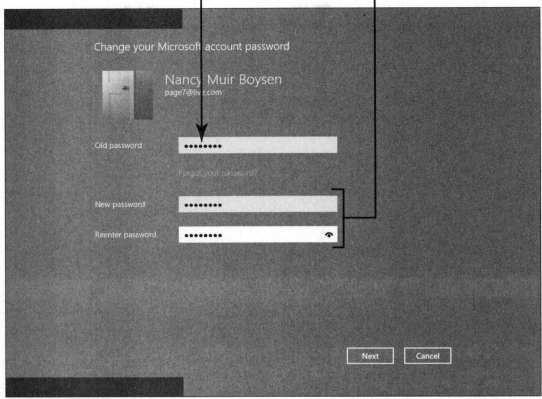

Change your Microsoft account password

Nancy Muir Boysen
page7@live.com

Old password

••••••••

Forgot your password?

New password

••••••••

Reenter password

••••••••

Next   Cancel

Figure 23-10

After you create a password, you can go to the PC
Settings window and change it at any time by clicking
Accounts⇨Sign-in Options⇨Change.

Allow Firewall Exceptions

1. When you have a firewall active, you can allow certain
programs to communicate through that firewall. For
example, you might want to allow live apps such as
Weather or Video to send information or content to your
computer. Right-click the Start button on the Desktop
and then click Control Panel in the menu that appears.
Click System and Security.

2. In the resulting System and Security window (see **Figure 23-11**), click Allow an App through Windows Firewall.

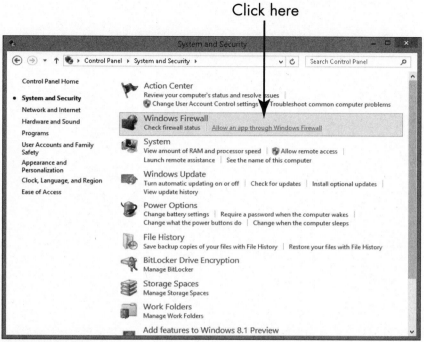

Figure 23-11

3. In the Allowed Apps window that appears (**see Figure 23-12**), click the Change Settings button, and then select the check boxes for apps on your computer that you want to allow to communicate over the Internet without being stopped by Firewall.

4. Click the Private and Public check boxes to narrow down whether you want only networks that are secure to allow this communication, or both secure and public and non-secure networks to do so.

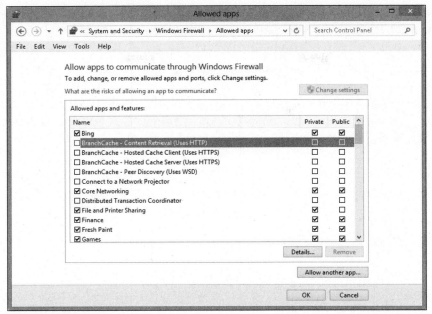

Figure 23-12

5. Click OK.

 If you allow apps to communicate across your firewall, it's very important that you do have antivirus and antispyware software installed on your laptop — and that you run updates to them on a regular basis. These types of programs help you avoid downloading malware to your laptop that could bother you with advertising pop-ups, slow your laptop's performance, damage computer files, or even track your keystrokes as you type to steal your identity. If you don't want to pay for an antispyware program, consider a free solution such as Spyware Terminator (www.spywareterminator.com/).

Use a Lock to Deter Thieves

When you travel with your laptop, you may have to leave it alone for a few moments now and then — perhaps in a cubicle in a branch office or a table at an Internet café while you step away to grab your latte.

When that happens, a lock that you clip to your laptop (usually on the back or side, identified by a lock icon) and wrap around a table or desk leg might make you feel more secure. These are similar to the lock you use to keep your bicycle safe as you wander into a store or gym.

Don't count on a laptop lock to keep your laptop safe during a lengthy absence. They are relatively easy to circumvent. But for a short period of time in a non-high-risk area, they can be useful.

Locks are relatively cheap, from about $5 to $30 or so. They're also usually pretty easy to tuck into a laptop case without adding much bulk.

Utilize a Fingerprint Reader

Fingerprint readers use *biometric* technology that identifies you by a unique physical characteristic. Here's what you should know about laptop fingerprint readers:

➡ Many laptops include a built-in fingerprint reader for security. This is useful to keep anybody but you from accessing data on your laptop because your fingerprint is unique. See your manual for instructions on using the reader.

➡ An option to using your fingerprint is using your finger to draw your password. Windows 8 has a picture password feature that works with touchscreen laptops and tablets. You enter onscreen gestures on a picture to log in to Windows. See Chapter 6 for more about using this feature.

➡ If your laptop doesn't have a built-in fingerprint reader, you can buy an external model such as the Microsoft Fingerprint Reader. These come in a wide price range (from about $40 to $200), but they are relatively portable. **Figure 23-13** shows one such device from Eikon.

Figure 23-13

➡ Some fingerprint readers allow you to log in to your laptop by simply swiping your finger over the reader, and some can also store passwords for your online accounts. Laptops or tablets with a touchscreen may allow you to press your finger to the screen to read your fingerprint.

Protect Your Laptop from Damage

Here are a few tips for protecting your laptop from physical damage or recouping some losses if damage does occur:

➡ A well-made laptop case is really a must when moving about with your laptop. It helps to protect the laptop if you drop it and protect it from things falling on it. Look for one with both good padding and pockets for storing USB sticks and cords and DVDs, a power cord, and possibly a fingerprint reader or lock.

➡ Your laptop screen is one of its biggest vulnerabilities. If it gets scratched or damaged in some way, short of attaching an external monitor (which doesn't do you much good if you're on a plane), your laptop is pretty much a goner. You can buy a fairly low-cost screen protector, a thin sheet of plastic that you place across your monitor that can help prevent scratches and, as a bonus, keep your screen from picking up dust or smudges.

➡ Because you can't prevent each and every possible disaster, always *back up* your data (copy it to storage other than your laptop's hard drive) so you don't lose it — and consider getting insurance for your laptop. If your homeowner's policy doesn't already cover it, companies such as Safeware offer special laptop insurance against damage and theft. If your laptop is essential to your work or hobby, or if you travel with it a great deal, you might want to get an insurance quote to see whether coverage is within your budget.

Use a Service to Find a Lost Laptop

Laptops are lost or stolen on a frighteningly regular basis. The biggest concern, aside from having to buy a new laptop (which may or may not be covered by your insurance), is what a thief might do with the data on the laptop. Stored passwords for financial and retail shopping accounts could be used to steal your identity or run up debt in your name.

Luckily there are software applications such as LaptopCop (`www.webwatcher.com/laptop-cop.html`) (see **Figure 23-14**) and CompuTrace (`www.absolute.com/en/products/absolute-computrace.com`), as well as free software such as Adeona (`http://adeona.cs.washington.edu`) or LaptopLock (`www.thelaptoplock.com`) that you can install on your laptop. Adeona, for instance, transmits regular messages as to your laptop's location as long as it's connected to the Internet. Other options offer a central service that tracks your laptop's whereabouts.

Figure 23-14

Using these programs and services, you can do several things, depending on software features — including these:

➠ Pinpointing where your laptop is whenever it connects to the Internet

➠ Remotely disabling the computer, deleting files from it, or locking out any would-be user

➠ Issuing a warning to the thief that the computer is now protected and useless

➠ Observing what activities the thief is performing on your computer in real time

Maintaining Windows

*T*hat wonderful laptop that you've spent your hard-earned money on doesn't mean a thing if the software driving it goes flooey. If any programs cause your system to *crash* (that is, it freezes up and you have to take drastic measures to revive it), you can try a few different approaches. You can also make an effort to keep your system in good shape to help you avoid those crashes.

In this chapter, you find out how to take good care of your programs and operating system in these ways:

➡ When a program crashes, you can simply shut that program down by using the Windows Task Manager. This utility keeps track of all the programs and processes that are running on your laptop.

➡ If you have problems and Windows isn't responding, sometimes it helps to restart in Safe Mode, which requires that Windows load only basic files and drivers. Restarting in Safe Mode often allows you to troubleshoot what's going on, and you can restart Windows in its regular mode after the problem is solved.

➠ Use the System Restore feature to first create a *system restore point* (a point in time when your settings and programs all seem to be humming along just fine), and then restore Windows to those settings when trouble hits.

➠ You can clean up your system to delete unused files, free up disk space, and schedule maintenance tasks.

➠ If you need a little help, you might run a trouble-shooting program to help you figure out a problem you're experiencing with a program. These walk you through several possible solutions and sometimes solve the problem for you.

Shut Down a Nonresponsive Application

1. If your laptop freezes and won't let you proceed with what you were doing, press Ctrl+Alt+Del.

2. In the Windows screen that appears, click Task Manager.

3. In the resulting Task Manager dialog box, click More Details and then click the Processes tab (see **Figure 24-1**).

4. Click on a task (typically the last app you were working in when Windows crashed), and then click the End Task button.

5. The app shuts down. Click the Close button to close Task Manager.

 If pressing Ctrl+Alt+Del doesn't bring up the Task Manager, you might need to press and hold your laptop's power button to shut down. You may, or may not, have lost documents you were working in at the time of your computer crash. Note that some

applications use an AutoSave feature that keeps an interim version of the document that you were working in — you might be able to save some of your work by opening the app and choosing to save that last version. Other programs don't have such a safety net, and you simply lose whatever changes you made to your document since the last time you saved it. The moral? Save, and save often.

Click the Processes tab

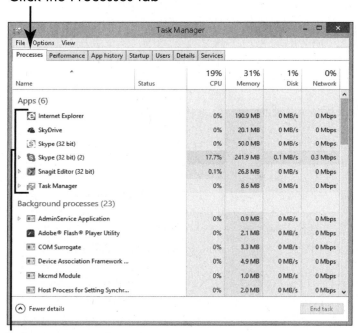

Select any application

Figure 24-1

You may see a dialog box appear when an application shuts down that asks if you want to report the problem to Microsoft. If you say yes, information is sent to Microsoft to help it provide advice or fix the problem down the road.

Create a System Restore Point

1. You can back up your system files, which creates a restore point you can later use to return your laptop to earlier settings if you begin to experience problems. Press Win+I from the Desktop and then click Control Panel.

2. Click System and Security and in the resulting window, click the System link.

3. In the System window, click the System Protection link in the left panel. In the System Properties dialog box that appears (see **Figure 24-2**) on the System Protection tab, click the Create button.

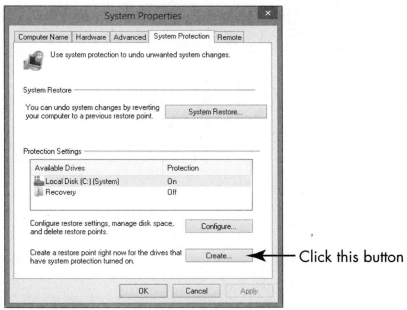

Figure 24-2

4. In the Create a Restore Point dialog box that appears, enter a name to identify the restore point, such as the current date or the name of a program you are about to install, and click Create.

5. Windows displays a progress window. When the restore point is created, the message shown in **Figure 24-3** appears. Click Close to close the message box, click Close to close the System Protection dialog box, and Close again to close the Control Panel.

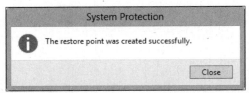

System Protection

The restore point was created successfully.

Close

Figure 24-3

 Every once in a while, when you install some software and make a few new settings in Windows, and when things seem to be running just fine, create a system restore point. It's good computer practice, just like backing up your files, only you're backing up your settings. Once a month or once every couple of months works for most people, but if you frequently make changes, create a system restore point more often.

Restore Your Laptop

1. From the Control Panel, click System and Security and then click System on the following screen.

2. Click the System Protection link on the left side of the window.

3. In the System Properties dialog box that appears, click the System Protection tab and then click the System Restore button, as shown in Figure 24-4.

4. In the System Restore window, click Next. In the window that appears, shown in **Figure 24-5,** choose the date and time of the restore point you want to restore to and then click Next.

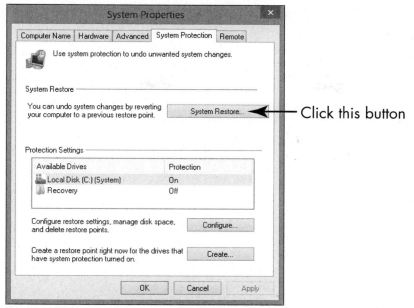

Click this button

Figure 24-4

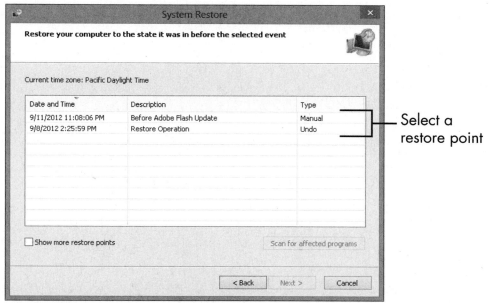

Select a restore point

Figure 24-5

5. Click the Finish button to start the restore.

6. A dialog box confirms that you want to run System Restore and informs you that System Restore cannot be interrupted and in most cases cannot be undone. Close any open files or programs, and then click Yes to proceed. The system goes through a shutdown and restart sequence.

 System Restore doesn't get rid of files that you've saved, so you don't lose your Ph.D. dissertation. System Restore simply reverts to Windows settings as of the restore point. This can help if you or some piece of installed software made a setting that is causing some conflict in your system that makes your laptop sluggish or prone to crashes. If you're concerned about what changes will happen, click the Scan for Affected Programs button shown in the window displayed in **Figure 24-6** before starting the restore.

 System Restore doesn't always solve the problem. Your very best bet is to be sure you create a set of backup discs for your laptop when you buy it. If you didn't do that, and you can't get things running right again, contact your computer manufacturer. They may be able to send you a set of recovery discs, though they may charge a small fee. These discs restore your laptop to its state when it left the factory, and in this case you lose applications you installed and documents you created, but you can get your computer running again.

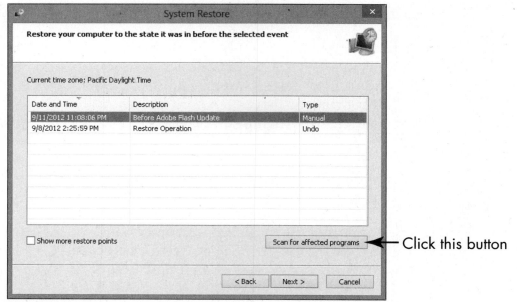

Click this button

Figure 24-6

Refresh Your Laptop

1. Refreshing your laptop is a way to get a sluggish device to perform better by resetting your system files to default settings, while leaving your personal files alone. Press Win+I to display the Settings charm panel.

2. Click Change PC Settings, and then click Update & Recovery.

3. In the left panel, click Recovery. Click the Get Started button under the Refresh Your PC without Affecting Your Files heading (see **Figure 24-7**).

4. A message appears explaining what will happen when you run Refresh. Click Next to proceed.

5. On the next screen (see **Figure 24-8**), click Refresh to proceed, or Cancel to cancel the Refresh. When the Refresh is finished, a list of the apps that were removed appears on your Desktop.

Click here

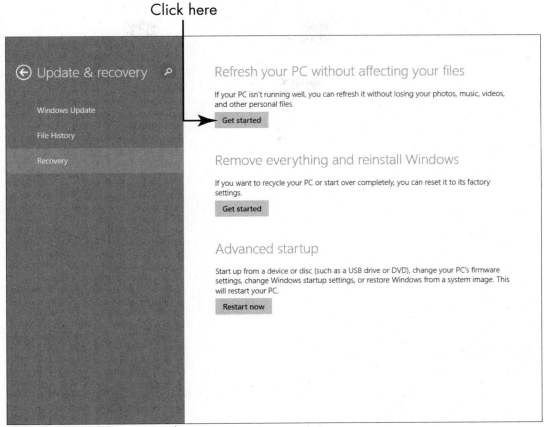

Figure 24-7

Figure 24-8

Warning: Remember that using the Refresh procedure retains apps you bought from the Windows Store, but you lose apps you installed from other sources, such as a DVD or an online site.

Reset Your Laptop

1. Where refreshing a PC resets system files to factory defaults and retains all your files and some apps, resetting your PC not only resets system files, it gets rid of all the personal files and apps that you installed. Resetting is for those times when nothing else has gotten your laptop working again. To begin, press Win+I and click the Change PC Settings link.

2. Click Update & Recovery and click Recovery.

3. Click the Get Started button under the Remove Everything and Reinstall Windows setting.

4. On the next screen, shown in **Figure 24-9,** read the description of what Reset will do, and then click Next.

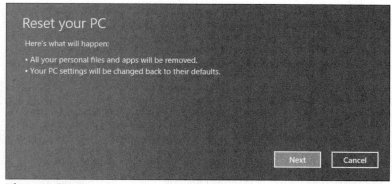

Figure 24-9

5. On the following screen, shown in **Figure 24-10,** choose which drive to remove files from: only the drive where Windows is installed or all drives.

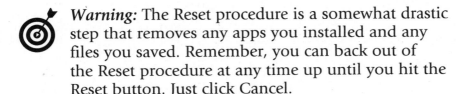

Figure 24-10

6. On the following screen, choose either a thorough or quick reset.

7. On the following Ready to Reset Your PC screen, if you're positive you want to proceed, click the Reset button.

> *Warning:* The Reset procedure is a somewhat drastic step that removes any apps you installed and any files you saved. Remember, you can back out of the Reset procedure at any time up until you hit the Reset button. Just click Cancel.

Defragment a Hard Drive

1. To clean up files on your hard drive, from the Control Panel, choose System and Security and then click Defragment and Optimize Your Drives in the Administrative Tools window.

2. In the resulting Optimize Drives window (see **Figure 24-11**), to the left of the Optimize button is the Analyze button. Use this to check whether your disk requires defragmenting. When the analysis is complete, click the Optimize button. A notation appears (see **Figure 24-12**) showing the progress of defragmenting your drive.

Click this button...

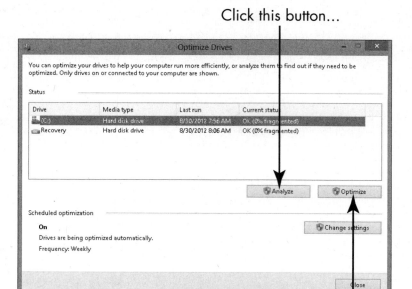

Figure 24-11

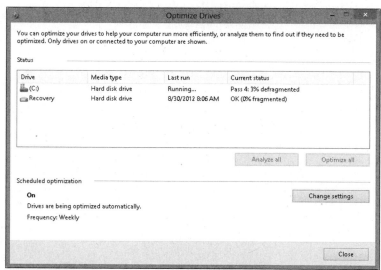

then click this button

Figure 24-12

3. When the defragmenting process is complete, the Optimize Drives window shows that your drive no longer requires defragmenting. Click Close to close the window and then close the Control Panel.

 Warning: Disk defragmenting could take a while. If you have energy-saving features active (such as a screen saver), they could cause the defragmenter to stop and start all over again. Try running your defrag overnight while you're happily dreaming of much more interesting things. You can also set up the procedure to run automatically at a preset period of time, such as once every two weeks by using the Change Settings button in the Disk Defragmenter window and choosing a frequency in the dialog box that appears.

Free Disk Space

1. To run a process that cleans unused files and fragments of data off of your hard drive to free up space, open the Control Panel.

2. Click System and Security and then click Administrative Tools.

3. Double-click Disk Cleanup. In the Disk Cleanup for Windows dialog box that appears (see **Figure 24-13**), click the files you want to delete and click OK. A message asks you to confirm that you want to delete this material. Click the Delete Files button.

Figure 24-13

4. The resulting dialog box, shown in **Figure** 24-14, shows
the Disk Cleanup progress.

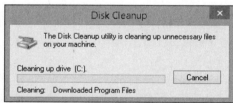

Figure 24-14

 Click the View Files button in the Disk Cleanup dialog
box to see more details about the files that Windows
proposes to delete, including the size of the files and
when they were created or last accessed.

Delete Temporary Internet Files by Using Internet Explorer

1. When you roam the Internet, various files may be downloaded to your laptop to temporarily allow you to access

sites or services. To clear these away, first open Internet Explorer from the Desktop.

2. In the upper-right corner, choose Tools⇨Internet Options.

3. On the General tab of the resulting Internet Options dialog box (see **Figure 24-15**), click the Delete button in the Browsing History section.

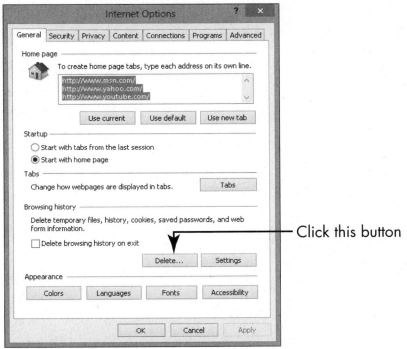

Click this button

Figure 24-15

4. In the resulting Delete Browsing History dialog box, shown in **Figure 24-16,** click the Temporary Internet Files and Website Files check box to select it if it's not already selected. Be sure other check boxes such as History are deselected if you want to keep them. Click Delete.

5. A confirmation message asks whether you want to delete the files. Click Yes. Click OK to close the Internet Options dialog box.

Temporary Internet files can be deleted when you run Disk Cleanup (see that task earlier in this chapter), but the process that I describe here allows you to delete them without having to make choices about deleting other files on your system.

Make sure this box is checked

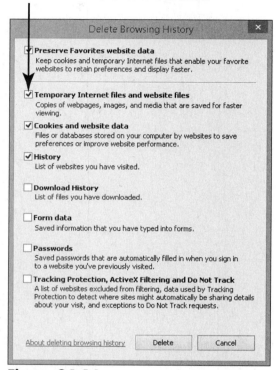

Figure 24-16

Schedule Maintenance Tasks

1. From the Control Panel, click System and Security and then click Schedule Tasks in the Administrative Tools window.

2. In the resulting Task Scheduler dialog box, shown in **Figure 24-17,** choose Action⇨Create Task.

Click this option

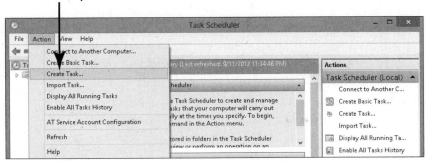

Figure 24-17

3. In the resulting Create Task dialog box on the General tab (see **Figure 24-18**), enter a task name and description. Choose when to run the task (either only when you are logged on or whether you're logged on or not).

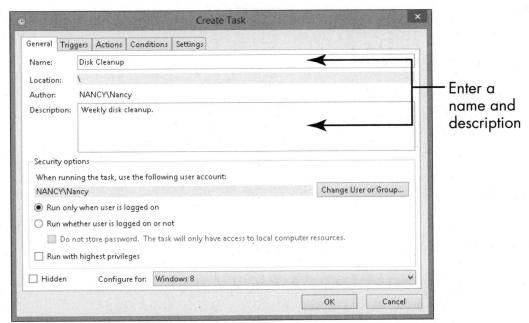

Enter a name and description

Figure 24-18

4. Click the Triggers tab and then click New. In the New Trigger dialog box, choose a criteria in the Begin the Task drop-down list and use the settings to specify how often to perform the task as well as when and at what time of day to begin. Click OK.

5. Click the Actions tab and then click New. In the New Action dialog box, choose the action that will occur from the Action drop-down list. These include starting a program, sending an e-mail, or displaying a message. Depending on what you choose here, different action dialog boxes appear. For example, if you want to send an e-mail, you get an e-mail form to fill in. Click OK.

6. If you want to set conditions in addition to those that trigger the action and those that control whether it should occur, click the Conditions tab of the Create Task dialog box and choose from the options there such as starting the task when the computer has been idle for a time or only if the laptop isn't running on a battery.

7. Click the Settings tab and make settings that control how the task runs (on demand, restart if the task fails, and so on). Click OK.

8. After you complete all settings, click OK to save the task and click the Close button to close the Task Scheduler dialog box.

 If you like a more wizard-like interface for building a new task, you can choose the Create Basic Task item from the Action menu in the task Scheduler dialog box. This walks you through the most basic and minimal settings you can make to create a new task.

Troubleshoot Software Problems

1. If you can't figure out why you're having problems with a piece of software, from the Control Panel, click Find and Fix Problems (under System and Security).

2. In the resulting Troubleshooting window (see **Figure 24-19**), click Programs.

Click to troubleshoot programs

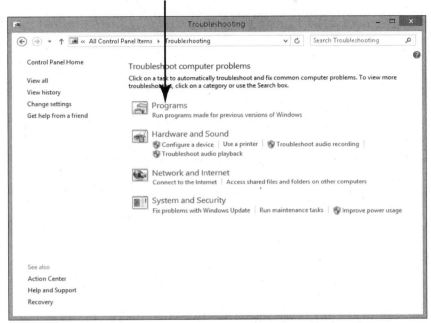

Figure 24-19

3. In the resulting Troubleshooting Problems–Programs window, choose what you want to troubleshoot:

- **Network** allows you to troubleshoot a connection to the Internet.

- **Web Browser** helps you figure out problems you may be having with the Internet Explorer browser.

- **Programs** is a good choice if you have an older program that doesn't seem to be functioning well with this version of Windows. Program compatibility is a common cause of problems running software.

- **Printing** allows you to find out why you're having difficulty with your printer, including checking for the correct printer driver software.

- **Media Player** troubleshooting can be used to pinpoint problems with general settings, media files, or playing DVDs.

4. Follow the sequence of instructions for the item you selected to let Windows help you resolve your problem (see **Figure 24-20**).

 In some cases, you'll be asked for administrator permission for the troubleshooter to perform an action, so it's a good idea to run the troubleshooting wizard through an administrator-level user account. See Chapter 3 for more about user accounts and administrators.

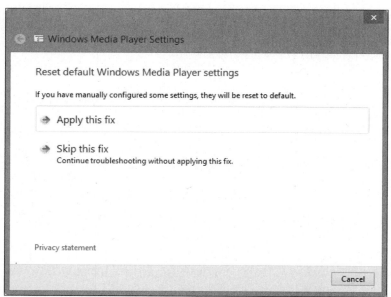

Figure 24-20

 **Index**

• *M* •

Notes

About the Author

Nancy Muir is the author of more than 100 books on technology and business topics. Prior to becoming an author, Nancy was acquisitions manager and then associate publisher at two major technology publishing companies and a software training manager at Symantec. Nancy is senior editor of the website `UnderstandingNano.com` and has taught technical writing at the university level. She has also been a regular contributor of articles on technology for `Retirenet.com`.

Author's Acknowledgments

Thanks to Katie Mohr for giving me the opportunity to author this book and others. Also, I'm grateful to my editor, Linda Morris, for making sure this project ran like clockwork. Thanks to Sharon Mealka for performing the technical edit on the book.

Publisher's Acknowledgments

Acquisitions Editor: Katie Mohr
Project Editor: Linda Morris
Copy Editor: Linda Morris
Technical Editor: Sharon Mealka
Editorial Assistant: Annie Sullivan
Sr. Editorial Assistant: Cherie Case

Project Coordinator: Patrick Redmond
Cover Image: ©iStockphoto.com/jpmediainc

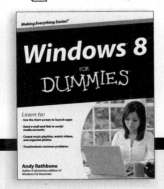

Math & Science

Algebra I For Dummies,
2nd Edition
978-0-470-55964-2

Anatomy and Physiology
For Dummies,
2nd Edition
978-0-470-92326-9

Astronomy For Dummies,
3rd Edition
978-1-118-37697-3

Biology For Dummies,
2nd Edition
978-0-470-59875-7

Chemistry For Dummies,
2nd Edition
978-1-1180-0730-3

Pre-Algebra Essentials
For Dummies
978-0-470-61838-7

Microsoft Office

Excel 2013 For Dummies
978-1-118-51012-4

Office 2013 All-in-One
For Dummies
978-1-118-51636-2

PowerPoint 2013
For Dummies
978-1-118-50253-2

Word 2013 For Dummies
978-1-118-49123-2

Music

Blues Harmonica
For Dummies
978-1-118-25269-7

Guitar For Dummies,
3rd Edition
978-1-118-11554-1

iPod & iTunes
For Dummies,
10th Edition
978-1-118-50864-0

Programming

Android Application
Development For
Dummies, 2nd Edition
978-1-118-38710-8

iOS 6 Application
Development For Dummies
978-1-118-50880-0

Java For Dummies,
5th Edition
978-0-470-37173-2

Religion & Inspiration

The Bible For Dummies
978-0-7645-5296-0

Buddhism For Dummies,
2nd Edition
978-1-118-02379-2

Catholicism For Dummies,
2nd Edition
978-1-118-07778-8

Self-Help & Relationships

Bipolar Disorder
For Dummies,
2nd Edition
978-1-118-33882-7

Meditation For Dummies,
3rd Edition
978-1-118-29144-3

Seniors

Computers For Seniors
For Dummies,
3rd Edition
978-1-118-11553-4

iPad For Seniors
For Dummies,
5th Edition
978-1-118-49708-1

Social Security
For Dummies
978-1-118-20573-0

Smartphones & Tablets

Android Phones
For Dummies
978-1-118-16952-0

Kindle Fire HD
For Dummies
978-1-118-42223-6

NOOK HD For Dummies,
Portable Edition
978-1-118-39498-4

Surface For Dummies
978-1-118-49634-3

Test Prep

ACT For Dummies,
5th Edition
978-1-118-01259-8

ASVAB For Dummies,
3rd Edition
978-0-470-63760-9

GRE For Dummies,
7th Edition
978-0-470-88921-3

Officer Candidate Tests,
For Dummies
978-0-470-59876-4

Physician's Assistant Exam
For Dummies
978-1-118-11556-5

Series 7 Exam
For Dummies
978-0-470-09932-2

Windows 8

Windows 8 For Dummies
978-1-118-13461-0

Windows 8 For Dummies,
Book + DVD Bundle
978-1-118-27167-4

Windows 8 All-in-One
For Dummies
978-1-118-11920-4

Available in print and e-book formats.

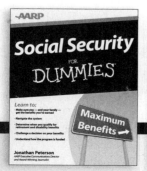

Take Dummies with you everywhere you go!

Whether you're excited about e-books, want more from the web, must have your mobile apps, or swept up in social media, Dummies makes everything easier .

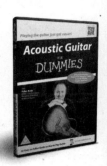